P9-CEN-179

YALE CLASSICAL STUDIES

YALE CLASSICAL STUDIES

EDITED FOR THE DEPARTMENT OF CLASSICS

by
JEFFREY HENDERSON

VOLUME XXVI

ARISTOPHANES:
ESSAYS IN INTERPRETATION

CAMBRIDGE UNIVERSITY PRESS

CAMBRIDGE
LONDON NEW YORK NEW ROCHELLE
MELBOURNE SYDNEY

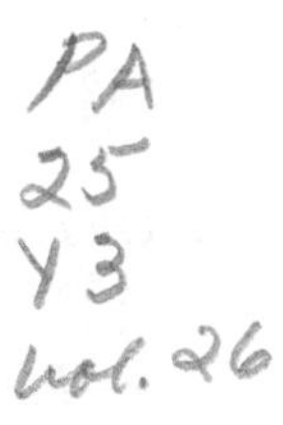

Published by the Press Syndicate of the University of Cambridge
The Pitt Building, Trumpington Street, Cambridge CB2 1RP
32 East 57th Street, New York, NY 10022, USA
296 Beaconsfield Parade, Middle Park, Melbourne 3206, Australia

First published 1980

Typeset in Great Britain at the
University Press, Cambridge
Printed in the United States of America by the
Murray Printing Company, Westford, Mass.

British Library Cataloguing in Publication Data
Yale classical studies.
Vol. 26: Aristophanes
1. Classical literature – History and criticism –
Addresses, essays, lectures
I. Henderson, Jeffrey
880'.09 PA3003 80–40042

ISBN 0 521 23120 5

Contents

Introduction

No special justification is needed for a new collection of interpretive essays on Aristophanes: of all the major writers of the fifth century he is surely (at least in the English-speaking world) one of the most neglected by classicists. The absence of up-to-date texts and commentaries for most of the plays exacerbates the problem. As anyone who has tried to teach Aristophanes in Greek or in translation will attest, the task of making the plays available to students is beset by many formidable problems not encountered in the case of other Greek authors. Aristophanes is a comic playwright composing in a defunct and often alien mode about topical subjects only imperfectly intelligible to a distant posterity. An ancient tragedian, historian, philosopher or orator has at least the advantage of writing in forms either still viable or made much more viable by extensive scholarly and critical exegesis. It seems to me that as a result an unfortunate trend has developed: Aristophanes, despite his own insistence to the contrary and despite his having written about the same topics as his contemporaries, has more and more been denied the status of a serious and/or intelligible spokesman for his times. Rather than perform the difficult job of establishing a methodology for deciding the matter one way or the other, many scholars have decided that Aristophanes is primarily a humorist of genius whose views about matters of perennial concern are either undiscoverable or, if discoverable, much less important and useful than those recoverable from other contemporary sources.

This volume is an attempt to reexamine such conclusions. Each contributor sets out from the assumption that Aristophanes' claim to be serious as well as humorous is sincere. Each attempts to discover the uniquely Aristophanic approach to topics of importance to students of Athenian history, literature and society. I hope that the result will go some way toward restoring Aristophanes to the list of those ancient voices still accorded an undivided and respectful hearing.

Ann Arbor J. H.
June 1979

Aristophanes' *Acharnians**

LOWELL EDMUNDS

ὁ δὲ βασιλεὺς τὸν Ἡσίοδον ἐστεφάνωσεν εἰπὼν δίκαιον εἶναι τὸν ἐπὶ γεωργίαν καὶ εἰρήνην προκαλούμενον νικᾶν, οὐ τὸν πολέμους καὶ σφαγὰς διεξιόντα.

The Contest of Homer and Hesiod, 322G

'Politics...are a stone attached to the neck of literature, which, in less than six months, drowns it. Politics in the middle of imaginative interests are like a pistol-shot in the middle of a concert. The noise is deafening without being emphatic. It is not in harmony with the sound of any of the instruments.'[1] Thus Stendhal. He spoke ironically; but critics of Aristophanes are dead serious when they make this same distinction between poetry and politics, and proceed to shut their ears to all those supposed pistol-shots that every Aristophanic concert contains. *Acharnians*, like the other 'peace plays', thwarts this muffling of the ears, because the whole play is deafening. Aristophanes has a clear 'program'. The play is thoroughly political, beginning with its title, the name of the most hawkish demesmen of the day (Thuc. 2. 21. 3), and with the name of the dove, Dicaeopolis, 'Just City'.[2]

* Full references for works cited in the footnotes are given in the Bibliography, pp. 34–6.

1. Beyle (1926), vol. 2, ch. 52 (p. 189). A similar statement is found in ch. 23 of *The Charterhouse of Parma*.

2. On the name, see Russo (1953) 133; de Ste Croix (1972) 365. 'Dicaeopolis' is not a comic compound, but is an historical name (*IG* II² 1622, line 685). It is one of 47 personal names ending in -πολις listed in Dornseiff (1957) 191–2. These names, as well as such adjectives as ἄπολις (Soph. *Ant.* 370), ὑψίπολις (Pind. *O.* 2. 8), and the adjectival use of δικαιόπολις (Pind. *P.* 8. 22), show that the name cannot mean 'Just *Citizen*'. Whether the first element in these -πολις compounds is verbal or adjectival, the second element is always 'city', not 'citizen'. If δικαιόω could mean 'to make just' (Pind. frag. 169S–M seems to be the only example), then 'Dicaeopolis' might mean 'He Who Makes the City Just'. But the analogies of such personal names as Εὔπολις, Καλλίπολις, Κλεόπολις, Νεόπολις, Ἀγαθόπολις, and others (in Dornseiff's list) suggests that the first element of 'Dicaeopolis' is adjectival, and that the name means 'He of Just City'. I shall call him 'Just City'.

'Just City' makes peace with Sparta – an act of whimsy, of puckish self-assertion, not necessarily tendentious, one might like to think. All that matters is the brief imaginative and imaginary triumph of the old farmer. His very name, however, his justification of his action, and other matters, show that far more is at stake than the supposedly private and selfish claims of the protagonist. The broader claims implicit in his private truce arise from the very poetic and dramatic means by which it is attained. In each major section of *Acharnians*, more or less the same poetic, and perhaps specifically comic, device can be found. A metaphor or figure of speech will be taken literally and reduced to the concrete.[3] Then it will be remade and given a new and better sense. This second step is intimately connected with dramatic action, sometimes only with by-play on stage, but, in the more striking cases, with the forward movement of the plot. The plot advances from the opening scene in the Assembly to geographically and temporally remote scenes – the Rural Dionysia, the house of Euripides, the trial, the private agora, the Choes; and these festivals and this new political order have issued from the unmaking and remaking of metaphor.

Acharnians, the play itself, is performed at a Dionysiac festival, the Lenaea. The dramatic performance, in carrying out the unmaking and remaking of metaphors, and in thereby creating Dionysiac festivals, is itself a metaphor for the process it describes. The play itself becomes, as it were, such a festival. The audience, through its enjoyment of the action, is thus reeducated in the metaphors that underlie the Dionysiac festival in which they are now participating as spectators. To an undoubtedly large extent, the audience's experience is a matter of identification with the protagonist, and yet the process of metaphor and dramatic action

3. Newiger (1957) has discussed this phenomenon at length, and his work is cited below more than once. As regards *Ach.*, my understanding of the phenomenon differs from his in two main ways. First, I regard it as pervasive, not occasional. Second, I regard it as not simply a comic/dramatic device, but as integral to Aristophanes' purpose, the restoration of peace. Newiger (1957) 122 provides a very useful diagram to illustrate Aristophanes' handling of metaphor. In terms of this diagram, what I add to Newiger is the notion that there should also be a system of arrows pointing from right to left, back to the subject of the metaphor; that the metaphor, once taken literally and dramatically deployed, is not dissolved, as it were, but is reconstituted, so that a sense of the reality underlying the metaphor is reawakened.

that I have adumbrated is not entirely in the hands of Dicaeopolis. Sometimes, for example, it is a matter of his making the appropriate use of what is given. As a dramatic character, he is much more complicated than is usually admitted, and it will be best to postpone discussion of this subject, even omitting, for now, an analysis of the remarkable opening monologue. I shall begin with the scenes in the Assembly immediately following the monologue, and continue through the play, commenting on its characteristic treatment of metaphor and related devices in each major section. Nothing like a full explication of each section or of the play as a whole has been attempted, and paraphrase has been kept to a minimum, since the intent of this study is to isolate a single, fundamental process, on which the action depends.

The two scenes in the Assembly are articulated by the movements of Amphitheos. He is the first to speak, or attempt to speak, in the Assembly (45–55). He is silenced in favor of the Athenian ambassadors returning from the Great King. At the end of the first scene, Dicaeopolis despatches Amphitheos to Sparta to make a private peace (129–32; cf. especially 131 with 52). In the second scene, Athenian ambassadors return from Thrace with Thracian mercenaries. Dicaeopolis causes the Assembly to be dismissed, and at the same time Amphitheos returns from Sparta with the truce (175). After Dicaeopolis accepts the longest of the truces the Spartans have offered, Amphitheos speaks the final line of the prologue and disappears, never to be seen again (203).

Most commentators followed Müller-Strübing in taking Amphitheos as a comical name for Hermogenes, son of Hipponicus, and brother of Callias.[4] In 1968, Sterling Dow showed that Amphitheos, whose name appears in an inscription on a cult-table, was an historical person, a fellow-demesman and probably an acquaintance of Aristophanes.[5] This fact is of greater consequence than might at first appear. The name Amphitheos means 'God on both sides', i.e. descended from a god on both sides. Thus the Herald greets Amphitheos' declaration of his name with derision:

4. Müller-Strübing (1873) 697–9.

5. Dow (1969) 234–5. Griffith (1974) attempts to defend Müller-Strübing's against Dow's identification of Amphitheos, and suggests that ἄνθρωπος in 46 is also a joke based on the name of a real person. There was an Olympic victor called Ἄνθρωπος in 456 B.C. (Arist. *EN* 1147b34).

'Not a mortal, eh?' (46). The Herald's scorn is the occasion for a genealogy in the Euripidean style, as Amphitheos unfolds the truth of his name (47–51).[6] The Herald assumes that Amphitheos is a lunatic and summons the police (54). But Dicaeopolis takes seriously the paratragic genealogy by which Amphitheos has asserted the literal truth of his name (47–51).[7] It is because of his belief that Dicaeopolis ventures to send Amphitheos to Sparta and thus secures a truce. He somehow knows that peace is of divine origin (cf. *Pax* 211–12). The whole action of *Acharnians* thus ensues from Dicaeopolis' taking literally the name Amphitheos.

In the first of the two scenes in the Assembly, the same sort of literalism is displayed. The Athenian ambassadors returning from Persia bring with them the King's Eye. The title is historical.[8] Aristophanes, however, dramatizes the metaphor in this official's title[9] and brings out the King's Eye in a mask covered with a single, huge eye (95–6; cf. schol.). The King's Eye, having been reduced to the eye painted on the mask, i.e., to an eye, is now remade into a new metaphor by Dicaeopolis, who takes the eye as the eye painted on the bow of a trireme. The King's Eye becomes a trireme, and the new metaphor is then extended to the nautical possibilities of the beard hanging from the mask.[10] The original metaphor implicit in the title has been unmade, reduced to the literal, and then remade. Similarly, the two eunuchs, attendants of the King's Eye, are perceived by Dicaeopolis to be Athenian effetes, Cleisthenes and Straton, in disguise. Although the nature of the by-play is not certain, Dicaeopolis apparently tears away their disguises and shows them for who they are, not Persian eunuchs but Athenians. In so doing, however, Dicaeopolis has dramatized the stock insult of barbarian effeminacy (cf. *Eq.* 1375). In showing that the two eunuchs are not eunuchs but Cleisthenes

6. On the parody of Euripides, see the commentators and Bakhuyzen (1877) 1–2. Rau (1967) 186 denies that this genealogy is paratragic.

7. Newiger (1957) 124: 'Es scheint, als hätte Aristophanes gerade Parodie mit seiner Technik der wörtlich genommenen Metapher gerne verbunden.' In fact, this combination occurs again and again in *Ach.*

8. Autran (1951) 287–91.

9. See Rennie (1909) on 94.

10. See the commentators. Although it is not exactly clear what Dicaeopolis is referring to in 97, it is clear that the trireme metaphor is being developed. *Lys.* 1072–3, which show that the mask might hang down below the waist, may shed light on this problem.

and Straton, he shows, in effect, that these two decadents are *like* eunuchs.

In the second scene, the Athenian ambassador returning from Sitalces brings with him Thracian mercenaries, who steal Dicaeopolis' garlic. Since the Assembly, in which only empty talk, *alazoneia* (63, 87, 109, 135, cf. 373) is practiced, affords him no redress, he resorts to another kind of language altogether. He asserts an omen, and causes the Assembly to disband. Hereupon Amphitheos appears (175).

In the last section of the prologue (174–203), the scene changes from the Pnyx, where the Assembly sat, to the country-side,[11] and here Dicaeopolis receives the private truce for which he sent Amphitheos to Sparta. The word for truce is σπονδαί, literally, 'libations'. Libations are made with wine. Thus the truce-offer comes to Dicaeopolis in the form of wine, and that of three ages, five, ten, and thirty years. He chooses the oldest wine, the longest truce. The truce is defined by the wine itself. What Dicaeopolis has done is to invert the synecdoche by which a truce is named after the final and consecrating element, the libation. Dicaeopolis has inverted the relation of whole and part, so that now libation has become the whole of which peace is a part. The wine of the libation becomes the very substance of peace. In 195, Dicaeopolis addresses Dionysus in accepting the thirty-year truce. This is the fourth and the central of the seven lines of his statement: ταύτας δέχομαι καὶ σπένδομαι κἀκπίομαι (199). The line is arresting, with its asyndetic opening and the parechesis of the verb-endings. The object must be understood differently with each of the three verbs: 'I accept this [truce] and I make this [libation][12] and I shall drink this [wine].'[13] The political (the truce) and the private (the drinking) are joined in the sacral (the libation). The central verb in the line is of central importance in the play as a whole. In order to fulfill his desire for a return to peace, his own estate,[14] and his own deme, Dicaeopolis must finally effect the transformation of the political into the sacral that was already intimated in his assertion of the omen (170–1), and he does so by unmaking the

11. Most commentators doubt a change of scene, but see Dover (1972) 79.
12. See Rennie (1909) on σπένδομαι.
13. For this interpretation of the line, see Newiger (1957) 52–3.
14. On the definite article in 32, see Starkie (1909).

metaphor of *spondai* into wine, and then remaking it into something else, namely, the Rural Dionysia. In the last line of his seven-line speech of acceptance, Dicaeopolis signifies his intention to celebrate this festival. It is therefore not simply as a private individual that Dicaeopolis achieves his longed-for peace with all its physical pleasures. These private pleasures are sacraments that come to him as Dionysiac celebrant.

Just after Dicaeopolis declares his acceptance of the thirty-year truce, the chorus of angry Acharnians appears on stage, in pursuit of the one who has made peace with the hated Spartans (204f.). They come upon Dicaeopolis marshalling his family and servants for the phallic procession, which will move through the crowd of fellow-demesmen (257). Here Dicaeopolis celebrates the sexual aspect of peace, which was already implicit in the pun in 198.[15] As in the case of wine-drinking, the goal of personal pleasure is mediated by a divinity. Dicaeopolis invokes Phales, the personified phallus, as the companion of Dionysus (263). Phales is invited to drink with Dicaeopolis (277–8), and in this way sexual desire is accommodated to the festival in honor of the god of wine.

The procession requires two things of Dicaeopolis. First, he must attend to the practical arrangements – the preliminary sacrifice, his daughter's carrying the basket, and the slaves' keeping the phallus upright. Second, he must sing the phallic song (261). The Dionysiac celebrant is a singer. Dicaeopolis' procession has sometimes been brought into relation with the passage in the *Poetics* (1449a f.) in which Aristotle states that comedy arose from the leaders of the phallic songs or processions (τὰ φαλλικά). Even if it is wrong to find a protocomedy in this scene in *Acharnians*,[16] it is not too much to regard Dicaeopolis as a protopoet. Just as the comic poet presents his work at a festival in honor of Dionysus – in the case of *Acharnians*, the Lenaea – so Dicaeopolis offers a song to Phales, the companion of Dionysus, as part of the Rural Dionysia. To the spectators of *Acharnians*, who are participating in a Dionysiac festival, Dicaeopolis presents in this ritual

15. In βαῖν' ὅπῃ θέλεις, the second word can be taken as a segmentation-pun, so that the dative of πέος will be heard (cf. Dickerson (1974) 181–2) and the whole will mean, 'Fuck whatever you wish with your cock.' The obscene sense of βαίνω would come from its use of the stud-function: LSJ⁹ s.v. A. II. 1.

16. So Pickard-Cambridge (1962) 134.

performance the epitome of another such festival, the Rural Dionysia.

The Acharnians interrupt the ritual (280–3). The ensuing section of the play, the parodos (284–346), reverts from the sacral to the political.[17] The question is whether the Acharnians will refrain from stoning Dicaeopolis to death and give him a hearing. ἀκούειν, λέγειν, or λόγος occurs in nearly every line (292–324). There is no escape for Dicaeopolis in this realm of language, any more than in the Assembly. The passionate Acharnians will not listen to reason.[18] Even his offer of speaking with his head on a chopping-block (317–18), which he of course means literally, is lost on the Acharnians, and he will later chide them for their indifference to this offer (352–7). He must liberate himself through metaphor, after his fashion. The first hint of his ruse comes in 321: οἷον αὖ μέλας τις ὑμῖν θυμάλωψ ἐπέζεσεν ('How your dark coal again flares up'). *Thymalops* must here mean a half-burned piece of charcoal (cf. *Thesm.* 729). There is a pun on θυμός, anger or spirit, and the verb ἐπιζέω is tragic usage for the surge of passions.[19] The pun identifies the passions of the Acharnians with their native product, charcoal. What was metaphorical, the oaken toughness of the Acharnians (180 πρίνινοι, 609 Μαριλάδη, 612 Πρινίδης; cf. frag. adesp. 75K Δρυαρνεῦ) – and oak is the wood from which charcoal is made (666) – has become literal, and, as in the case of the name Amphitheos, it is the paratragic style (here the verb just mentioned) that secures the identity of the two things which would otherwise remain merely similar. Since tragedy permits one to speak of a passion 'boiling over', it becomes possible to substitute, by means of a pun, 'ember' for 'anger', and the passion of the Acharnians becomes identical with their native product. Once Dicaeopolis has made this identification, it magically becomes binding on the Acharnians themselves. For now a charcoal-basket can serve Dicaeopolis as hostage. 'This basket is my fellow-demesman', say the chorus (333). Dicaeopolis forces them to listen to him, and returns again to wine: they are sour wine and

17. On the metrical and formal characteristics of this section, see Gelzer (1960) 157–8. This section has some affinities with the epirrhematic agon, but diverges from the type in important respects.

18. On the meters, see Rennie (1909) on 284ff.

19. For references, see Starkie (1909) *ad loc.*

he is the good wine that can be mixed half and half with water (352–7).

The portion of the play following the hostage-scene and preceding the parabasis, comprises, in the traditional terminology of scholarship, a syzygy (347–92), the proagon (393–488), and the agon (490–625), but this portion as a whole comprises a single action centering on the speech of self-defense that Dicaeopolis has been trying to deliver ever since the Acharnians first appeared. First, there are the preparations – the chopping-block (358–67) and the borrowing of the beggar's rags from Euripides (383–488). He can now deliver the ῥῆσις μακρά (416). The choral ode (490–5) just preceding this long speech resumes in several points 359–65: once again they express eager curiosity. Then the long speech (496–556) divides the chorus. The half that is not won over summons Lamachus as its champion (566–71). Dicaeopolis insults him (575–92) and restates the grievances of the opening monologue and the first two scenes of the play (593–619).

Although the construction of this entire portion of the play from line 280 up to the parabasis bears some affinity to the epirrhematic agon of a *diallage*-scene,[20] the typical agon of Old Comedy is missing in *Acharnians*, as commentators have often pointed out.[21] The reason must be that, under the historical circumstances of January 425 B.C., a debate on the subject of making peace with the Spartans – a debate between two characters, such as the typical agon presents – would have been intolerable.[22] Peace must be argued for in a more indirect manner. Aristophanes has so contrived matters that Dicaeopolis appears as a defendant at a trial (634), at which he must plead the justice of the peace he has made with Sparta. As defendant, he wishes to make a pitiable appearance (383–4), according to the custom of the Athenian law-courts (cf. Plato *Apol.* 34c).

In order to make himself pitiable, Dicaeopolis goes to Euripides to borrow the rags of Telephus, one of the tragic poet's several ragged kings (cf. *Ran.* 1063). The parody of Euripides' *Telephus*

20. See Gelzer (1960) 47–8 for the definition of *diallage* and 166–8 on this portion of *Ach.*

21. The solution of Russo (1953) 172–82 is simply to expand the definition of agon so as to include this part of *Ach.*

22. So Mazon (1904) 25–6; Starkie (1909) on 496ff.

that was implicit in the hostage-scene and in the use of the chopping-block[23] now becomes explicit in the costume, in the long speech, and perhaps also in the entry of Lamachus following the speech.[24] The *Telephus* of 438 B.C. was Aristophanes' favorite butt. He parodied it more often and more fully than any other Euripidean tragedy, taking over whole scenes from it in both *Acharnians* and *Thesmophoriazusae*.[25] Paratragedy in Aristophanes is not simply polemical and not simply a laugh-getting device but has different purposes in different places.[26] The parody of the *Telephus* in *Acharnians*, at any rate, serves a particular dramatic purpose, replacing as it does the typical agon. The rags and other accoutrements of Telephus (the conceit of the trial and the defendant's rags is dropped) are a disguise.

But before Dicaeopolis adopts this disguise he sheds another. Having brought out the chopping-block (and having thus rendered literal the figure of speech in *Tel.* frag. 706N²), and being now about to give his speech of self-defense, he hesitates, and he explains his fear of the old rustics who are going to judge him (370–6). As an example of their litigiousness (375–6, cf. 630), he cites his own experience (377–82). At this point, Dicaeopolis identifies himself as Aristophanes. As the scholiast in the Ravenna manuscript says: ὡς ἀπὸ τοῦ προσώπου τοῦ ποιητοῦ ὁ λόγος. It is not necessary to assume that Aristophanes played the role of Dicaeopolis,[27] only that Dicaeopolis speaks for him.[28] There can be no doubt about the true identity of Dicaeopolis, for he speaks in the person of Aristophanes once again in 496–508, and for a third time, I believe, in 885–7. Although it is hardly unusual for a character in Aristophanic comedy to overstep the boundaries of his role and address the audience directly, these are the only places in extant comedies of Aristophanes in which a character speaks for the poet. Elsewhere this function belongs exclusively to the chorus in the parabasis (cf. however, Ar. frag. 471K).

Dicaeopolis, 'Just City', proves to be Aristophanes, the comic poet. Just as the metaphorical name of Amphitheos was taken

23. Rau (1967) 27–8.
24. Rau (1967) 40 thinks not.
25. Rau (1967) 19–50; Miller (1948) 174–83.
26. Rau (1967) 182–4.
27. On this question, see Bailey (1936) 231–40.
28. de Ste Croix (1972) 363–7 has argued well against Dover (1963) 15 on this matter.

literally, so that the real Amphitheos, Aristophanes' fellow-demesman, became the magical agent of peace, so here, inversely, the name Dicaeopolis ceases to be that of a dramatic character and is claimed as his own title by the comic poet. In effect, Aristophanes makes the assertion that 'the Just City is really I, the comic poet'. As he will say when he again asserts the true identity of Dicaeopolis, 'Comedy, too, knows justice (τὸ δίκαιον). I shall say what is terrible but just (δίκαια)' (500–1). The justice of the comic poet is thematic (317, 406, 561–2, 645, 655, 661, cf. *Eq.* 510). Once 'Just City' is revealed as the comic poet, he can be remade into something else, namely, Telephus. In the mode of paratragedy, the comic poet can be what he is, while seeming something else (441), and can assert the justice of his cause.

Why must Aristophanes 'be who in fact I am' (441) in order to argue his case? First of all, Aristophanes has a personal reason for identifying Dicaeopolis as himself and for the burlesque of the *Telephus*. In his comedy of the previous year, *Babylonians*, Aristophanes had criticized Athens' treatment of its allies, and he had done so at the City Dionysia, when foreigners were present. Cleon 'indicted him for wrongdoing (ἀδικίας) against the citizens, as if he had written these things as an act of outrage against the Boule' (schol.). It is apropos of this indictment that Dicaeopolis is revealed as Aristophanes (377–82). Dicaeopolis refers to it a second time when he again speaks in the person of Aristophanes (502–3, cf. 630–1, 659–60). Aristophanes anticipates and removes the possibility of a similar charge (502–8), something he could not have done through Dicaeopolis speaking in character.

Furthermore, having revealed himself behind Dicaeopolis, Aristophanes can divide the chorus from the audience. From the point of view of Dicaeopolis, the chorus is the Acharnians; from the point of view of Aristophanes, it is simply the chorus (443 χορευτάς). The audience (442 θεατάς) is enticed by means of this long, delightful scene at the house of Euripides (395–479) to consent to the division. The bellicose and anti-Spartan passions of the Acharnians are now separated from the audience, and the paratragic play-within-the-play insulates the justification of peace with Sparta, which might otherwise be offensive, no matter how laughably presented. The audience, which has thus been 'distanced' from the dramatic situation, is also freer to accept the ensuing division of the chorus and the partial victory of Dicaeopolis. In sum, when Dicaeopolis as it were unmasks himself, and Aristophanes then, before the very eyes of the audience, dons the rags of Telephus, a new drama is created. The question of peace is transposed into a new sphere. What was to have been a trial according to the Acharnians' expectations (364 δίκην) becomes something else. Once again Dicaeopolis, or Aristophanes, has left the hostile political milieu behind in order to make a political statement.

Aristophanes has another purpose, too, in speaking as 'who in fact I am' (441). What would have been impossible for Dicaeopolis speaking in character is natural for Aristophanes: to make assertions about the nature of comic poetry. The word that Aristophanes uses for comedy in this passage is τρυγῳδία (499, 500, cf. 886, *Vesp.* 650–1, 1537) instead of the more usual κωμῳδία, and perhaps with a play on τραγῳδία, a term just heard at the house of Euripides (400, 411, 465). τρυγῳδία comes from τρύξ, raw wine or lees of wine, and ᾠδή, song. It is not clear which sense of τρύξ is to be understood in the compound, but it is clear that for Aristophanes comedy is in some sense wine-song. Thus in asserting the claim of comedy to counsel the city (499, cf. *Ran.* 686–7), in asserting comedy's knowledge of justice (500), Aristophanes has this special understanding of comedy in mind: comedy as wine-song. Paradoxically, the political function of comedy rests on its association with wine. This conclusion appears less paradoxical, however, when one remembers that Aristophanes has already dramatized the same point. Dicaeopolis, 'Just City', makes peace with Sparta. Peace is wine. Wine is the occasion of festivals in honor of Dionysus. These festivals include poetic forms of celebrating Dionysus – in Dicaeopolis' case, there was the song in honor of Dionysus' companion, Phales. Peace, which began as a political issue, is finally achieved by the Dionysiac celebrant. 'Just City' is the Dionysiac celebrant. When Aristophanes then asserts the didactic, political claim of wine-song, in a statement prefatory to the *rhesis* justifying peace with Sparta, he has only stated more directly what has already been enacted by Dicaeopolis.

More directly, but still indirectly, for Aristophanes has donned the rags of Telephus. He begins the passage on wine-song thus:

Bear me no grude, spectators, if, a beggar,
I dare to speak before the Athenian people
About the city in a Comic Play (τρυγῳδία).[29]

Of these three lines, the first two are largely a quotation from the *Telephus* (frag. 703N²). The third line introduces the polis as the subject of the speech, with the admission of making a wine-song. In virtue of the paratragedy, he speaks as the beggar Telephus. Aristophanes thus in these three lines conflates the function of the comic poet and the role of nobleman disguised as beggar. This conflation shows why the parody of the *Telephus*, of this Euripidean tragedy in particular, was chosen to replace the typical agon. The nobleman disguised as beggar is the fitting image of comedy. Although comedy comes before the people with a just claim and with a didactic mission, it can do so only in disguise. The dilemma of comedy vis à vis the Athenians is summed up by the half of the chorus which is not persuaded by the *rhesis*: 'Even if what he says is just, ought a beggar to have said it?' (562, cf. 558).

The *rhesis* is one of the best known passages in Aristophanes, not for any specifically Aristophanic qualities, but because of its reference to Megarean decrees.[30] For this reason, it has been, with *Pax* 606–11, central in the continuing discussion of the origins of the Peloponnesian War.[31] Yet Aristophanes has not set out to make a statement about these origins. He, or rather Dicaeopolis, since Aristophanes recedes into the character of Dicaeopolis at the beginning of the speech (509–12), is defending the justice of his truce with Sparta (cf. 317). The truce is just if the Spartans are the offended party (cf. 310, 313–14, 356, 369, 482). It is for this reason that Dicaeopolis argues that the Athenians started the war (515 ἡμῶν γὰρ ἄνδρες); that they did so for trivial and ludicrous reasons; that the Spartans were naturally provoked by the Megarean decree; that the Athenians would have reacted the same way with even less provocation. The principal cause of the war was the rape of the Megarean prostitute Simaetha by drunken cottabus-players, which provoked the retaliatory rape of two of Aspasia's prostitutes by the enraged Megareans (524–9). Dicaeopolis implies that it was only to satisfy the grievance of his mistress,

29. 496–8. The translation is that of Rogers (1910).
30. Apparently 517–22 and 523–38 refer to two different decrees.
31. See de Ste Croix (1972) 231–44; cf. Kagan (1969) 254–5.

Aspasia, that Pericles, the 'Olympian', passed the Megarean decree that became the *casus belli*. The 'Olympian' acted like Zeus himself, who caused the deaths of thousands of Greeks and Trojans to satisfy Achilles' grievance concerning the seizure of his concubine, Briseis. Parody of Homer is not impossible. Parody of Herodotus 1. 1–5 in the account of the mutual rapes is quite certain, parody, that is, within parody.[32] The formal argument[33] is only the occasion for the characteristic devices of *trygodia*, by which political issues are transposed into some other realm. Here the parody of Herodotus is a way of transposing the question of 'war-guilt' into an absurd and meaningless series of events, so that the Athenian grievances are shown for what they really are, vacuous. The conclusion of the *rhesis* uses another device of *trygodia*. Dicaeopolis argues that if the Spartans had done something similar, something far less provocative, the Athenians would have launched three hundred ships, and the city would have been full of —. The next six lines (546–651) contain nothing but genitives and genitival constructions depending upon 'full of' and describing preparations for war. The proposition that 'the city would have been full of —' is thus not simply stated but is rendered as concrete as possible by the accumulation of genitives. So far as possible, words become things. This device is like the treatment of metaphor already observed in several places, in that comedy concretizes or exposes a meaning which is obscure or perverted or lost in ordinary discourse, as, for example, the meaning of peace is lost in the *alazoneia* of the Assembly.

The *rhesis* is successful enough to win over half the chorus.[34] The unpersuaded half summons Lamachus as its champion. With his opening words, paratragic or perhaps para-Homeric,[35] he becomes the *miles gloriosus*, just as Amphitheos was transformed by paratragic genealogy from a mortal into a divine emissary. Perhaps it was the very name, Lamachus (λα- intensive + μαχ- 'battle') which

32. Seel (1960) 31f. on *Ach.* 578ff. as parody of *Il.* 6. 467ff. C. W. Fornara, 'Evidence for the Date of Herodotus' Publication', *JHS* 91 (1971) 25–34 at 28 suggests that in *Ach.* 523–9 the parody is of the *Telephus* rather than of Herodotus. He points out (pp. 28–9) that parody of Herodotus in Aristophanes (e.g. *Av.* 1124–38) is much more obvious.

33. On which see Murphy (1938) 101–4.

34. On the division of the chorus, see Gelzer (1970) col. 1422.

35. See Rennie (1909) on 573, 574, 575 and van Leeuwen (1901) on 574.

caused him to be chosen for this role.[36] If so, the comparison with Amphitheos is even closer: the implicit metaphor of the name is taken literally and dramatized by parodistic style. It is as a type, then, and as the representative of certain attitudes, and not as the historical person, that Dicaeopolis attacks Lamachus.[37] When he appears on stage, Lamachus is also extravagantly costumed as this type, and Dicaeopolis borrows a feather from his crest in order to vomit into his shield (584–7). Dicaeopolis thus makes literal (586) the figurative nausea inspired in him by Athenian politics, the nausea which caused him to make his private truce (599). Like the hostile half of the chorus, Lamachus rebukes Dicaeopolis as a beggar (578, 594), and now Dicaeopolis throws off the rags of Telephus and reveals himself as πολίτης χρηστός, 'a good citizen' (595). He further identifies himself as such by the comic patronymic στρατωνίδης, Son of a Gun (596). His ilk have done the fighting,[38] while Lamachus and his have been profiteering in the various military and ambassadorial offices created by the war (597–619). As the scene ends, Lamachus vows undying hostility to the Peloponnesians (620–2) and Dicaeopolis announces his intention to open a market to the Peloponnesians, Megareans and Boeotians, to them but not to Lamachus.[39] Dicaeopolis thus in effect rescinds the decree which had closed the markets of the Athenian empire to the Megareans (533, 535) and which he had named as the cause of the war. Since it is useless to be a just citizen in the Athens of Lamachus, Dicaeopolis must become, with his truce (cf. 599) and now with his agora, a city unto himself. He has now taken his own name literally, just as he had done with the names Amphitheos and Lamachus.

In the anapests, the parabasis (626–718) does not contain the characteristic devices of comedy that have been observed heretofore. Yet the anapests in themselves constitute such a device. The chorus says in the kommation: ἀλλ' ἀποδύντες τοῖς ἀναπαί-

36. So Bruns (1896) 153–4 and Larsen (1946) 93–4 suggest.

37. Gelzer (1970) col. 1423; Bruns (1896) 152–4. The comment of Graves (1905) on 619 is worth quoting as an example of a still prevalent sort of misreading of Aristophanes: 'this imputation of greed and favouritism is grossly unjust to Lamachus...'

38. Gelzer (1970) col. 1423.

39. I follow the interpretation of the syntax of the dative in 625 given by Rogers (1910).

στοις ἐπίωμεν (627). Whether ἀποδύντες, 'stripping', is literal, of removing the himation, or whether it is metaphorical,[40] the chorus is doffing its persona in order to speak for the comic poet, just as Dicaeopolis has already done. And the anapests continue themes that Dicaeopolis/Aristophanes has already broached: the justice of the poet (645, 655, 661) and the didactic value of his poetry (633–5, 641–2, 646–51, 655–6). The anapests use again the unusual term for comedy, this time in its adjectival form, τρυγικός (628, cf. 655). In short, the anapests themselves constitute one of those transformations of which *Acharnians* has already provided notable examples.

In the epirrhema, the antode, and the antepirrhema, the chorus speaks in character as old men on the plight of old men (cf. 179–80, 210–20, 600–1, 610)[41] but they do not speak as Acharnians any longer. In fact, the words for 'Acharnian' are not heard again after the parabasis, as the chorus' persona is generalized to that of old farmers.[42] It is in the ode that the chorus speaks as Acharnians for the last time, invoking the fiery Acharnian muse, which they pray to come like a spark springing from oaken charcoal (665–75). The ode is the conventional invocation hymn usually found in the epirrhematic syzygy.[43] This hymn invites the gods or the muse to join the chorus or the festival.[44] The intent of such invocations is made clear in *Knights* 581–94, where Pallas is invoked to come with Victory (cf. *Eq.* 586 λαβοῦσα with *Ach.* 675). So in the ode in *Acharnians* the chorus is asking for the inspiration that will bring victory. The subject of the invocation is, however, unusual. The Acharnians invoke the Acharnian muse, which is of the same nature with themselves. This muse is compared with a spark (667); Dicaeopolis has compared the Acharnians' spirit with an ember flaring up (321). The spark springs from charcoal made of oak (666); the Acharnians themselves are oaken (180, 612, and the hostage-scene). The simile is developed: the charcoal fire from which the spark springs is the scene of preparations for a rural feast. Amongst other things, a Thasian sauce is being prepared. The

40. On this question, see Dale (1969) 289–90; Sifakis (1971) 103–8.

41. Note that the antode exceptionally continues the theme of the epirrhema, as Dover (1972) 51 points out.

42. Sifakis (1971) 28–9.

43. Sifakis (1971) 41–4.

44. The Muse is invoked or addressed in *Pax* 774–92, 815; *Ran.* 675–85; *Av.* 737–51; cf. frag. 334K.

sauce is called 'of bright fillet' (671). This is Pindar's epithet for Mnemosyne, the mother of the Muses (*N.* 7. 15). This echo of Pindar implies an analogue in the scene described in the simile: the mother of the Acharnian muse is the rural festival. Hence springs the spark of song, and, in its implicit prayer for victory in this ode, the chorus asks for 'a more rustic song' (674, reading ἀγροικότερον). The success of the comedy, *Acharnians*, will be the victory of the poetry that arises from the rural festival, such a festival as Dicaeopolis has already celebrated as his first act of peace, and this is the poetry of peace.

In the part of the play following the parabasis (719–end), the triumphant Dicaeopolis celebrates the peace he has won. Resuming what he has said just before the parabasis (623–5), he opens a market to the Peloponnesians, Boeotians and Megareans. This is poetic, or comic, justice, since it was, in Dicaeopolis' view, the closing of the markets to the Megareans that had brought on the war. Dicaeopolis' market is closed to Lamachus (722), i.e. to the hawks, and of course to sycophants (725–6). 'Just City' has at last contrived a just city, which, with its international market, has all the advantages of Athens herself, but which for the rest is presumably identical with the rural deme to which he has returned. This one aspect of the larger polis is retained in his just city because the just city requires various imported delicacies as the accoutrements of festivals.

In the two symmetrical scenes following the parabasis (729–835, 860–958), Dicaeopolis enlarges the material foundations of peace in food and sex. These are material pleasures, but, like wine, they are also sacraments, as will soon appear. Dicaeopolis' means of establishing and running his market are a free and joyous exercise of the peculiar powers already demonstrated in the Assembly and in the face of the hostile Acharnians. To establish the agora, he creates aediles out of three leather straps (724). If this line is to be explained from the fact that the aediles carried straps, then it is a matter of synecdoche, not of a simply rhetorical sort, but also, as usual, practical. By this fancy, the action is carried along.[45]

45. Similarly, the ὅροι (719) may well be some objects already on stage, which become boundary-stones when Dicaeopolis names them so. See the observations of Newiger (1957) 125.

It is fitting that a Megarean, from a city starving to death because of Athens (535), should be the first to approach Dicaeopolis' market.[46] The Megarean, as an act of kindness to his daughters (734, 742–3), offers them for sale to Dicaeopolis, after disguising them as pigs with hooves and snouts and putting them in a sack (740–5). The Megarean offers them first of all as sacrificial victims for the Mysteries (747, 764). They would thus be a suitable contribution to the new sacral and gustatory state of things. Dicaeopolis sees through the disguise, however; these are human females (cf. 774). The word for pig that Dicaeopolis and the Megarean have used up to now is χοῖρος, 'piglet' (as distinguished from δέλφαξ, 'sow'), which is also slang for the female genitals.[47] Thus Dicaeopolis can say of one of the girls – he is being pressed to agree that she is a pig – '*Now* she appears to be a piggy (χοῖρος), but when she's grown up, she'll be a – cunt' (781–2).[48] Dicaeopolis then objects that she is unsuitable as a sacrificial victim because she lacks a tail.[49] The Megarean assures him that when she grows up, she'll have a large, thick red one (786–7). Since Dicaeopolis is now scrutinizing the genitals of the girls, it is possible that 'tail' here stands for clitoris,[50] although the usual obscene sense refers to the male member.[51] The Megarean goes on to promise, in language that suggests the growth of pubic hair,[52] that this piggy will be an excellent sacrifice to Aphrodite. Dicaeopolis, now affecting to take 'piggy' literally, objects that pigs are not sacrificed to Aphrodite. Of course they are, says the Megarean, and the flesh of these pigs is sweetest fixed on the spit (795–6).[53] The image makes it clear once for all what the sacrifice is and what the dish is. The transposition of food into sex is continued in 801 in the obscene sense of 'chickpea'[54] and in the double entendre

46. For an explication of this scene, see Dover (1972) 63–6.

47. Taillardat (1962) 75; Henderson (1975) 131–2; Radermacher (1940) 236–8.

48. Dicaeopolis uses κύσθος, which is what Henderson (1975) 35 calls a 'primary obscenity'. For this type of joke ἐκ τοῦ παρὰ προσδοκίαν see Starkie (1909) lxvii–lxviii.

49. On the importance of the tail, see Starkie (1909) on 785.

50. N.b. 789, cf. *Lys.* 87–9, and Vaio (1973) 379 n. 48 on the costume of Diallage (*Lys.* 1114ff.) – 'exaggerated female σωμάτια with painted genitals'.

51. Taillardat (1962) sect. 98; Henderson (1975) 128.

52. Henderson (1975) 136.

53. On the obscene image, see Henderson (1975) 170.

54. Henderson (1975) 116, 119, 143.

of the Megarean's closing words. He tells his daughters to eat their bread with salt, but his words also mean 'bang your cunnus against the phallus' (835).[55]

The fate of the girls in this scene corresponds to the development of the central image of the play. Peace can come only through a truce. 'Truce' is literally 'libation', and libation is wine. Peace thus comes to Dicaeopolis in its literal form, as wine, and Dicaeopolis then uses the wine for the libation and drinking at the Rural Dionysia. Similarly, the girls are at first only disguised as pigs and are pretended victims for Demeter and Kore. They are reduced to their literal humanity by Dicaeopolis and then remade and reconsecrated as pigs in the sense of *cunni*. As such, they will be sacrifices to Aphrodite and will have a role to play in the city of peace, the just city. One recalls the hopes of Dicaeopolis for his own daughter, expressed on the occasion of the Rural Dionysia (254–6).

The two scenes following the parabasis are separated by a stasimon (836–59) in which the chorus enumerates various undesirables who are excluded from Dicaeopolis' agora. The negative, selfish aspect of the just city has already been proclaimed in the prohibition of Lamachus (625, 722) and will be more fully developed later. After the stasimon, there appears a Boeotian, the personification of Boeotia, with his flutes[56] and with every conceivable Boeotian export (871, 873–6, 878–80). Dicaeopolis begs leave to address the Copaic eels, the favorite Athenian delicacy (881–2, cf. *Pax* 1003–5, *Lys.* 35–6). His paratragic tone (in 882) is continued in the Boeotian's reply, which parodies Aeschylus (frag. 174N²) in summoning 'the chief of the Copaic maidens' to come forth and oblige Dicaeopolis. In 'oblige', in certain words in Dicaeopolis' address to this maiden[57] and finally in his parody of Euripides' *Alcestis* (893–4, cf. *Alc.* 367–8)[58] the reception of the eel takes on an erotic overtone. This sexualization

55. Henderson (1973) 289–90.

56. See Rennie (1909) and Starkie (1909) *ad loc.* on the flute as the national instrument of Boeotia.

57. With the Boeotian's ἐπιχαρίζομαι Starkie (1909) *ad loc.* compares *Eq.* 517. Cf. LSJ⁹ s.v. χαρίζω I. 3. Dicaeopolis uses ποθέω (885, 890) and ποθεινός (886). For an erotic sense of the former, see Theoc. 12. 2; of the latter, Xen. *Lac.* I. 5.

58. With 893–4, cf. Eubulus, frag. 64K, where the image of a maiden clad in beet also appears.

of food obviously corresponds to the development of the preceding scene; but the implied union of Dicaeopolis and the eel has a further meaning. As previously, Dicaeopolis drops his persona and speaks as Aristophanes. He addresses the eel as 'longed for by comic choruses (τρυγῳδικοῖς χοροῖς)' (886). The adjective 'comic' recalls the other places in which Dicaeopolis spoke as Aristophanes (499–500, cf. 628 in the parabasis). It is Aristophanes who gives instructions for the eel to be taken inside (893), where she will be part of the banquet provided by the choregus after the performance.[59] The pleasures of the peace secured by Dicaeopolis and the victory of the comic poet's 'wine-song' come together in the paratragic image of the eel-maiden.

Dicaeopolis takes the eel as a market-tax and then arranges a price for the rest of the Boeotian's merchandise. It is a matter of trading something which Athens has but Boeotia lacks (900). Dicaeopolis has an inspiration: a sycophant wrapped up like pottery (904–5). The Boeotian likes this idea, because he can exhibit the sycophant as a curiosity, like a monkey.[60] Dicaeopolis' simile (a sycophant is like a pot: 904–5, 927–8) is the basis of a lyric intermezzo sung by him and the chorus as they wrap up the sycophant. This creature sounds like a cracked pot (932–4, 940–2) and is the container of various ills (936–9). Dicaeopolis' feat of simile and metaphor thus rids the agora of its plague and foists it on Boeotia. There is apparently some selfish cynicism in this (956–8). The just city is not necessarily just toward other cities.[61]

Just as the Boeotian departs, the servant of Lamachus appears. Lamachus bids Dicaeopolis sell him some thrushes and a Copaic eel for the celebration of the Festival of the Pitchers (Choes) (960–2). Dicaeopolis' brief exchange with the servant, which concludes the scene, serves three purposes. First, it announces the change in the temporal setting to the time of the Festival of the Pitchers in early March, whereas the Rural Dionysia took place in December. Second, Dicaeopolis reasserts the selfishness (especially 969–70) already noticed. Finally, his refusal of Lamachus prepares for the scene laid before the houses of Dicaeopolis and Lamachus in which the one prepares for a banquet and the other

59. So Rennie (1909) on 886, I believe correctly.
60. So Rennie (1909) on 906.
61. Cf. Plato *Rep.* 422a4–423b4, with Bloom (1968) 371–2.

for a campaign (1071–1142). Dicaeopolis' refusal to sell any of his goods to Lamachus is a preliminary indication that their positions are absolutely irreconcilable (cf. 1144).

There follows a song (971–99).[62] The main point of ode and antode (971–5, 987–99) is to felicitate Dicaeopolis on the advantages he has gained through his truce (974 σπεισάμενος). The antithesis of war and peace already adumbrated in the opposition of Dicaeopolis to Lamachus is expressed in the personification of War, the drunken guest who disrupts the banquet, burns up the vine-stakes and pours the wine out of the – vines (979–87). The cutting down of the vines by the invading Spartans was a particular grievance of the Acharnians, as Dicaeopolis well knew (512). This grievance is not simply economic, however. Since Dicaeopolis has made peace through a truce in the radical sense, through wine, and since Aristophanes speaking through Dicaeopolis has defined comedy as wine-song, the characterization of War as the enemy of wine and of the vine implies the charge that War is the enemy of the festival, of the sacral basis of the pleasures of peace. Peace is the goddess 'most loving of the vine' (*Pax* 307, cf. 520, 596–7, 706–8) because the vine is the very foundation of peace in its sacral aspect. Thus the chorus here in this song addresses Reconciliation, i.e. the truce secured by Dicaeopolis, as the foster-sister of Aphrodite and the Graces. The pleasures associated with Aphrodite and the Graces can flourish only in peace, and peace is, as Dicaeopolis has shown, wine. The scholiast in the Ravenna manuscript comments: 'That peace is dear to Aphrodite and the Graces is well said, because marriages and festivals take place upon the occasion of peace.'

Even the fertility of the land under peace is conceived in sacral terms. The persona of the chorus, the old man, still has the virility to take Reconciliation (cf. *Pax* 336), and he would even 'bang out' two rows of vine, cultivated and uncultivated, a row of fig shoots, and olive trees in a circle all around (994–9). With the oil from the olives he and she will annoint themselves on festival days (999). The union of Trygaeus and Opora in *Pax*, the union of the old man and Reconciliation, is the union of a mortal and a divinity. The mythological type of this *hieros gamos* is the union of Demeter

62. It is sometimes referred to as the second parabasis, incorrectly. See Rennie (1909) on 971–99; Gelzer (1970) col. 1426.

and the hero Iasion (Homer, *Od.* 5. 125–8; Hesiod, *Theog.* 969–74). From this example and from comparative evidence, it is clear that this sacred marriage is in origin a fertility ritual, designed to promote the growth of the crops.[63] In Athens there was a ritual marriage of the wife of the Archon Basileus with Dionysus.[64] This ritual took place during the night after the second day of the Anthesteria, which was called the Pitchers.[65] Immediately following this passage, in which the old man desires to unite with Reconciliation, the Pitchers is proclaimed (1000–2).

This festival is dramatized in two scenes (1003–68, 1069–1149), and then, following a stasimon (1150–73), in the exodus (1174f.). In the first scene, the eccyclema reveals the interior of Dicaeopolis' house,[66] where women and servants under his supervision are preparing a feast and plaiting crowns.[67] These preparations are twice interrupted, once by a farmer and then again by a bridesmaid and groomsman. The rebuff of the farmer, who only wants to have his eyes salved with peace, since he has worn them out weeping for the oxen that the Boeotians drove off, has seemed mere selfishness on Dicaeopolis' part. Dicaeopolis' motives are not selfish, however. As soon as the farmer identifies himself as an ἀνὴρ κακοδαίμων, Dicaeopolis says, κατὰ σεαυτόν νυν τρέπου (1019 = *Nub.* 1263) – 'Keep your misfortune to yourself.'[68] He means to avert the bad omen of the farmer's misfortune, to preserve the proprieties of the festival day. The principle is *procul este profani!*, just as in his agora, which aimed to do justice to the Peloponnesians, Megareans and Boeotians, Dicaeopolis would not do business with a representative of the Athenian war-party (966–70, cf. 620–2).

The chorus believes that Dicaeopolis would not give a share of his private peace to anyone (1036–9), but the advent of the bridesmaid and the groomsman proves them wrong. Each makes the same request, but in different terms (1052, 1060). Dicaeopolis'

63. See Frazer (1911) 97ff. and, for bibliography, Schwabl (1967).
64. Hesychius, s.v. Διονύσου γάμος; Arist. *Ath. Pol.* 3. 5; Dem. 59. 73.
65. In assigning the marriage to this night, I have followed Burkert (1972) 258.
66. On the eccyclema, which rolls back in at 1096, see Dale (1969) 291–2 and Dover (1972) 84.
67. On the importance of crowns at the Pitchers, see Burkert (1972) 255–6.
68. So Starkie (1909) *ad loc.*

refusal of the first request, the groom's, conveyed by the groomsman, is a foil for his acceptance of the second, the bride's, conveyed by the bridesmaid. The bride's request has the merit of being laughable (1058) and thus can win over Dicaeopolis. She earnestly begs him ὅπως ἂν οἰκουρῇ τὸ πέος τοῦ νυμφίου (1060) – 'that the bridegroom's member guard the house (or: stay at home)'. What is laughable here is the use of the tragic word οἰκουρέω with πέος as subject, and perhaps also, depending on how the actor pronounced the word, a pun on οὐρέω, 'urinate'. Dicaeopolis is also moved by the consideration that 'she is a woman and unable to bear the ills of war' (1062).[69] In so far as marriage is integral to peace, as the *hieros gamos* of Reconciliation and the old man implies, Dicaeopolis must acknowledge the bride's request. Again one recalls the hopes of Dicaeopolis for his own daughter (254–6).[70]

In the second scene, two messengers arrive. One brings marching orders to Lamachus, who is thus prevented from participating in the Pitchers (1071–83). The other summons Dicaeopolis to a feast at the house of the priest of Dionysus (1084–94; cf. *Ran.* 297). The eccyclema now rolls back (1095) and the scene is laid before the houses of Lamachus and Dicaeopolis. The one prepares for guard-duty in the mountains, the other for the feast. In this way, the antithesis between war and peace, on which the whole of the play after the parabasis is built – an antithesis already prepared in the appearance of Lamachus just before the parabasis – is brought into sharper form.

The preparations consist mainly of orders given by Lamachus and Dicaeopolis to their servants, who are to bring one thing or another from their respective houses, or to help their master in some way. The exchanges between the two are mostly in stichomythia, which gives even sharper point to the antithesis, and take

69. This is the translation of Rennie (1909) *ad loc.*, reading ἀξία of the MSS. See also Elliott (1914) 175–6 and latterly Erbse (1954) 88: digna non est quae hac peste vexetur. The adjective could also be interpreted to mean 'not deserving of the war': LSJ[9] s.v. ἄξιος II. 2 and Graves (1905) *ad loc.*

70. Consider Newiger (1975) 189 on *Lys.* (for translation, see below, p. 233): 'Die Sehnsucht nach den Frauen – und damit nach dem Frieden – ist allerdings tiefer angelegt, als man gemeinhin erkannt hat, denn es handelt sich um die eigenen Ehefrauen, und die Sehnsucht is gegenseitig, so daß dieses tolldreiste Stück geradezu eine Beschwörung der ehelichen Liebe und Lebensgemeinschaft ist.'

the form of mockery of Lamachus by Dicaeopolis. The technique of the mockery is clearly displayed in the opening exchange:

> Λα. παῖ παῖ φέρ' ἔξω δεῦρο τὸν γυλιὸν ἐμοί.
> Δι. παῖ παῖ φέρ' ἔξω δεῦρο τὴν κίστην ἐμοί.
> Boy, bring me out my soldier's knapsack here.
> Boy, bring me out my supper-basket here.[71]

Dicaeopolis, while preserving the form of Lamachus' command, substitutes a culinary for a military term. By this travesty, the martial is transfigured into the peaceful, the grim into the joyous. Towards the end of their exchanges, Lamachus calls for his breastplate, Dicaeopolis for his pitcher (1132–3). They continue:

> Λα. ἐν τῷδε πρὸς τοὺς πολεμίους θωρήξομαι.
> Δι. ἐν τῷδε πρὸς τοὺς συμπότας θωρήξομαι.
> With this I'll arm myself against the foe.
> With this I'll warm myself against the feast.[72]

Dicaeopolis plays on the secondary meaning of θωρύσσεσθαι, 'fortify with drink'. His pitcher is the breastplate with which he defends himself, just as the bridegroom's member was to be the weapon with which he would guard his house. Dicaeopolis here alludes to the drinking contest at the Pitchers, which the herald has already proclaimed (1000–2), and in which Dicaeopolis will be the victor (1203, 1224–5). Dicaeopolis transforms martial struggle into the peaceful ritual competition of the drinking contest. The travesty on which the whole exchange between Dicaeopolis and Lamachus rests corresponds to what, we are told, are the historical–psychological dynamics of the Pitchers. The drinking contest, the central ritual of this festival day, has the character of a solemn blood-sacrifice, and even retains some of the formal traits of such a sacrifice; yet the ritual has been transmuted into a fundamentally joyous one, as this passage in *Acharnians* shows clearly enough.[73]

71. 1097–8. The translation is that of Rogers (1910).
72. The translation is that of Rogers (1910).
73. I refer here to the argument of Burkert (1972) 236–69. On the underlying somberness of the drinking ritual, see especially 244, 254. One can object that Burkert's description of the drinking-contest is colored by his analysis of the ritual in terms of the 'Jäger-Opfer-Komplex' (256), i.e., that he tends to confuse the historical-psychological dynamics of the ritual with its actual mood. If it really

After Lamachus and Dicaeopolis depart on their 'unlike paths' (1144), the chorus sings a song cursing a certain Antimachus who had failed to provide a feast for the chorus when he was a producer at the Lenaea (1150–73).[74] The allusion is obscure in most respects but it is at least clear that Antimachus had omitted an obligatory and important part of the festival. Against the background of the Pitchers and Dicaeopolis' feast, Antimachus must appear especially contemptible. The curse corresponds to the chorus' earlier 'banishment' of undesirables from the agora (836–59), and to Dicaeopolis' exportation of the sycophant. It is a matter of purifying the ritual atmosphere.[75]

The exodos begins with a parody of a Euripidean messenger-speech.[76] The servant of Lamachus calls for water and bandages, and describes the wounds of his master. Then the wounded hero is brought on stage, again in tragic style.[77] Lamachus' opening 'speech' is reminiscent of the dying Hippolytus (1190–7, cf. Eur. *Hipp.* 1347–52). Dicaeopolis' mocking reply is antistrophical, and his replies continue to correspond metrically to Lamachus' lines, though Dicaeopolis' sentiments and diction are comic, Lamachus' tragical. The antithesis between their positions is now even more sharply stated; on the one side, the pain of Lamachus, wounded by a vine-pole,[78] on the other, the pleasure of the revelling Dicaeopolis. In the first encounter, it was Dicaeopolis the banqueter against Lamachus the soldier. Now, in the exodos, Dicaeopolis transposes into sexual terms all the suffering of Lamachus. Finally, Lamachus asks to be carried off to the doctors; and Dicaeopolis asks to be taken to the judges and to the Archon Basileus, the presiding official of the Pitchers, and he demands the wine-skin

was an dismal as Burkert suggests (n.b. 254: 'so begegnet man im Unheimlichen dem Heiligen'), the end of *Ach.* would flagrantly contradict the audience's experience of the Choes. Such a contradiction would have defeated Aristophanes' purpose. In his discussion of the association of wine and blood (248–50), Burkert omits what may be the most direct fifth-century evidence: the oath scene in *Lys.* 181–239. The sacrifice of the dark red Thasian wine is a parody of a blood-sacrifice (n.b. 196).

74. I follow the interpretation of the passage by Rennie (1909); cf. Dover (1963) 23.

75. Perhaps the chorus speaks here in the spirit of θύραζε Κῆρες/Κᾶρες. See Burkert (1972) 250–5 on the expulsion of unwelcome guests from the festival.

76. See Rennie (1909) on 1174. 77. See Starkie (1909) on 1174ff.

78. 1190. Cf. Henderson (1975) 62.

he has won (1222–5). His lines are ambiguous: the Archon Basileus was also the presiding official at the Lenaea, at which *Acharnians* was performed. The judges are those of the Pitchers but also those of the comic competition.[79] Dicaeopolis appropriates the victory chant sung to Heracles and Olympic victors (1227–34, cf. Archil. frag. 120D³, Pindar, *Ol.* 9. 1–2). The ultimate prize, then, is the wine-skin, and the ultimate victory is in the ritual drinking contest, and, because of the ambiguity of 1222–5, these become metaphors for the success of the poet himself, the success of the wine-song. In this way, the ritual basis of the comedy itself is reasserted and restored, and the place of comedy in the festival, in this case, the Lenaea, is reconsecrated.

The ambiguity of the lines of Dicaeopolis just mentioned also gives a glimpse once again of the comic poet behind the dramatic character. Indeed, Dicaeopolis never was the dramatic representation of a person, and the intervention of Aristophanes does not constitute a rupture of characterization any more than the parabasis ruptures 'dramatic illusion'. There is no 'dramatic illusion' in the first place,[80] nor is there any portrayal of a unique, individual character. Who is Dicaeopolis after all? Consider his opening monologue. It contains poetic (23 οὐδ'; 5 κέαρ), neologistic (9 τραγῳδικόν), and paratragic (27 ὦ πόλις πόλις, cf. Soph. *OT* 629; 8 ἄξιον γὰρ 'Ελλάδι, cf. Eur. *Tel.* frag. 720N²) usages. Furthermore, colloquialism (12, 24 πῶς δοκεῖς) and items of diction shared by poetry and Ionic prose, which may reflect the older, spoken Attic of an old (1129) farmer (2 βαιά, 10 ἐγανώθην, 29 νοστῶν).[81] Dicaeopolis wears a verbal motley that is not the costume of a particular person.[82]

79. Rennie (1909) on 1224 states: 'The nominal reference is to the judges in the drinking-contest and to the Archon Basileus as the President of the Anthesteria. The real reference is to the judges in the dramatic competition and to the Archon Basileus as the President of the Lenaea.'

80. Sifakis (1971) 7–14.

81. On these matters, see Dover (1970) 7–23. The diagram is an amplification of his observations, too. For further development of Dover's observations see now H. Diller, 'Zum Umgang des Aristophanes mit der Sprache – erläutert an den *Acharnern*', *Hermes* 106 (1978) 509ff.

82. Cf. Bruns (1896) 149; Dicaeopolis is not the 'Wiedergabe eines wirklichen Menschen'. The similarities between the opening monologues of Dicaeopolis and of Strepsiades in *Nub.* (Gordziejew (1938) 331–4) might suggest that to some extent Dicaeopolis is presented as a comic *type*.

Finally, one must consider the almost categorical fashion in which Aristophanes has composed the opening monologue (see the diagram, p. 33). He has laid out the sentences in units of two and four lines (first column of diagram). In the speaker's mood, there is a sharp alternation between pleasure and pain (second column), which is emphasized by the repetition of aorist passives and the καρδία-expressions (1, 12). The subject alternates between poetry and politics (fourth column). The opening monologue as a whole is in the form of a priamel. All the pleasures and pains of the first sixteen lines are simply foils to one greatest pain, which is the failure of the Assembly to concern itself with peace (17–27). The extraordinary formality of this composition, taken with the varied stylistic traits already mentioned, does nothing to characterize Dicaeopolis as a unique individual whose desire for peace has some individualistic basis. On the contrary, Aristophanes presents the character of Dicaeopolis in such a way that it already embodies the principal antithesis of pleasure and pain, from which peace will emerge. The escape from the political circumstances indicated in the monologue and dramatized in the two succeeding scenes, and the creation of a new order of things by 'Just City' – these are a feat of poetry, of the peculiar capacities of wine-song, and not simply individual self-assertion. Politics is transfigured through poetry, and in thus elaborating the poetry of politics, Dicaeopolis also secures a victory for the politics of poetry, which are peace. All the passivity of the opening lines is left behind, and the antithesis of pain and pleasure, at first insulated in the passivity of Dicaeopolis, is objectified in the clash with Lamachus, in which it attains ever more precise form. In the exodos, the wounded Lamachus embodies pain, and Dicaeopolis, full of wine and bound for an erotic night, embodies pleasure, and pleasure triumphs.

Dicaeopolis is also characterized as a type in the opening monologue by his very assertions. He describes himself as

ἀποβλέπων ἐς τὸν ἀγρὸν εἰρήνης ἐρῶν,
στυγῶν μὲν ἄστυ τὸν δ' ἐμὸν δῆμον ποθῶν

with my eyes fixed wistfully upon my farm and my heart hungering for Peace; abhorring the city, and home-sick for my own country parish.[83]

83. 32–3. The translation is that of Starkie (1909).

He is one of those who have been forced to move into the city, which he loathes (cf. *Eq.* 805–7, 1394–5; *Pax* 536, 552, 563, 569). Thucydides has given a sympathetic description of this type, a description that has implications for the understanding of the character of Dicaeopolis:

Thus for a long time the Athenians partook of a free way of life in the country, and after they were united in a single city, still most of them, the old-timers and their descendants, down to the time of this war, customarily were born and lived on their farms (ἐν τοῖς ἀγροῖς, cf. *Ach.* 32). Reluctantly did they move their whole households, especially since they had just restored their property after the Persian Wars. They were aggrieved, and they took it hard, leaving behind them their houses (οἰκίας) and the ancestral shrines (or rites: ἱερά) which had been theirs continually from the time of the ancient constitution. They were about to change their way of life (δίαιταν), each of them leaving behind what was, in effect, his own city (πόλιν).[84]

Dicaeopolis returns to the country, he celebrates the Rural Dionysia with his family, and restores his former way of life. Each of the main regrets singled out by Thucydides is a prime concern of Dicaeopolis, who thus conforms to Thucydides' general description. Dicaeopolis' desires are not unique but reflect the plight of a whole segment of the Athenian population.

In securing his private peace and returning to his deme, he even recovers, in Thucydides' phrase, 'what was, in effect, his own city'. And it is implicit in his name that this is the just city, since he is 'Just City'. Can Aristophanes mean that Dicaeopolis' return to his deme and his activities there constitute a just city? What is the justice of such a city? The scene of the Rural Dionysia shows that it consists merely of the immediately family; even the demesmen are barely noticed, as the crowd through which the family procession passes (257). The extreme narrowness of this 'city' is shown in the conditions of Dicaeopolis' agora. The main purpose of this 'city', furthermore, seems to be eating, sex, and the drunken worship of Dionysus. Is it possible that Aristophanes is suggesting that this is the just city?

The outrageousness of this possibility is somewhat palliated by a passage in the *Republic*. It is a description of a city, the first in the

84. 2. 16, cf. 2. 14. 2–15. 1, 65. 2. The translation is based on that of Jowett (1900).

series of cities conjured up by Socrates, Glaucon and Adeimantus. This first city is called by Socrates the most essential city (369d10 ἀναγκαιοτάτη), the true city or the city of truth (372e6 ἀληθινή) and the healthy city (372e7 ὑγιής), and he describes it thus:

They will feed on barley meal and flour of wheat, baking and kneading them, making noble cakes and loaves; these they will serve up on a mat of reeds or on clean leaves, themselves reclining the while upon beds strewn with yew or myrtle. And they and their children will feast, drinking of the wine which they had made, and hymning the praises of the gods, in happy converse with one another.[85]

The scene resembles that of the Rural Dionysia celebrated by Dicaeopolis – the family, wine, praise of the gods. For Plato, this is not the just city but the most essential one. For Aristophanes, it is conceivable that this is indeed the just city. Although in the fourth century justice became a specifically human virtue,[86] there is an earlier and well-attested sense of δίκαιος, 'just', and that is 'righteous', 'observant of duties to gods and men'.[87] In the fifth century, Sparta was known for being just in this sense, and, indeed, juster to gods than to men. Herodotus characterized this city in an oft-quoted apophthegm: τὰ γὰρ τοῦ θεοῦ πρεσβύτερα ἐποιεῦντο ἢ τὰ τῶν ἀνδρῶν (5. 63. 2, cf. 9. 7. 1). This was the city that would return home to celebrate a religious festival in preference to following up a victory,[88] but which practised justice towards other cities only if it coincided with her self-interest (cf. the Athenians' comment at Thuc. 5. 105. 4). The just city secured by the private truce of 'Just City' is similarly characterized by a narrow piety, specifically Dionysiac, and by self-interestedness. The primary aim of Dicaeopolis' new order of things, which is founded on the Dionysiac sacrament, is to celebrate the Dionysiac festival. It is to preserve the piety of this order that Dicaeopolis is selfish. His selfishness, in terms of the play, is primarily the result of pious justice, and only an ethic external to the presuppositions of the play can find fault with him. It would be odd if Aristophanes had

85. 372b1–8. The translation is that of Jowett (1881).

86. I.e., justice became the social and political virtue *par excellence*; see Aristotle, *EN* 1129b14–1130a13.

87. LSJ⁹ s.v. δίκαιος A. 2. Consider Homer, *Od.* 3. 52 and context.

88. Whereas, according to the Corinthians, Athenians consider a festival nothing but the discharge of duty: Thuc. 1. 70. 8. Cf. Edmunds (1975) 93.

portrayed as morally reprehensible a protagonist named 'Just City' whose goals are clearly Aristophanes' own.[89] One can observe in passing that it would be no less odd if this protagonist had been portrayed so as to represent the individual as against the city. The whole humor of the play – and the whole serious point of the play – is that *pro virili parte* Dicaeopolis impersonates the city.[90]

It might be objected that the agora of Dicaeopolis has nothing to do with the requirements of piety, and that the selfishness and cynicism displayed here deserve to be judged as such. This agora is, however, integral to the scheme of piety defined by the two festivals, the Rural Dionysia and the Pitchers. The latter includes feasting, which requires the delicacies imported by Dicaeopolis. Lamachus wanted to buy thrushes and a Copaic eel to celebrate the Pitchers (960–2). This agora simply furnishes the material prerequisites of Dionysiac piety, while at the same time doing justice to those who had been excluded by the war. The two scenes laid in the agora are concerned the one with sex and the other mainly with food: these are the imports. The two Pitchers scenes with Lamachus at the end of the play are concerned the one with sex and the other with food. Only pedantry would demand that the two girls with whom Dicaeopolis will spend the night after the Pitchers be the Megarean's two daughters or that the food for his feast be exactly the food brought by the Boeotian. It is enough that the scenes in the agora have shown what was required by the pious justice of Dicaeopolis.

When Aristophanes names his protagonist Dicaeopolis and dramatizes the name to show what the Just City would do, his

89. Dover (1963) 21–2 and (1972) 87–8 is mistaken.

90. Therefore the 'city' achieved by 'Just City' is most precarious, and, in this regard, critics are right to speak of fantasy, etc. apropos of Dicaeopolis. The type of comedy represented by *Ach.* is the second type defined by Hegel (1971) 315 (= C. III. 3. a. β. ββ). (This section of Hegel (312–17) must be read if one is not to be misled by what he later says (337–41) concerning subjectivity in Old Comedy.) On the tendency to personification in the heroes of Aristophanes, consider this statement by Newiger (1957) 108: 'die komischen Hauptfiguren vieler Stücke sind Menschen, Personen immer nur in dem höheren Sinne, daß sie zugleich Träger and Vollzieher eines Gedankens sind. Sie sind zweifellos viel "symbolischer", viel stärker erdachte Wesen allen Helden des Epos und der Tragödie; anders gesagt: ihre Idee steht ihnen deutlicher im Gesicht geschrieben.'

purpose is to argue the case for peace. The Just City is the city at peace. Aristophanes' contemporary Athens, the city at war, will of course appear only in the worst light. The contrast between the two cities is presented especially in terms of language. The city at war is a city of *alazoneia*, sycophancy, ludicrous decrees, and malicious dicastic rhetoric (676–718), whereas *trygodia*, wine-song, which knows what justice is (500), returns to a plain sense of the fundamental metaphors – wine is Dionysus, love is Aphrodite (794, cf. *Lys.* 551–4, 833–4, 888–9, 1290). These are the foundation of the city, Aristophanes seems to claim.

Has Aristophanes been just to his contemporary Athens, the city at war? Even granting the exigencies of comedy, one may well wonder. At any rate, this city does not lack its own eloquent defender. The Thucydidean Pericles, in the Funeral Oration, describes an Athens 'most self-sufficient both for war and peace' (2. 63. 3). It is this principle of self-sufficiency which most distinguishes Pericles from a Dicaeopolis (cf. 2. 60. 2–4), for the self-sufficiency of the polis entails the primacy of the polis.[91] The individual should feel that he is first and foremost a citizen, and should freely choose the city's ends as embodying his own highest purposes.[92] The primacy of the city is thus, in modern terms, a secular principle, and is implicitly opposed to the sacral, private concerns of a Dicaeopolis, for whom the city is not self-sufficient but rests on transpolitical or infrapolitical grounds.

To compare Dicaeopolis and the Thucydidean Pericles may seem like trying to go Aristophanes one better, but the comparison will in fact help to bring the concerns underlying *Acharnians* into sharper focus. The main concerns of Dicaeopolis in seeking peace with Sparta are food and drink, sex, and the festivals. What does Pericles have to say on these matters? Although he, like Dicaeopolis, frames his understanding of festivals in terms of the antithesis between pain and pleasure, he paradoxically associates the pleasures of festivals with *gnome* (2. 38. 1). For Dicaeopolis, the pleasures of festivals are of course physical. In the Funeral Oration, the varied imports that Dicaeopolis brought back to Athens – or to some Athenians – are simply examples of the greatness of the city (2. 38. 2). Pericles regards food under a strictly political aspect,

91. Edmunds (1975) 76–88.
92. See Hegel (1923) 599–615 on Greek democracy.

just as Thucydides himself observes: 'In peace and prosperity both states and individuals are actuated by higher motives, because they do not fall under the dominion of imperious necessities; but war, which takes away the comfortable provision of daily life, is a hard master and tends to assimilate men's characters to their conditions.'[93] There is not the slightest consideration of the fact, so clearly dramatized by Aristophanes, that food and drink are also sacramental.

What of eros? Again Pericles is paradoxical. The citizens should become lovers (ἐραστάς) of the city (2. 43. 1).[94] The private goals of eros, those sacrifices to Aphrodite on which Dicaeopolis is bent when last seen, are implicitly denied. From the political and military perspective of the *History* as a whole,[95] eros can appear only as something negative, as in the excursus on Harmodius and Aristogeiton (6. 54–60).[96]

The basis of Pericles' consistently political view of festivals, food and drink, and eros is the notion that the city is a perfect conjunction of private and political. 'The same men have a care for private and political matters at the same time, and the rest, who are tending to their own affairs,[97] have no deficient understanding of politics. We alone consider the one who takes no share in politics not as unmeddlesome but as useless...' (2. 40 .2). Aristophanes doubts such a conjunction. He believes in the *apragmon* scorned by Pericles (cf. 2. 63. 2–3, 64. 4). For Aristophanes, the piety of the *apragmon* constitutes the true city, on which the city praised by Pericles rests. Yet such are the difficulties of reading Aristophanes and such are the charms of Thucydides that the historian's account of Athens now prevails, and the Athens known to Dicaeopolis is most obscure to us. From a sophisticated

93. 3. 82. 2, cf. 2. 65. 2, 4. 62. 2. The translation is that of Jowett (1900). Cf. Edmunds (1975) 96 n. 10.

94. Cf. *Ach.* 143 and context, where Aristophanes makes fun of the notion of loving a city.

95. Thucydides' perspective is clearly revealed in his aside at 5. 60. 3, where he says that the army of the Lacedaemonians and their allies was the κάλλιστον of Greek armies up to this time. With this aside, compare Sappho frag. 16. 1–4, where the fairest thing (κάλλιστον) on earth is not an army but that which one loves.

96. On Thucydides' judgment on the 'rash undertaking' of Harmodius and Aristogeiton, see Edmunds (1975) 194–5.

97. For this interpretation of the Greek, see Edmunds (1972).

twentieth-century perspective, 'the Greek polis', i.e. Athens, was the home of civic and military pursuits.[98] The Athenian would issue forth from the obscurity of the household into the bright light of the political arena, there to compete for honor and fame. Privacy had only a privative meaning. Intelligence, energy and the moral virtues necessary to success in politics and war were admired. To this concept of Athens, which derives in some measure from Thucydides, there is allied another, which is equally remote from and antagonistic to Aristophanes', and this is of Athens as the birth-place of tragedy. The Athenians held a 'tragic view of life'. Although this view has never been defined in such a way as to secure general agreement, we are content that the Athenians were preoccupied with the doomed but ennobling exertions of heroic personages. At any rate, a comic view of life is not ascribed to fifth-century Athens.

In *Acharnians*, in the figure of Dicaeopolis, Aristophanes has shown another Athens, which differs profoundly from the two related Athenses presently most familiar to us. Aristophanes has shown that in the midst of the city at war there is the city of peace, the righteous city, which is characterized by its privacy, its devotion to family and locale, and to the festivals.[99] In the festivals, in which the objects of private desires are transmuted into sacraments,[100] the city is regenerated, and for this reason the 'city' achieved by 'Just City' is the essential city. Ultimately the city survives not through military victory but through its righteousness, through the festivals of regeneration. Comedy has a special place in the larger city, since it restores the essential city. Comedy is wine-song, and, as such, it has the peculiar power to reinvigorate the central metaphor of the festival: wine is Dionysus.

98. Arendt (1958) 24–37, 192–9.

99. For this complex of interests, cf. Thuc. 7. 69. 2, where men going into battle are exhorted to remember their wives, children and ancestral gods.

100. Cf. Eliade (1958) 31: 'Indeed one of the major differences separating people of the early cultures from people to-day is precisely the utter incapacity of the latter to live their organic life (particularly as regards sex and nutrition) as a sacrament.' On the religious value of food, see Eliade (1963) 43 and n. 6.

The composition of the opening monologue

	Sentence type	Mood	Repetition	Subject
1	exclamation a	a pain	δεδήγμαι...καρδίαν	unspecified
2	continuation b	b pleasure	ἥσθην	
3	continuation b	a pain	ὠδυνήθην	
4	question a	b pleasure	ἥσθην	
5–6	answer	pleasure b	ηὐφράνθην	politics (Cleon)
7–8	exclamation		ἐγανώθην	
9–12	assertion ending in question (12)	pain a	ὠδυνήθην	poetry
			ἔσεισε...καρδίαν	
13–14	assertion	pleasure b	ἥσθην	poetry
15–16	assertion	pain a	διεστράφην	
17–39	priamel			politics
		18	ἐδήχθην	

Bibliography

Arendt, Hannah (1958). *The Human Condition.* Chicago.
Autran, C. (1951). 'L'œil du roi', *Humanitas* 3, 287–91.
Bailey, C. (1936). 'Who Played Dicaeopolis?', in *Greek Poetry and Life*, Essays presented to Gilbert Murray on his seventieth birthday, 231–40. Oxford.
Bakhuyzen, W. H. van de Sande (1877). *De parodia in comoediis Aristophanis.* Utrecht.
Beyle, Marie-Henri (de Stendhal) (1926). *The Red and the Black*, trans. C. K. S. Moncrieff. The Modern Library: New York.
Bloom, Allan (1968). *The Republic of Plato.* New York and London.
Bruns, Ivo (1896). *Das literarische Porträt der Griechen im fünften und vierten Jahrhundert.* Berlin.
Burkert, Walter (1972). *Homo Necans: Interpretationen altgriechischer Opferriten und Mythen. Religionsgeschichtliche Versuche und Vorarbeiten*, ed. Walter Burkert and Carsten Colpe, 32. Berlin and New York.
Dale, A. M. (1969). *Collected Papers.* Cambridge.
Dickerson, G. W. (1974). 'Aristophanes' *Ranae* 862', *HSCP*, 177–88.
Dornseiff, F. and B. Hansen (1957). *Rückläufiges Wörterbuch der griechischen Eigennamen.* Berichte über die Verhandlungen der sachsischen Akademie der Wissenschaft zu Leipzig, Phil.-hist. Kl. 102, 4. Berlin.
Dover, K. J. (1963). 'Notes on Aristophanes' Acharnians', *Maia* 15, 6–25.
Dover, K. J. (1970). 'Lo stile di Aristofane', *Quaderni Urbinati di Cultura Classica* 9, 7–23 = 'Der Stil des Aristophanes', in *Aristophanes und die alte Komödie*, ed. H.-J. Newiger (Darmstadt 1975) 124ff.
Dover, K. J. (1972) *Aristophanic Comedy.* Berkeley and Los Angeles.
Dow, Sterling (1969). 'Some Athenians in Aristophanes', *American Journal of Archaeology* 73, 234–5.
Edmunds, L. (1972). 'Thucydides ii. 40. 2', *CR* NS 22, 171–2.
Edmunds, L. (1975). *Chance and Intelligence in Thucydides.* Cambridge, Mass.
Eliade, Mircea (1959). *Patterns in Comparative Religion.* Repr. as a Meridian Book, New York, 1963.
Eliade, Mircea (1963). *Myth and Reality.* New York and Evanston.
Elliott, Richard T. (1914). *The Acharnians of Aristophanes.* Oxford.
Erbse, H. (1954). 'Zu Aristophanes', *Eranos* 52, 76–104.
Frazer, J. G. (1911). *The Golden Bough*³, Part I: The Magic Art and the Evolution of Kings, vol. 2. London.

Gelzer, Thomas (1960). *Der Epirrhematische Agon bei Aristophanes. Zetemata* 23. Munich.
Gelzer, Thomas (1970). 'Aristophanes', in *RE*, Suppl. vol. 12, cols. 1392–1569.
Gordziejew, V. (1938). 'De prologo Acharnensium', *Eos* 39, 321–50, 449–76.
Graves, C. E. (1905). *Aristophanes: The Acharnians.* Cambridge.
Griffith, J. G. (1974). 'Amphitheos and Anthropos', *Hermes* 102, 367–9.
Hegel, G. W. F. (1923). *Vorlesungen über die Philosophie der Weltgeschichte*, vol. 2, ed. G. Lasson. Leipzig.
Hegel, G. W. F. (1971). *Vorlesungen über die Ästhetik*, Part 3 (Die Poesie), ed. R. Bübner. Stuttgart.
Henderson, Jeffrey (1973). 'A Note on Aristophanes *Acharnians* 834–5', *CP* 68, 289–90.
Henderson, Jeffrey (1975). *The Maculate Muse.* New Haven and London.
Jowett, B. (1881). *The Republic of Plato²*. Oxford.
Jowett, B. (1900). *Thucydides²*. 2 vols. Oxford.
Kagan, Donald (1969). *The Outbreak of the Peloponnesian War.* Ithaca and London.
Larsen, J. A. O. (1946). 'The *Acharnians* and the Pay of Taxiarchs', *CP* 41, 91–8.
van Leeuwen, J. (1901). *Aristophanis Acharnenses.* Leiden.
Mazon, Paul (1904). *Essai sur la composition des comédies d'Aristophane.* Paris.
Miller, Harold W. (1948). 'Euripides' *Telephus* and the *Thesmophoriazusae* of Aristophanes', *CP* 43, 174–83.
Müller-Strübing, Hermann (1873). *Aristophanes und die historische Kritik.* Leipzig.
Murphy, C. T. (1938). 'Aristophanes and the Art of Rhetoric', *HSCP* 49, 69–113.
Newiger, Hans-Joachim (1957). *Metapher und Allegorie. Zetemata* 16. Munich.
Newiger, Hans-Joachim (1975). 'Krieg und Frieden in der Komödie des Aristophanes', in ΔΩΡΗΜΑ *: Hans Diller zum 70. Geburtstag.* Griechische Humanistische Gesellschaft: ZR: Studien und Untersuchungen, 27. Athens. [Translated in this volume, pp. 219ff.]
Pickard-Cambridge, A. (1962). *Dithyramb, Tragedy and Comedy*, rev. T. B. L. Webster. Oxford.
Radermacher, L. (1940). 'Χοῖρος Mädchen?' *RM* 89, 236–8.
Rau, Peter (1967). *Paratragodia: Untersuchungen einer komischen Form Aristophanes. Zetemata* 45. Munich.
Rennie, W. (1909). *The Acharnians of Aristophanes.* London.
Rogers, Benjamin B. (1910). *The Comedies of Aristophanes*, vol. I (I. The Acharnians; II. The Knights). London.
Russo, Carlo F. (1953). *Aristofane: Gli Acarnesi.* Bari.
Schwabl, Hans (1967). 'Hieros Gamos', in *Der Kleine Pauly*, vol. 2, ed. K. Ziegler and W. Southeimer, cols. 1139–41.

Seel, Otto (1960). *Aristophanes oder Versuch über Komödie*. Stuttgart.
Sifakis, G. M. (1971). *Parabasis and Animal Chorus*. London.
Starkie, W. J. M. (1909). *The Acharnians of Aristophanes*. London.
de Ste Croix, G. E. M. (1972). *The Origins of the Peloponnesian War*. London.
Taillardat, Jean (1962). *Les images d'Aristophane*. Paris.
Vaio, John (1973). 'The Manipulation of Theme and Action in Aristophanes' *Lysistrata*', *GRBS* 14, 369–80.

Appendix

Several notes on individual lines and passages in *Ach.* have appeared since the time of the survey provided by K. J. Dover, 'Aristophanes 1938–1955', *Lustrum* (1957), vol. 2, 52–112. These notes are summarized in this appendix.

13–14 Manfred Landfester, 'Aristoph. Ach. 13f.', *RM* NF 113 (1970) 93–4: in 13, μόσχῳ is not a proper name. ἐπί here should be understood on the analogy of λέγειν ἐπί τινι. Translate: 'er sang ein boiotisches Lied auf ein bzw. das Kalb'.

63 Victor Coulon, 'Beiträge zur Interpretation des Aristophanes', *RM* NF 105 (1962) 11–12: no peacocks are brought on stage; cf. H. Weber, *Aristophanische Studien* (Leipzig 1908) and Starkie *ad loc.* Dicaeopolis simply associates peacocks with ambassadors sent to Persia.

68–9 Coulon 12: 'παρὰ in R und διὰ in AΓ sind von Erklärern zum Text hinzugefügt worden und dann in den Vers eingedrungen.' On the local genitive, Coulon cites his discussion in *REG* 43 (1930) 60–1.

70 Denys Page, 'Some Emendations in Aristophanes' Acharnians', *WS* 69 (1956) 116–17: for μαλθακῶς read μάλα κακῶς. K. J. Dover, 'Notes on Aristophanes' *Acharnians*', *Maia* 15 (1963) 6: μαλθακῶς should not be emended. The envoy's statement blends complaint with pleasurable reminiscence.

Coulon 12–13: ἐφ' ἁρμαμαξῶν is to be construed with κατακείμενοι.

78 Coulon 13: retain καταφαγεῖν, contrary to Morell. The proceleusmatic (τα δυναμε) is sound (cf. H. J. Newiger, *Hermes* 89 (1961) 175, who questions this and the other supposed proceleusmatics in Aristophanes.) In this phrase (καταφαγεῖν καὶ πιεῖν), the preverb of the first verb should be understood with the second verb. (For more examples, see Robert Renehan, *Greek Textual Criticism* (Cambridge, Mass. 1969) 84–5 and *Studies in Greek Texts* (Göttingen 1976: Hypomnemata 43) 62.)

82 Coulon 13–14: The scholiast's ὄρος δὲ ἀμίς is incorrect. For the Persian mountains of gold, see Weber, *op. cit.* (on 63), 19, who cites Plautus, *Mil.* 4. 2. 73 and Varro at Nonius, p. 379.

83–4 Coulon 14–15: for the genitive, see Weber, *op. cit.* (on 63), 21 and van Leeuwen on *Eq.* 1079; Eupolis, *Marikas* fr. 181 (= Plut. *Nik.* 4); for the juxtaposition of genitive and dative of time, see Hdt.

2. 47. 10. τῇ πανσελήνῳ should be assigned to Dicaeopolis, not to the ambassador. The expression is proverbial for 'never'. Cf. 'am Sankt Nimmerleinstag', 'tous les 36 du mois', and ἡ 'Ακεσαίου σελήνη (Herond. 3. 61, Zenobius).

95 Page 117–19: for βλέπεις read βλέπων, and set the phrase off with commas.

100 K. J. Dover 7–8: read 'Ιαρτα ναμα Ξαρξαα or Ξαρξαια or Ξαρξασα πυσσα σατρα, meaning 'Iarta by name, son of Xerxes, satrap'.

111 Dover 8–9: τουτονί must be Dicaeopolis' stick.

158 Dover 12–13: this line refers to circumcision, even though the Thracians did not practice circumcision. It was something the Greeks found comical, and 'in the case of the Odomantians Aristophanes used an established humorous device to emphasize their barbarous character'.

228f. Page 119–20: for τῶν ἐμῶν χωρίων, read τῶν ⟨τ'⟩ ἐμῶν χωρίων.

271–5 Dover 13–14: cf. Priapos and Theocr. 5. 116f.

338–9 Page 120–1: for τε, read γε. For τῷ, read χῷ.

344–6 Dover 14: σειστός means what it does in Hellenistic and Byzantine Greek: 'pendant', 'feminine ornaments'. 'The chorus gyrate and make their cloaks...fly out and come to rest hanging down, in front or behind, like useless pendants.'

341–7 E. K. Borthwick, 'Three Notes on the "Acharnians"', *Mnem.* 20 (1967) 409: 'as the chorus twirled around, some concealed stones *did* fly out from the folds of their cloaks and...σειστός alludes to the vocabulary of dice-throwing'. 'ὅδε γε (346) does not even refer to τρίβων as generally supposed'; rather, sc. λίθος.

348 Dover 14: Παρνάσ(σ)ιοι may not be corrupt; Aristophanes may have coined it 'on the analogy of the equally unexpected Φυλή/Φυλάσιοι (1028)'.

377–8 and 501–2 Dover 15: the first person here is 'I, the comic hero' or 'I, the comic protagonist'. (Cf. n. 28 above.)

393–4 Hugh Lloyd-Jones, 'Aristophanes, *Acharnians* 393–4', *CR* NS 8 (1958) 15: for ἆρά μοι R or ἤδη ΑΓS, read ἁρμοῖ, meaning 'now'.

446 Dover 15–16: for the dative, cf. Dem. 23. 50.

483 Alan H. Sommerstein, 'Notes on Aristophanes' *Acharnians*', *CQ* 28 (1978) 383ff. γραμμή at 483 means 'goal' not 'starting line'.

501–2 See on 377–8.

523–9 See Fornara, cited in n. 32 above.

530–1 Dover 16: these lines refer not to Pericles' oratorical technique but to his Olympian anger.

578ff. Seel, cited in n. 32 above: these lines are a parody of *Il.* 6. 467ff.

593 M. V. Molitor, 'Aristophanes, *Acharnians* 593 and 1073–4', *CR* NS 19 (1969) 141: in 425/4 B.C. the election of *strategoi* may have taken place, exceptionally, before the Lenaea, at which *Ach.* was performed. 'It is...possible...that Aristophanes meant to represent Lamachus...as *strategos*-elect who, because he had not

yet been officially installed in office, was still in fact subject to the orders of the *strategoi* then in office.'

Nan V. Dunbar, 'Three Notes on Aristophanes', *CR* NS 20 (1970) 269–70: line 593 does not prove anything about the status of Lamachus. κελεύειν in 1073 does not necessarily imply that Lamachus was not a *strategos*. On the basis of these passages, nothing can be concluded about the date of Lamachus' election.

709 E. K. Borthwick, 'Aristophanes, *Acharnians* 709: An Old Crux, A New Solution', *BICS* 17 (1970) 107–10: read οὐδ' ἂν αὐτὸν Ἀρταχαίην ῥᾳδίως ἠνέσχετο. This is the Artachaies of Hdt. 7. 117.

731–2 Dover 17–18: from these lines, it can be inferred that initial and intervocalic digamma had disappeared from the dialect of Megara by 425 B.C.; loss of postconsonantal digamma in καλός, ξένος, μόνος was 'the norm throughout much of the Greek mainland'. But κόριχον retained a long first syllable.

775 Dover 18: the infinitive ending is not Boeotian, but Lesbian; and the form as a whole is nowhere attested. Aristophanes is 'concocting a bizarre form'.

777 Page 121–2: for the MSS' χοιρίδιον read χοίρινον: '"Quick, you, give us a pig-squeal."'

830–1 Page 122–3: for χοιρίδι' ἀπέδου, read χοιρι' ἀπεδίδους.

832–3 Page 123–4: in 833, read πολυχαρμοσύνη for πολυπραγμοσύνη and assign this and the next word to the Megarian. Dicaeopolis' reply begins with ἐς.

Dover 19: 'The joke...turns upon the fact that in the latter part of the fifth century πολυπραγμοσύνη or πολλὰ πράττειν in the sense "interference with the internal affairs and interrelations of other states" was a well-known reproach against Athens... Dicaeopolis apologizes gracefully for his interference...'

834–5 See Henderson, cited in n. 55 above.

868 Dover 19–20: accept Elmsley's Θείβαθε.

893 Borthwick (1967) 411–12: the reading of R (ἔκφερ') is correct and is used here in the sense, 'carry out a corpse for burial'.

905 Dover 20–1: 'σιώ is a distortion in transmission caused by the familiarity of the Spartan oath'; θ>σ is not Boeotian but Laconian.

910–11 Dover 21: read Θείβαθε (cf. on 868) and interpret ἵττω as ϝίττω.

965 Sommerstein: a dig at Lamachus for having given his son the archaic warrior-name Tydeus (*IG* II². 1556. 30), cf. A. *Sept.* 384.

1003ff. Sommerstein: the eccyclema comes out at 1003 with Dicaeopolis, his slaves and the banquet paraphernalia; at 1003–6 Dicaeopolis calls back into the house for other slaves who do not appear; then he does cooking himself, speaking with various visitors while he does so. At 1096 the house is closed up, the paraphernalia withdrawn on the platform and the relationship of 'inside' and 'outside' returns to normal. It is highly probable that the eccyclema was used also in a similar scene in *Birds* (1579).

1018ff. Dover 21–2: 'The dominant element in Dicaeopolis is a selfishness so pure that it exists only in fictional characters; he is the real hero of popular comedy, through whom the spectator vicariously escapes from duties and discomforts and commitments and takes refuge in a world of fantasy...'

1065ff. Dover 22–3: 'In telling the bride to take a course of action which will naturally tempt the bridegroom to stay at home... Dicaeopolis models his instructions on those of a magician or quack-doctor.'

1073–4 See on 593.

1078–84 Coulon 15–16: 1078–9 should not be divided between Lamachus and Dicaeopolis; both should, with Elmsley and ΑΓ, be assigned to Lamachus.

1095 Sommerstein: a lacuna must be posited before 1095 (with an unpublished suggestion by D. S. Robertson). καὶ γάρ means 'yes, for you likewise...' (a colloquial usage found elsewhere in Aristophanes and in Euripides). Sommerstein suggests for the missing line e.g. ⟨ὡς μεγάλα περιβάλλει με δυστυχήματα⟩.

1096 Coulon 16: for σύγκλῃε, read, with Willems, *Aristophane*, vol. I (1919) 70, n. 4 and H. van Herwerden, *Vindiciae Aristophaneae* (Leyden 1906) 13, σὺ κλᾶ'.

1154ff. Dover 23: 'ἐμέ means "me, the comic choreutes"'; that choreutes and the choreutes of *Ach.* are not necessarily the same.

1168–72 Borthwick (1967): with the missile which hits not its intended victim but someone else, cf. Homer, *Il.* 4. 489f.; 13. 518f. 'This theme, with variations, occurs also at 8. 311; 11. 233; 13. 605; 15. 430; 23. 865.'

1174–88 Page 125–7: it is probable that these lines 'are indeed the work of an alien hand'.

A. M. Dale, 'A Heroic End', *BICS* 8 (1961) 47–8: in 1181–3, πτίλον is the subject of the verb. The following speech is made by the feather, not by Lamachus.

Dover 23–5: the last three lines of this passage can be made theatrically acceptable by exaggerated miming; the difficulty often felt in 1181 is illusory; 1182 is the real problem. Dale's solution could be accepted if the line were not suspect on other grounds. Our present 1182 may represent a gloss that has ousted the original line.

M. L. West, 'Aristophanes, *Acharnians* 1178–86', *CR* NS 21 (1971) 157–8: as for ἐξήγειρεν in 1181, 'the truth is probably that scribal memory has brought the verb back in place of some word like ἐξέτριψεν (Dobree), ἐξέκρουσεν, or...ἐξεκοττάβισ''. In 1182, for πεσών, read Weber's (*op. cit.* on 63) κλάσας. In 1185, read λείπω φάος καὶ θυμόν.

1178–89 Sommerstein translates, 'The man's been wounded by a stake in jumping over a trench, and wrenched his ankle backwards and put it out of joint, and broken his head falling on a stone, and woken up the Gorgon from her sleep on his shield. And (when he saw) the great feather had fallen (out of his helmet) onto the rocks, he intoned a terrible cry: "My glorious treasure, now I look upon you for the last time and leave you, the light of my life. I am no more." These were his words when he fell in a ditch; then he rose and came face to face with his fleeing men as he "chased and repelled the raiders with his spear". Here he is. Open the door!' Details: 1181 is genuine and comically repeats 574. 1182: read πεσὸν; κομπολακύθου is a gloss. Perhaps πτίλον δὲ τὸ μέγ' ⟨ὡς εἶδεν ἐκ κράνους⟩ πεσόν. 1184f.: addressed by Lamachus to his feather. 1186f. πεσών is subordinate to λέξας: Lamachus made his speech after having fallen into the ditch (1178); δραπέταις refers to Lamachus' own routed troops. 1188 is a tragic quotation ludicrously unsuited to its immediate context.

1208–9 Page 124–5: for τί με σὺ read τί μ' οὐ (*bis*).

Dover 25: Dicaeopolis' question is not really a question, but a kind of teasing, by which he pretends surprise when they do what he has told them to do.

Aristophanes and Socrates on learning practical wisdom

MARTHA NUSSBAUM

'Well then,' said I, 'when a man of this kind is met by the question, "What is the honorable?" and on his giving the answer which he learned from the lawgiver, the argument confutes him (*exelenchēi*), and by many and various refutations (*pollakis kai pollachēi elenchōn*) upsets his faith and makes him believe that this thing is no more honorable than it is base, and when he has had the same experience about the just and the good and everything that he chiefly held in esteem, how do you suppose that he will conduct himself thereafter in the matter of respect and obedience to this traditional morality?'

'It is inevitable,' he said, 'that he will not continue to honor and obey as before.' Plato, *Republic* 538d–e (tr. P. Shorey)

Two conceptions of moral and civic education confronted each other in the Athens of the late fifth century, competing for the allegiance of parents and young men. On one side (observes the Stranger from Elea in Plato's *Sophist*) was

the time-honored (*archaioprepes*), traditional (*patrion*) way, which men used to adopt with their sons, and still do adopt very often. It consists partly in anger and partly in a gentler sort of exhortation, and the best name for it as a whole is admonition (*nouthetētikēn*).[1]

On the other is the claim of the expert: moral education is useless unless it is guided by a precise practical skill, akin to scientific knowledge. The supporter of the traditional way views moral training as a process of habituation and acculturation in which all adult citizens can play a role, a straightening and guiding of green branches of the civic tree. His opponent argues that the method of acculturation and the civic values it imparts have no special

1. Pl. *Soph.* 229e–230e (see the comments on this passage in R. Robinson, *Plato's Earlier Dialectic* (Oxford 1953) 12f.; cf. the sympathetic description in *Protag.* 325c–26e and the hostile remarks of Callicles, *Gorg.* 483e–484b. For a historical reconstruction of traditional education see H.-I. Marrou, *Histoire de l'éducation dans l'antiquité* (Paris 1960), ch. 4; F. A. G. Beck, *Greek Education, 450–350 B.C.* (London 1964).

claim to respect merely because of their time-honored place in our lives. He demands an account of values that embodies precise knowledge, akin to the knowledge available in medicine and natural science. He insists that the only competent moral teacher is the man who has such knowledge and can impart it.[2] One insists on the authority of the many; the other asks us to disregard them and follow the wise.

When we think of this debate over moral training, two texts immediately come to mind as central. One is Plato's *Protagoras*; the other is the *Clouds* of Aristophanes. Both have Socrates as their central character, and both portray Socrates as an opponent of traditional methods and values. I wish in this paper to examine Aristophanes' portrait of alternative approaches to education for practical wisdom, and later to examine its relationship to the Platonic portrait of Socrates' views and aims. I shall argue that the play develops interesting criticisms of both the traditional and the intellectualistic models, posing difficult questions about the relationships between morality and culture, and the still more problematic relationship between rationality and democracy.

In trying to treat the *Clouds* as a source of interesting moral reflection, we immediately encounter an obstacle: our reverence for Socrates. The nineteenth century regarded his achievements with a highly critical eye – witness both Hegel's and Kierkegaard's remarks about his 'negative' dialectic, and Nietzsche's profoundly ambivalent portrait.[3] Ours, by contrast, has been a time of comfortable acceptance, even adulation. Socrates, in the popular mind, is an early apostle of the liberal ideals of sincerity and self-realization; few contemporary parents would not gladly trust their children to him. It does not seem acceptable to suggest that Socratic teaching might be genuinely dangerous, or subversive of

2. For further remarks on some implications of a scientific view, and Aristotle's reasons for opposing it, see my *Aristotle's De Motu Animalium* (Princeton 1978), Essay 4, 'Practical Syllogisms and Practical Science'.

3. Hegel, esp. *Gesch. d. Philos.* II, 89: 'Aristophanes hat durchaus nicht unrecht, ja man muss sogar seine Tiefe bewundern, die Seite des Dialektischen des Sokrates als eine Negative erkannt und (nach seiner Weise freilich) mit so festem Pinsel dargestellt zu haben'; Kierkegaard, *The Concept of Irony*, tr. L. Capel (Bloomington 1965). Nietzsche wrote (in the fragment 'Wissenschaft und Weisheit im Kampfe'), 'Socrates stands so close to me that I fight a battle against him every day.' His many discussions of Socrates and his effects are now collected and analyzed in W. Dannhauser, *Nietzsche's View of of Socrates* (Ithaca 1974).

important values.[4] One well-known writer on moral development has even made Socrates (along with Martin Luther King) the paradigm of the highest human developmental stage. The logic of this theory implies that one cannot understand Socrates without agreeing with him: to criticize him is to give evidence of being 'stuck' at a lower level of development.[5]

The reputation of the *Clouds* has suffered as a consequence of this uncritical adulation. Here is a daring and abrasive comedy in which the great teacher makes his first appearance dangling in a basket, babbling some nonsense about watercress. In the course of the drama he is charged with corrupting youth and contributing to social disintegration. Socrates himself ranks this play among the 'early slanders' which he considers to be indirectly responsible for the charges brought against him – hence, ultimately, for his death.[6] How, in view of this accusation brought by a figure whom we revere, are we to assess the irritating work?

There are on the surface some striking discrepancies between the Platonic Socrates and the figure in the *Clouds* which might seem to support the charges of the *Apology*. Plato's Socrates tirelessly exhorts those he meets – whether citizens or sophists – to pursue virtue and the health of the soul rather than worldly success. The Aristophanic teacher helps students trick their creditors, win court cases, gain fame and power; he says nothing about virtue or the soul. Moreover, the Platonic figure, while critical of the justifications ordinary men offer for their beliefs, does not appear to be radically critical of the content of the beliefs. The Aristophanic Socrates mocks ordinary beliefs in both religion and morals; he teaches a new religion and a disdainful attitude towards law.

4. An important recent philosophical exception was Wittgenstein, who wrote, 'I cannot characterize my standpoint better than by saying that it is opposed to that which Socrates represents in the Platonic dialogues' (*Nachlass* 110, 157, cited in Garth Hallett, *A Companion to Wittgenstein's 'Philosophical Investigations'* (Ithaca 1977) 771); his reasons for saying this appear to be remote from our present concerns but in fact are not. Cf. also the pertinent remarks in S. Cavell, *Must We Mean What We Say?* (New York 1969) xxviii.

5. Lawrence Kohlberg, in many of his publications, including 'From Is to Ought', in *Cognitive Development and Epistemology*, ed. T. Mischel (New York 1971), pp. 00–0, and 'Education for Justice: a Modern Statement of the Platonic View', in *Moral Education*, ed. N. F. and T. R. Sizer (Cambridge, Mass. 1970) 57–83; an interesting critique of Kohlberg's views is Kurt Baier's 'Moral Development', *The Monist* 58 (1974) 601–15.

6. *Apol.* 18a–e.

Plato's Socrates, interested primarily in morals, expresses dissatisfaction with the methods and aims of natural science; in Aristophanes we find a quibbling scientist discoursing on the physiology of flea intestines. In short, 'Socrates' in the *Clouds* may seem to be a jumbled type-portrait of the fifth-century sophist-scientist, made in a way that conceals the opposition of the historical Socrates to much of fifth-century thought.[7]

Most modern criticism of the *Clouds* is based on the assumption that if Aristophanes does in fact attack Socrates in a way which assimilates him to sophistic teaching, this attack is wrong and unfair to Socrates.[8] The two most common responses have been (1) to malign Aristophanes, charging him with obtuseness or worse, and (2) to deny that he in fact does attack Socrates in this play. The attraction of the second line of argument[9] lies less in its

7. This point will be developed further below, pp. 71–76.

8. There are, of course, many exceptions among writers about the play: in the last century, the philosophers mentioned in n. 3, and H. T. Rötscher's *Aristophanes und sein Zeitalter* (Berlin 1827), on which Kierkegaard relies heavily; more recently, W. Schmid, 'Das Sokratesbild der *Wolken*', *Philol.* 97 (1978) 209–28 (though he later veers over to the Gelzer–Murray thesis, cf. below n. 9) and Leo Strauss, *Socrates and Aristophanes* (New York 1966). Eric Havelock's 'The Socratic Self as it is Parodied in Aristophanes' *Clouds*', *YCS* 22 (1972) 1–18, contains a good discussion of the vocabulary of Socratic intellectualism. There are others. It is my feeling that none of these writers has given a persuasive reading of the play as a whole or raised the most telling issues about the teaching of the Platonic Socrates that prompts me to add my attempt to theirs.

I shall not take up two other suggestions: (1) that Aristophanes accurately portrays the interests of the historical Socrates, while Plato presents a whitewashing, falsified account; and (2) that both are accurate portrayals of Socrates at different stages in his career. See the good discussion in K. J. Dover, *Aristophanes Clouds* (Oxford 1968) xlvi–xlix (hereafter Dover, *C*). I shall assume for the purposes of this paper that the methods and aims of Socrates were substantially those he announces in the *Apology* and which are ascribed to him in such early Platonic dialogues as *Euthyphro*, *Laches*, *Lysis*, *Charmides* and *Protagoras*. For a full discussion of the relationship between Socratic and Platonic moral thought, see now T. H. Irwin, *Plato's Moral Theory: The Early and Middle Dialogues* (Oxford 1977), esp. chs. III–VII (hereafter Irwin, *PMT*). The *Gorgias* appears to be a transitional dialogue: cf. G. Rudberg, 'Protagoras–Gorgias–Menon: eine platonische Übergangzeit', *Symb. Oslo.* 30 (1953) 30–41, and E. R. Dodds, *Plato Gorgias* (Oxford 1959) 16f., 20f., 296ff. Any full treatment of the Socratic problem would of course have to deal at length with the evidence of Xenophon; I shall not attempt that here.

9. This line of argument is, as presented here, a composite; but its main tenets are endorsed by T. Gelzer, 'Aristophanes und sein Sokrates', *MH* 13 (1956) 65–93; H. Erbse, 'Sokrates im Schatten der aristophanischen *Wolken*', *Hermes* 82 (1954) 385–420; G. Murray, *Aristophanes: A Study* (Oxford 1933).

internal plausibility, which is slim, than in its conclusion that we may continue to respect the intelligence of the author. Furthermore, it has the good sense to offer a new reading of the play itself, relying on this rather than on biographical and psychological conjecture for its support. Socrates, the argument goes, is not being attacked here for subverting the moral education of Athenian youth; at worst he is being gently mocked as an idle chatterer. The fault is ascribed entirely to Strepsiades, who wishes to use the new education for immoral purposes. Socrates never urges him to cheat: Socrates' deities, the Clouds, at last reprove the old man for his wicked desires. The instruction given Pheidippides by the Wrong Speech is not to be read as expressing the Socratic point of view; indeed Socrates clearly dissociates himself from this teaching by leaving the stage before the debate between the Speeches. In short, this interpretation makes on behalf of the Socrates of the *Clouds* much the same defense that Gorgias the sophist offered the Platonic Socrates when asked to justify the teaching of rhetoric:

> In my opinion, if a man becomes a rhetorician, and then uses this power and this art unfairly, we ought not to hate his teacher and cast him out of our cities. For he imparted that skill to be used in all fairness, while this man puts it to an opposite use. Thus it is the man who does not use it aright who deserves to be hated and expelled and put to death, and not his teacher. (*Gorgias* 457b–c)

The parallel points to a difficulty with the proposed solution. For the Platonic Socrates considers this a totally inadequate defense. He asserts repeatedly, here and elsewhere (1) that a teacher of rhetoric ought to have knowledge of right and wrong and to be capable of imparting it to his pupils (otherwise his profession will not be a *technē*); (2) that knowledge is sufficient for right action – it is impossible to act against real knowledge of the good. Hence, if a pupil does act badly, the teacher must have failed. Gelzer and Erbse, in order to show that the Aristophanic Socrates is not too unlike the Platonic Socrates, have presented the Aristophanic teacher with a defense which he could never use were he the proponent of the Socratic paradoxes. The gap between the two is not really closed.[10]

10. Note also that Aristophanes would have to be ignorant of a basic principle of Socratic teaching closely connected to one ('nobody does wrong willingly')

An even more pressing problem is that despite some useful observations the theory does not make sense of the evidence. First, Socrates' absence from the stage during the debate of the two Speeches cannot be taken as evidence that he disapproves of the victor's immorality: the same actor who played Socrates was, by theatrical convention, required to play one of the Speeches. It is Socrates, furthermore, who is said to keep the two Speeches on the premises for educational purposes (112) and who stages the debate for Pheidippides. More important still, although Pheidippides is still skeptical at the conclusion of the debate (1112), he emerges some time later as a thorough partisan of the new education and appeals to the authority of Socrates to justify beating his father (1432). Whether it was the Speech or Socrates himself who instructed him in the interim, he was made aware of no opposition between the two. And Socrates himself expresses satisfaction with Pheidippides' progress: he will be able to escape from any legal charge (1151). Throughout the play Socrates makes no attempt to teach justice or to urge the just use of rhetorical skill. His attitude is at best morally neutral; at worst he condones deceit.[11]

The play, then, does not exempt Socrates from the abuse it heaps on the new education. How can we now account for the violence of its attack? Aristophanes, critics all concede, cannot have been thoroughly ignorant about Socrates. He must have known that his parody could not succeed unless the figure presented was recognizable to his audience as Socrates. Indeed the play frequently parodies, in telling fashion (cf. pp. 71–73ff. below), the verbal and physical mannerisms of the figure familiar from Plato. Most critics therefore (unwilling to base an interpretation on an unfounded attribution of malicious intent to defame)[12] conclude that the fault lies with the author's powers of discrimination. Aristophanes assimilates Socrates to the sophists because he cannot tell the difference. The play presents a generalized attack on intellectuals;

that he seems to parody at *Birds* 603–5. The Athenians who convicted Socrates appear to have been convinced that Socrates was guilty of this sort of failure in teaching; and, as I shall argue, Plato's discussion of the dangers of public dialectic in the *Republic* support this indictment.

11. Cf. esp. 260, 874ff.; for the stance of the Chorus, 316–18, 331–4, 418f., 435f.

12. This view is endorsed by W. Arrowsmith in the introduction to his translation (New York 1962) 13.

Socrates is chosen as a familiar figure whose grotesque physiology and well-known manner afford many occasions for humor. The comic playwright speaks from the position

> of someone to whom all philosophical and scientific speculation, all disinterested intellectual curiosity, is boring and silly. To such a person, distinctions which are of fundamental importance to the intellectual appear insignificant, incomprehensible and often imperceptible.[13]

Just as there are many people to whom the difference 'between Bach and Rachmaninow, the Labour Party and the Communist Party, Oxford and Cambridge, or England and Scotland' is of no interest, so the distinction between Socrates and the sophists was available to Aristophanes, but he simply did not grasp it.

Insofar as this theory is not merely a psychological conjecture, it must base itself on something in the play. It must be a summary of an investigation which has determined (1) that in the *Clouds* Socrates is assimilated to the sophists; (2) that in the respects in which he is assimilated, that assimilation is mistaken. An initial difficulty in assessing Dover's charge is that there appears (to me at least) to be no such thing as 'sophistic thought'. On the issues treated by the play one could hardly imagine thinkers more at odds than Protagoras and Antiphon, Critias and (Plato's) Thrasymachus.[14] But the crucial difficulty in the accusation is its failure to be precise about the *respects* in which the allegedly misleading comparison is being made. If we take any of the pairs Dover offers us, we can find *some* respect in which assimilation would be useful, and even fruitful. (In the case of the second pair, the interval between Dover's writing and our reading has shown that assimilation then might have been a shrewd prophecy.) We certainly would not want to dismiss a work as confused without first asking much more about the positions allegedly being

13. Dover, *C* lii; cf. also his *Aristophanic Comedy* (Berkeley/Los Angeles 1972) 116–20 (hereafter Dover, *AC*), and his discussion of the use of comedy as evidence for the history of Greek morality in *Greek Popular Morality* (Oxford 1974) 18ff., 35ff. (hereafter Dover, *GPM*). None of what follows should be taken to deny the importance of Dover's admirable work both on comedy and on popular morality.

14. See for example the arguments of G. Grote, *A History of Greece*[6] (London 1888) ch. 67; T. Gomperz, *Greek Thinkers*, tr. L. Magnus (London 1901), I, 415; and H. Sidgwick, 'The Sophists', in *Lectures on the Philosophy of Kant and other Lectures and Essays* (London 1905) 323–71, from *JPh* 4 (1872) 288–307, and 5 (1873) 66–80. The history of this controversy is summarized by W. K. C. Guthrie, *The Sophists* (Cambridge 1971), chs. 1 and 3.

conflated and the points on which the author is conflating them. (Which wing of the Labour Party is being portrayed as proto-Communist? On what issues? Under what hypothetical circumstances? We might be dealing with anything from a vicious libel to a revealing truth – we cannot possibly tell without a careful sifting of the evidence.) Dover's hypothesis, then, can too easily serve as an excuse to stop interpreting the play; this is the most dangerous thing about it.

In the case of the *Clouds* the key will be to focus on the issue of moral education and the opposition, on this issue, between a traditional and an expert-centered conception. If we look at the play with careful attention to those issues, I believe we shall find (1) that, in respects essential to the play, the assimilation of Socrates to some of his contemporaries suggests an interesting criticism of his thought; (2) that the interesting criticism can legitimately be found in the play; and (3) that, far from being irrelevant to our understanding of the Platonic Socrates, the *Clouds* anticipates the main lines along which Plato, in the *Republic*, modifies the Socratic program of moral education. An analysis of the debate between the two Speeches will bring us most directly to the central issues of the play.

Right and Anti-Right[15]

A young man is brought by his father to Socrates' school. Socrates, who is reputed to offer instruction in right and wrong discourse (99), does better still in this case: he arranges for Pheidippides a direct confrontation with Right Discourse itself, and its opponent,

15. I have chosen these names as translations of the Greek *kreittōn* and *hēttōn* (lit. 'stronger' and 'weaker' or 'superior' and 'inferior') rather than the more usual 'Right' and 'Wrong' both because the second Speech offers less a defense of immorality than an *elenchos* of morality (see below) and because he himself points to his negative or elenctic function in explaining how he came to have his name: 'I am called *hēttōn logos* for this reason: because I was the first one who devised ways to refute customs and court cases with opposing arguments' (1038–40). *kreittōn* suggests that the strength of custom and convention are the backing for that Speech's position (see below, and cf. Dover, *C* lvii–lviii); I have therefore chosen 'Right' to indicate this in the hope that it will be understood that he is 'right' only relatively to a certain set of conventions and institutions. (Devlin's use of the phrase 'the right-minded man' (see below) is something like what I have in mind.) Anti-Right's name indicates that his is the case which opposes traditional morality and hence does not have its backing.

Anti-Right. Socrates offers his pupil no mere second-hand instruction: the young man will see the two *logoi* face to face, and thereby come to know them both (882 4, 886–7). The way to become a good speaker is, apparently, not to practice speaking but to become acquainted with paradigms of discourse – just as, for Plato's Socrates, the way to become virtuous is less to practice goodness than to seek out, and 'look to', paradigmatic forms of the virtues.[16] The personification of the two *logoi* is a handy dramatic device. But when they appear before the pupil in person, ready to tell the Chorus what their natures are (960), we may also be seeing a telling and particular representation of Socratic epistemology at work.

The debate is introduced as a training in rhetoric (874f.). But once the paradigmatic *logoi* appear on the scene, it becomes a competition between two systems of moral training for the allegiance of the young man. The *logoi* display themselves as incompatible alternatives; each urges Pheidippides to follow him rather than his despised rival.

We notice, however, as we read the debate, that this initial appearance of rhetorical evenhandedness is merely superficial. The debate is not really an argument between proponents of rival programs, but something much more unusual in the rhetorical tradition: an *elenchos* of the moral views of one speaker by the arguments of the other. Anti-Right yields the first, expository place to his rival, announcing that he will debate 'from the things he will say' (942) – starting only from the views expressed by his opponent. Using these he will 'shoot him down' (944) using new and inventive (*kainois*, 943) arguments. These two are not *logoi*

16. For some remarks about the role played by a picture of knowing as seeing or touching in presocratic thought see M. Furth, 'Elements of Eleatic Ontology', *JHistPhilos.* 6 (1968) 111–32, and in *The Presocratics*, ed. A. P. D. Mourelatos (Garden City, N.Y. 1974) 241–70. There is general agreement that the Socrates of Plato's early dialogues emphasizes knowledge rather than practice or habituation; most critics would also agree that the notion of acquaintance plays at least some role in his picture of knowing (cf. esp. *Meno* 97 and the repeated talk of 'looking to a paradigm' or 'form' – e.g. *Euthyphro* 6e, *Meno* 72c). There is a great deal of disagreement about how important or central acquaintance really is in the moral epistemology of the early and middle dialogues; but we do not need to resolve this question in order to be able to consider the possibility that this passage is a reference (1) to the visual metaphors so prominent in Socrates' talk of knowledge, however we interpret them, and, more importantly, (2) to his stress on intellectual learning rather than on practice.

in the same sense. One expounds, the other argues; one sets out a view, the other speaks against it (cf. *enantiais gnōmaisi*, 1037, cf. 1314; *antilexai*, 1040). And, as it will turn out, the aim and achievement of this negative procedure will be to show Right that he himself does not really believe in the education he defends. This is not to say that there is no positive content to the position of Anti-Right; it will turn out both to embody substantial moral assumptions and to produce tangible results. But in form and spirit it is much less like a contest in rhetoric than like another kind of debate that also conceals its positive contribution: the Socratic *elenchos*.

The contest proper opens with a request from the Chorus to Right: 'O you who crowned our elders with many excellent habits (*ēthesi chrēstois*),...tell us your *physis*' (959–60). To anyone versed in the contemporary arguments over morality and moral education, this request, with its mention of both habit and nature, is a reminder of the ongoing debate about the relative merits of convention (*nomos*) and nature (*physis*) in human life.[17] The debate in fact pervades the play. '*Nomizein*' is used more often in the *Clouds* than in any other play of Aristophanes; '*physis*' more than twice as frequently.[18] A closer examination shows us that '*physis*' is associated only with Socrates and his followers: it is used three

17. For general discussions of the *nomos–physis* antithesis see F. Heinimann, *Nomos und Physis* (Basel 1945, repr. 1965); Guthrie, *Sophists*, 55–134; M. Pohlenz, '*Nomos* und *Physis*', *Hermes* 81 (1953) 418–83; A. W. H. Adkins, *From the Many to the One* (London 1970) 110–26; Dover, *GPM*, 74–95, 256ff. On *physis* itself see also E. Benveniste, *Noms d'agent et noms d'action en indo-européen* (Paris 1948) 18; D. Holwerda, *Commentatio de vocis quae est* ΦΥΣΙΣ *vi atque usu in graecitate Aristotele anteriore* (Groningen 1955); C. Kahn, *Anaximander and the Origins of Greek Cosmology* (New York 1960) 200–3; A. P. D. Mourelatos, *The Route of Parmenides* (New Haven 1970) 60–3. While it is true that the request, 'Tell me about your *physis*' would not have to raise the more general *nomos–physis* issue, it turns out that, in the play's terms, at any rate, the recognition that individuals have a real nature, or *physis*, is always accompanied by a recognition of and interest in a more general distinction between human nature and socially imposed habits: no non-Socratic speaks of the *physis* of an individual (cf. below). The Clouds' request thus serves to reveal their intellectual orientation. A more general study of appeals to *physis* at this period appears to substantiate the view that to raise the question of *physis* is usually (1) to oppose it implicitly to convention or to appearance, and (2) to reveal a general theoretical interest in the underlying reality of a kind, or of the world.

18. Cf. Todd, *Index Aristophaneus* (Cambridge 1932) and Heinimann, *Nomos und Physis*, 77ff., 107, 121ff., 131ff., 140ff.

times by Socrates, once by Anti-Right, twice by the Chorus, by Strepsiades and Pheidippides only after they have been subjected to Socratic education (877, 1187).

The belief that there is a *physis* as distinct from *nomos*, human nature and natural preferences as distinct from conventional or social values and preferences, need not lead to an attack on *nomos*. Some fifth-century philosophers who emphasized the distinction also insisted on the gratitude due to *nomos*, which has raised our lives above the existence of the beasts.[19] But nonetheless, the very concession that there is an opposition between *nomos* and *physis* immediately weakens the hold of law and convention, however beneficial they are seen to be. If morality is after all only a human artifact, not grounded in natural necessity or divine law, then we seem to have a choice: the power of *nomos* over us will depend now upon our assessment of its usefulness. (There will be no reason to obey a harmful law.) And even if the general benefits of *nomos* are seen as justifying our continued support of it in general, they will never give me reason for following *nomos* at cost to my self-interest, whenever the gratification of my self-interest would neither result in punishment nor threaten the overall stability of society.[20]

These were some of the familiar arguments about morality and its justification that form the background of the *Clouds* debate. Even before the debate begins, we are aware that Socrates and his school are somehow involved in the debate over the status of *nomos*; and we soon see that their interest in *physis* is not the sort that goes with a contented praise of social convention. Religious *nomoi* have already been attacked (247f., 329, 423, 819); the kingship of Vortex, in place of Zeus, deprives justice of its extra-human backing. The second Logos will introduce himself by saying that he got his name because of his persistent opposition to the claims of *nomos* in the city (1038–40). His injunction is, 'Use your *physis*', and this is further spelled out, "Skip, laugh, consider (*nomize*) nothing shameful' (1077f.). Pheidippides summarizes the results of his education, an education which, as we remember, he ascribes to Socrates (1437) as well as to the *logos*, by saying, "How

19. Salient examples are Protagoras' long speech in the Platonic dialogue; Critias, *DK* 88B25; the fragments of the 'Anonymus Iamblichi' (*DK* 89); there are many others.

20. Critias (B25) presents an argument that this problem was the motivation for the invention of gods: men would now fear doing wrong, even in secret.

pleasant (*hēdy*) it is to associate with new and clever matters, and to be able to look down on the established conventions (*tōn kathestōtōn nomōn*). He rejects his father's appeal to *nomos* (1416, 1420) by proclaiming the freedom of his *physis* (*ephyn eleutheros ge kāgō*, 1414). Since it was only a man who made the *nomoi* in the first place, he, a man, can freely do just the same, and is in no way bound to respect the other man's product (1421ff.).[21]

Thus the appearance of Right as spokesman falls between an initial challenge to *nomos* and its final scornful rejection. We might expect that the invitation to tell about his *physis* will prompt a significant contribution to the *nomos/physis* debate – possibly an attempt to connect traditional morality with the facts of nature, or at least with substantial benefits to human life. Right, however, simply begs the question. When asked about nature, he replies:

I shall tell you, then (*toinyn*), about education as it was customarily practiced in former times (*hōs diekeito*), when I, saying what was right (*dikaion*), flourished, and moderation had its customary respect ('*nenomisto*). 961f.).

There follows a long speech detailing the methods of conventional education; nowhere is there even a remark about human nature or extra-conventional human needs. Right evidently (cf. the *toinyn*) thinks of this speech as an answer to the Chorus' suggestive question. But he can do so only if he is either completely insensitive to the opposition between *nomos* and *physis* or determined flatly to reject it. Either he believes that enumeration of *nomoi* is a fitting answer to a sophistic question about *physis* or he is aware of what the Chorus insinuates but is determined to deny their breach between *nomos* and *physis*. (*Nomos* just *is* what is natural and right, questioning or deviation from *nomos* perverse and unnatural for man.) He does not grant that human nature and needs might clash with custom, or even that an agreement among men might stifle the natures of individuals within the group. The story of his own *physis* is told entirely with plural nouns (or indefinite singulars) and with verbs in the imperfect: his individual nature is an education remaining the same over time, and the same for all.

21. On this passage and the role of conventionalism about human beliefs in Presocratic epistemology, see my 'Eleatic Conventionalism and Philolaus on the Conditions of Thought', *HSCP* 83 (1979).

The program of education defended by this upholder of *nomos* is a program of acculturation and assimilation to time-honored civic tradition.[22] The goal of this 'most renowned, noble-towered wisdom' (1024f.) is the production of sturdy, reliable citizens, distinguished in health, strength, courage and self-control (962, 1009f., 1026–8). Its tools are stern discipline and rote repetition. The values which have sustained the polis in the past (a justification in terms of communal utility is implied) are to be passed on to the young without opportunity for questioning or discussion. Beginning at an early age, boys are sent for group training. They walk together in a well-ordered line (964). At no time, either at home or in school, is a child to speak up spontaneously or alone (963). The physical regimen is stern, promoting health, strength and endurance (965, 981–3, 986, 1002, 1012–14); warm baths, even warm clothing, are disdained as encouraging a degenerate softness (987, 991). Bodies thus trained are guaranteed to look very much alike (1012ff.). Training in music and poetry emphasizes the repetition of traditional songs with inspiringly patriotic words and simple melodies; severe penalties follow attempts at improvisation (969–72), which is called an insult to the Muses. Throughout, elders receive unwavering respect, as do the tenets of traditional religion (906–7). The virtues given most emphasis are courage (986, 967), moderation (*sōphrosynē* 962, 973ff., 996ff., 1006, 1027, 1060) and the sense of shame (992, 973ff., 994f., 1020f.).

In this defense of traditional training we notice an anomalous element that leads us to wonder whether Right does not, after all, recognize some distinction between convention and nature. This is his marked degree of interest in sexual attractiveness and sexual pleasure, his rather prurient fascination with the anatomy of young boys.[23] Homosexual feeling is indeed strong in Right's speech. But there appears to be no clear concession to bodily hedonism. The speaker not only upholds the traditionally expected reticence on the part of the boy,[24] but also endorses some restraint on the part of the lover – for he imagines the ideal boy as sitting chastely with

22. See the illuminating summary in Dover, *C*, lvii ff.

23. Cf. Dover, *AC*, 115f.; C. H. Whitman, *Aristophanes and the Comic Hero* (Cambridge, Mass. 1964) 123–5.

24. Cf. the speech of Pausanias in Pl. *Smp.* and Dover, 'Eros and Nomos', *BICS* 11 (1964) 31–42.

companions of his own age and later praises the *sōphrosynē* of Peleus. The ideal body is one which is suited to military and athletic pursuits, apparently less so to the pursuit of sexual pleasure (1010ff.). The youth learns to regard his personal attractiveness as inseparable from civic virtue and reputation; hedonistic pursuits that injure the good name (996f.) are not only discouraged, they are also intimated to be fatal to the youth's attractiveness in the eyes of his elders. The strongest terms of opprobrium in Right's arsenal are those charging his opponent with shameless devotion to passive pleasure (*katapygōn*, *anaischyntos*, 908; *euryprōktos*, 1084ff.); to be a passive homosexual is for him the greatest evil that can befall anyone (1085f.). One might say that bodily pleasure, whether in baths or in intercourse, is not, for Right, something that can be separated from the active pursuit of civic virtue and decently pursued on its own: if one tries that, one turns the pleasure into something mean and contemptible. The only worthwhile pleasure supervenes, as it were, on military manliness, *sōphrosynē* and *aidōs*. Peleus wins Thetis only by honoring the obligations of hospitality above the temptations of a seductress.

But there are two ways in which we might understand, on Right's behalf, the connection between restraint and pleasure. He might indeed be holding that there is no pursuit of pleasure apart from the pursuit of conventional virtue: it supervenes on *nomos*-serving activity and cannot be sought in isolation from it. Right could, however, be saying instead that virtue is the best *source* of a pleasure which is independently identifiable as the product of activity: manly *sōphrosynē* (as the Peleus case strongly suggests) is chosen as a *means* to a reward which is separable from it. Only the conclusion of the debate will decide between these alternative readings; but we must notice them from the start, since they suggest that Right's refusal to distinguish between *nomos* and *physis* may be only superficial, belying an underlying admission of their separateness.

Since we have mentioned Right's abusive denigration of the sexual tastes of his opponent – and of the audience[25] – it is worth

25. Right's evident contempt for sexual softness and innovation is accompanied by a parallel view of poetry: innovation is an affront to the Muses, and the pleasure of poetry is inseparable, apparently, from its patriotic content. By contrast, his opponent's muse is tricky and innovative (*kompsoprepē* 1030f.). The *Frogs* exploits the parallel between poetic and sexual values in a similar way:

remarking briefly on his conduct during the debate as a whole. Never, either in the initial exposition of his program or in the interchange that follows, does he present a reasoned argument for his position. He reminisces in sentimental fashion about the happiness of the days of his predominance but says little to Pheidippides himself about why he should, or even how he could, adopt this way of life; what he does say (at 1002ff.) is so vague and remote as to be very little help. In the exchange with Anti-Right, he cannot for a minute hold his own in argument; he allows himself to be upset by moves so obviously specious that we wonder at his credulity (esp. 1050ff.). He is clearly indifferent to reason and to the reasoned justification of his opponent's proposals. His weapons are abuse, intolerance and disgust. One claim is answered by a threat (899); others by name-calling and unsubstantiated slurs (909–11, 916–18, 925–9, 1046, 1052–4, 1016–23); a hackneyed argument, easily answerable, by vomiting into a basin (904–6, cf. *Ach.* 584–7). This behavior is an important part of the Aristophanic portrait of traditional education – as vital to our understanding of the poet's criticism as the content of Right's speech.

Right's was the education which most adult males in the audience would have received.[26] His feeling that the basis of morality is time-honored *nomos*, and that *nomos* need not justify itself by argument, was a feeling no doubt broadly shared.[27] It is a view which has not left much of a mark in moral philosophy – as we might expect, since philosophy's *raison d'être* seems to have something to do with the importance of producing arguments for what we believe. (Thus the closest Greek philosophical parallel, the speech of Protagoras in Plato's dialogue of that name, becomes

the prostitute who allegedly inspires Euripidean poetry (1327ff.) is notorious for her ability to assume a large number of different sexual positions. Aeschylus' abuse of this muse-figure assumes that innovation is a sign of corruption: in sex as in poetry it is right and natural to do things the conventional way. In both plays, again, the poet's plea for poetic tolerance is not unconnected with a fear of political repression of a more general kind (see below). The two plays should, ideally, be studied together (cf. Dover, *C* at 209f., 252, 254f.).

26. Cf. Marrou, *Histoire de l'éducation*, ch. 4; Beck, *Greek Education*; Dover, *AC*, 111.

27. We should not see Plato's Cephalus (cf. below) as atypical of men of his generation; I shall argue below that the influence of Socrates may have been important in upsetting the hold of this view.

enmeshed in difficulties over justifying the claim of the philosopher to teach better than the average man.) It is nonetheless a common view of moral matters, in our time as well as then. There is in fact a contemporary analogue to Right's position which brings out more explicitly than any ancient philosophical defense of *nomos* the role of irrational passions in maintaining the fabric of convention. Because of its explicitness about both its backing and its consequences, it may help us to see better some of the implicit criticisms of Right made by the debate and by the *Clouds* as a whole.

In his now famous lecture, *The Enforcement of Morals*,[28] – an attack on the Wolfenden Report's arguments in favor of legalizing homosexual relations among consenting adults – Lord Devlin insists that morality is entirely conventional – a system of beliefs built up over time and passed on by tradition. Any society must, to endure, have certain shared beliefs about how its members ought to live their lives; on many important and sensitive issues, any society 'has to make up its mind one way or another'[29] about what it will and will not tolerate. These decisions a budding member of society must learn to accept as binding on his behavior. 'If he wants to live in the house, he must accept it as built in the way in which it is.'[30] It is crucial to the maintenance of *nomos* that it should not see itself as *nomos*: a defender of monogamy says, 'This is right' – not 'This is what my society has chosen.' As in Right's speech, we see that the opposition between *nomos* and *physis* must either be concealed or denied if *nomos* is to continue to offer its benefits.[31]

Lord Devlin continues to echo Right's position when he speaks of the reaction of *nomos* to questioning and the demand for

28. Patrick Devlin, *The Enforcement of Morals* (Oxford 1965); parts reprinted under the title, 'Morals and the Criminal Law', in *The Philosophy of Law*, ed. R. M. Dworkin (Oxford 1977) 66–82; page references will be from this selection. Telling criticisms of Devlin's position are made by H. L. A. Hart, 'Immorality and Treason', *The Listener* (30 July 1959) 162–3, repr. in Dworkin, 83–8; and by Dworkin, 'Lord Devlin and the Enforcement of Morals', *Yale Law Journal* 76 (1966) 986–1005, repr. in Dworkin, *Taking Rights Seriously* (Cambridge, Mass. 1977) 240–58 under the title, 'Liberty and Moralism'.

29. Devlin, 'Morals', 73 (the example in question is the practice of polygamy).

30. *Ibid.*

31. This point has been developed in a much more subtle and interesting way by Nietzsche, esp. in the fragment 'Über Wahrheit und Lüge im aussermoralischen Sinn', and in the *Genealogy of Morals*, Second Essay.

change, and of the place of reason in dealing with these demands. Much more in the spirit of Right than in that of Protagoras or the Anonymus Iamblichi, he insists on the small importance of reason in civic morality, finding the basis of morality in irrational feeling. The lawmaker is to use as his standard not the arguments of the philosopher, but a different norm:

It is that of the reasonable man. He is not to be confused with the rational man. He is not expected to reason about anything and his judgment may be largely a matter of feeling. It is the viewpoint of the man in the street – or to use an archaism familiar to all lawyers – the man in the Clapham omnibus. He might also be called the right-minded man... Every moral judgment, unless it claims a divine source, is simply a feeling that no right-minded man could behave in any other way without admitting that he was doing wrong. It is the power of common sense and not the power of reason that is behind the judgments of society.[32]

To a challenge or an argument the Right-minded Man opposes not reasoned consideration of principle but his 'intolerance, indignation and disgust' – feelings that Lord Devlin believes to be 'the forces behind the moral law'.[33] In the case of homosexuality, the overwhelming indignation of right-minded men is sufficient reason to 'eradicate' the practice from society. Like Right, Devlin's Right-minded Man would vomit into a basin when confronted by someone whose habits he did not like; and, like Right, he would try to claim that his disgust was sufficient to justify both the perpetuation of that disgust by teaching and the punishment of current 'offenders'.

The parallel is striking. Devlin's lecture, whatever one may think of it as moral philosophy, certainly could read like a good piece of literary criticism expounding the position of this Aristophanic character. (This may be no accident. It was not stressed until recently that Right is far from being the hero of this play: and it is a play that one might expect a person with these views to remember, even while forgetting Aristotle and Plato.) It is also an instructive parallel, which will help us to a deeper understanding

32. Devlin, 'Morals', 78.

33. *Ibid.*, 80. (In fairness to Devlin one must note that he does not believe that public feeling on the issue of homosexuality did at the time of writing pass the bounds of tolerance; but critics are right to ignore this empirical point and concentrate on the argument).

of the play. Both Devlin's view in our time and Right's in the Athens of the fifth century are broadly shared views; both reflect much in traditional educational practice. And yet both flourish in societies in which one of the basic values to which 'right-minded' men are deeply attached is personal autonomy and freedom. Thucydides' Pericles boasts that 'we' refuse to interfere in the private lives of citizens; and we respect each man, no matter what his private lot, as a potential contributor to the public good.[34] This attachment to personal liberty may be loved as irrationally as any other principle; Athenians are *erastai* of their city and its laws.[35] But it appears that this principle, unlike some others, requires reason for its defense against the intolerance that is endemic to democracy. If we have a traditional morality which accords considerable weight to personal liberty and self-respect, together with a moral education which teaches Right's disdain for reasoned argument, the educational system will be very likely to lead to acts of prejudice and intolerance that threaten what is basic to that morality itself.[36] If we wish to object to the prejudices of Right, or of Devlin's man on the Clapham omnibus, we can, of course, do so by appealing to *physis* – by insisting that there are extra-conventional human rights, such as the right to the social conditions of self-respect, that are violated by public attacks on citizens because of their private sexual practices. But we can also criticize Right *within* the sphere of *nomos* itself by showing him that his society, and he himself, value rights and freedoms that are endangered by his rage. If, however, like Right, our interlocutor is encouraged by his education to trust irrational feeling and disdain reasoned argument, he will be unlikely to perceive the danger his own intolerance poses for his cherished way of life. It may be that we cannot so lightly dispense with reason, in education and in public life, if we are to preserve our *nomoi* and our heritage.

This question about the connection between *nomos*-education and the *nomos* of liberty is not raised explicitly within the Aristo-

34. Thuc. 2. 37. 1–3. There is a valuable analysis of Pericles' emphasis on subjectivity and choice in A. Lowell Edmunds' *Chance and Intelligence in Thucydides* (Cambridge, Mass. 1974) ch. 1.

35. Thuc. 2. 43. 1.

36. Consider the ominous sound of the American political slogan of 1964: 'Extremism in defense of liberty is no vice.'

phanic debate itself. But it is nonetheless powerfully present in the play and would raise itself as a question for any sensitive watcher of the debate. The comic poet of the parabasis has claimed the right 'to speak the truth without constraint' (*eleutherōs*, 518) before the audience. We are fully aware that the first version of this play was badly treated at the hands of an irrational and intolerant group of spectators. The danger that the audience will not tolerate the poet's freedom, or hear his truths, is a recurrent theme in Aristophanic Comedy – from the *Acharnians*, where the poet, as Dicaeopolis, must put his head on a chopping block as he prepares to tell the truth to men unwilling even to hear him, to the *Frogs*, where the Chorus must pray to the gods for protection in speaking on serious, as well as comic, matters (384ff.).[37] The parabasis of the *Clouds* mordantly shows how a mob must be bribed and wheedled into granting an artist his creative liberty. And we may assume that the poet is no less acutely aware of their intolerance in other areas of private and political life. Just as in Right's speech sexual intolerance and poetic intolerance are closely linked, so Aristophanes' plea for poetic freedom and tolerance is accompanied throughout his work by an implicit plea for tolerance of sexual and political diversity.[38] And the remedy urged again and again in the comedies is the cultivation of rational judgment. Dicaeopolis urges the hot-headed Acharnians to *listen* closely to his argument. 'Pay close mental attention' or 'turn your intellects this way' (*prosechēte ton noun*) urges the Chorus of the *Clouds* (575), beginning an argument about civic utility. 'It is just', says the Chorus of the *Frogs*, 'that the holy chorus both advise and teach (*symparainein kai didaskein*) the appropriate things (*chrēsta*) to the city' (686f.); they urge the citizens of Athens, 'most wise by nature', to have good sense (*eu phronein*, 704) and not to resign their wisdom before the onslaught of irrational passion (*tēs orgēs anentēs*, 700). This tension between freedom and the intolerance that is nourished in freedom,

37. On the *Acharnians* passage see Lowell Edmunds' paper in this volume; on the first version of the *Clouds* cf. Dover, *C*, lxxx ff.; on the *Frogs* and poetic freedom see C. Segal, 'The Character of Dionysus and the Unity of the *Frogs*', *HSCP* 65 (1961) 207–30; Whitman, *Aristophanes*, ch. 7.

38. Cf. n. 22, above, and J. Henderson, *The Maculate Muse* (New Haven/London 1975) 30ff. (hereafter Henderson, *MM*). It will become evident below (esp. pp. 92ff.) that Aristophanes is not optimistic about the possible coexistence of this tolerance with democratic freedoms.

and the deep need for reason, if freedom is to prevail over constraint, are vividly present to us both in the *Clouds* and throughout Aristophanes' work. They suggest a telling criticism of Right's views, and one which would occur to any sensitive Athenian who watched him vomit and hurl abuse.

Right's disdain for reason makes him vulnerable in another way as well. Because it leaves him without the ability to argue or improvise, he is ill equipped to compete with his sophistical opponent in a contest of words. The contest that superficially presents itself as an even debate is actually conducted on the terms of Anti-Right with his chosen weapon, words, and in a place where he and not Right would feel at home: a school of philosophy and rhetoric. For Right to appear as Right Speech is for him to be immediately at a disadvantage. He must even give a verbal praise of being inarticulate, and not only in words, but 'with exceedingly clever speeches and contrivance and carefully crafted phrases' (950–2). Although the contest will prove only 'which is the better speaker' (953f.), this 'trial of cleverness' (955f.) is treated by the Chorus as 'the greatest contest' and as by itself sufficient to determine which education is the better. Socrates, the Chorus and, very likely, the audience, waiting as they do for the newest wrinkle in verbal artifice (cf. the parabasis), all assume that education is incomplete unless it can justify itself, that Right could not do a satisfactory job of training young citizens without being able to defend his procedure against a radical challenge by the use of words. (Why do we not feel that Anti-Right is deficient because he clearly could not resist Right in a wrestling match?)

But the oddest thing about the contest is not just that Socrates and we (who are all, in this respect, his heirs) regard Right as defeated unless he meets his opponent on his opponent's terms. It is that Right himself shares our view. Far from protesting that the terms of the contest are manifestly unfair to him, and that verbal skills are irrelevant to the training he advocates, he participates with enthusiasm. He concedes the vulnerability of his position to argument; and yet, as we saw, he is unable to detect even the grossest fallacies. The result is that he regards himself as having been thoroughly defeated, despite his apparent contempt for the tools of reason, and abandons his position altogether. The concluding exchange, more an extended pun than an argument, proves so devastating to him that he concedes defeat, takes off his cloak and runs off into the audience crying, 'I am defeated, *ō kinoumenoi*...I am deserting to your side' (1102–4).

In the first book of Plato's *Republic* the old man Cephalus, secure in his faith and in the traditional morality, refuses to compete with Socrates on Socrates' own terms. He leaves the argument to attend to his religious duties. His son, Polemarchus, takes up the defense of traditional beliefs and is at once upset by a number of swift and questionable moves. Like Right, he admits he is mistaken before the opponent has even presented a decent case. We wonder what Polemarchus would have thought about justice had the rest of the *Republic* not followed. Would he have become the man described so graphically by Plato in the epigraph to this paper? Right has Cephalus' values without his old-world serenity. He is a more ridiculous Polemarchus, entering eagerly into debate with no intellectual armor, then changing beliefs because of some transparent sophistry. The debate reveals the impotence of the old morality in a time of social ferment.[39] If there were a broad consensus about values, challenges might possibly be suppressed or ignored; in a time of social upheaval, education of the young must either produce a compelling justification of the traditional virtues or desert to the enemy.

The enemy, as portrayed here, confronts his opponent's loving description of *nomos* with a praise of unbridled *physis*. Right spoke of the traditions that held society together; he tended to speak in the plural, describing the upbringing of an unspecified average young man. Anti-Right addresses his opponent directly, *ad hominem*, assuming that he has needs as an individual which may differ from and lead him to disregard the needs of society as a whole. His moral proposals, based on what he holds are the facts about 'the necessities of nature' (1075), end with the injunction to pursue the promptings of *physis* without feeling the constraint of moral norms. And he believes that what nature prompts in a man is the self-centered pursuit of maximal pleasure. His example of a

39. J. Henderson has pointed out to me that '*physis*' is used in comedy as a euphemism for 'penis' (cf. Henderson, *MM*, 5); the invitation from the Chorus to Right to reveal his *physis* might have been the occasion for a visual joke which would underline my point. Cf. also 908, 983f. on Right's old age, and the hedonist's advice to the young man to 'use your *physis*' at 1078.

natural necessity is a need for sexual intercourse without regard to the convention of marriage. The 'pleasures' he acknowledges include homosexual and heterosexual sex, eating, drinking, laughing, gambling; it is not worth living, he says, if these are taken away (1074). For all of Peleus' vaunted moral virtue, he lost his wife (hence pleasure, the thing that makes life most worth the living) because he was not 'pleasant' enough as a lover (1068–70). Moral virtue is portrayed as a time-consuming pursuit which prevents one from achieving expertise in what really counts. (When Anti-Right enjoins young men to ignore *sōphrosynē* and to develop the use of the tongue (1058–62) it is not only as an instrument of speech.[40]) And the concluding series of jokes about *euryprōktoi* urges us to see our leaders, our poets and ourselves as passive hedonists waiting to be stimulated.

Anti-Right seems to believe in hedonism (and a fairly simple bodily hedonism, whose only concession to qualitative distinctions is the reminder to become skilful in bed) both as a psychological theory of actual human pursuits and as a theory of the good. The former is evident from his remarks about the audience, his analysis of the motives of Thetis, his description of nature and its necessities, the whole tenor of his appeal to the as yet unknown young man; the latter from his mockery of Peleus, his superior attitude towards the chastity and restraint of the old system, his assumption that nothing but *hēdonē* makes life worth living. Oddly enough, his psychological assumption about human nature receives confirmation, within the debate itself, by the responses of his opponent. By the end of the exchange, Right is clearly taking the instrumental view of virtue which does permit a distinction between *nomos* and *physis*. He pleads the superiority of the old ways in terms of bodily pleasure: chaste Peleus got an attractive wife for his pains, the casual adulterer risks getting his pubic hair plucked out and suffering the infamous radish treatment (1083f.). (Even Right's original appeal to Pheidippides stressed the *pleasure* of a life of leisured moderation, cf. esp. *chairōn*, 1008 – as much as, or more than, its *rightness*.) When these appeals to overall pleasure fail, Right, as we have seen, gives up, confessing himself an *euryprōktos* like the rest of us.

40. This is shown by the fact that he adds this *after* his praise of talking as a separate point (*aneimi dēt' enteuthen eis tēn glōttan*, 1058), and immediately before his criticism of Peleus' sexual ineptness.

Belief in hedonism (both as a theory of actual conduct and as a normative theory) might still be compatible with a limited defense of *nomos*. For it is evident that without any social order there would be a chaos in which the pursuit of pleasure would become much more difficult than it is in a well-ordered city. Anti-Right nowhere disputes this. He proposed not the overthrow of *nomos* but its exploitation by a smart minority. Pheidippides is not urged to bring about social change; he is simply invited to become a 'free rider' on the existing system – to break the moral and civil law and be smart enough to escape the penalty. Anti-Right's moral advice resembles that of Thrasymachus in *Republic* I: he ridicules conventional justice as constraining to the natural desires of the ruled citizen and urges the ordinary man to see that his *agathon* (1062) is in a prudent disregarding of conventional limits of shame and right.[41] *Hybris*, in Attic law, was the offence of treating a fellow-citizen as if he were a slave or foreigner.[42] In the world of Anti-Right, this lack of respect in the service of personal satisfaction becomes an ideal, displacing *sōphrosynē* (cf. 1068–70).

Right's opponent appears, then, to be an immoralist of a familiar type – close to Thrasymachus and not far from Callicles. If Socrates is here being assimilated to men whom, as Plato tells us, he was anxious to oppose, we must examine the assimilation carefully to find out whether we must indeed judge Aristophanes 'a dissolute, mendacious Alcibiades of poety',[43] or whether, as Nietzsche himself believed, we should see here a 'profound instinct' about Socrates and his effects.[44] First we must be precise about the relationship between the Socrates of the play and Anti-Right. We have seen Socrates so far only as stager of the debate. This is already significant, since it is a debate rigged

41. Unlike Polus in the *Gorgias* he does not distinguish between the advantageous and the *kalon*; unlike Callicles he gives advice to all, and not only to the extraordinarily gifted few; and he does not introduce a standard of the naturally *dikaion* to compete with conventional norms while preserving the status of justice as a conventional virtue.

42. Dem. 21. 180, cf. Dover, *C*, 226.

43. F. Nietzsche, *The Birth of Tragedy*, tr. W. Kaufmann (New York 1967), section 13.

44. *Ibid.* This phrase nicely captures what this paper will try to establish: not that Aristophanes was in possession of a fully elaborated philosophical critique of Socratism but that he had a deep intuitive insight into the dangers of this method.

against the old education, in which only a master of verbal argument could emerge victorious. But how far does Socrates endorse its hedonistic conclusion? Pheidippides goes indoors to receive instruction from Anti-Right.[45] He later emerges claiming the authority of Socrates for father-beating (1432). We are given no way of distinguishing the contribution of Socrates from that of his employee. When Pheidippides goes inside he is still skeptical; when he emerges he is a thorough partisan of the new education. The result is what we might have expected of a prolonged instruction from Anti-Right – or, rather, an Anti-Right with charm, since Pheidippides is more personally impressed with Socrates than with his spokesman. We can say provisionally that if Socrates *did* attempt not simply to echo Anti-Right's criticism of inarticulate *nomos*, but also to provide some more solid justification for virtuous action, this attempt was lost on his pupil.

Aristophanes' Socrates and Anti-Right are in striking ways different. One has scientific and contemplative interests; the other is interested only in rhetoric. One is ascetic, cheerfully enduring poverty, want and cold; the other advertises the delights of warm baths. One is chaste, the other self-indulgent. In what respects *would* an assimilation of these two disparate figures be justified? As we shall see further in the next section, Socrates throughout the play scorns the traditional gymnastic and moral education, together with the piety that sustained it. He clearly believes that the question, 'How should I live?' can best be answered by an expert and cannot be left to the many. In staging the debate Socrates clearly announces his demand for justification by argument, and participates with Anti-Right in the humiliation of the figure who has beliefs but no *logoi*. There are conspicuous differences between the two figures; but they may be differences of personal style – made from a position which attacks the tradition of communal uniformity and urges each individual to think out his own course of action and the reasons for it. The difference between a sybaritic, self-indulgent sophist and a restrained, serene, contemplative sophist was both seen and depicted by Aristophanes; but the play argues that these differences conceal a more basic sameness: an underlying intellectualism that dedicates itself to

45. Cf. Dover's notes on 1105–12.

exposing the inadequacies of traditional moral justification, and argues that what cannot justify itself has no reason for being. And we see that the teachings of both have the same (or rather a cumulative) result: traditional values are undermined and nothing enduring is put in their place. With this suggestion in mind, let us now examine the story of Strepsiades and his son to see to what extent the play as a whole bears out the suggestions of the debate concerning human nature and Socrates' effect on it.

Strepsiades and Pheidippides

The *Clouds* begins with a cry of distress, followed by an invocation of Zeus the King (1f.). In the midst of social and political upheaval, certain 'facts' about the world have not changed for Strepsiades. The war has made his slaves rebellious (7); the choice of an aristocratic wife has forced him to abandon the tranquillity of rural life for the exhausting financial and sexual demands of an urban marriage; the son of this marriage is a disobedient spendthrift and idler (42ff., 73f.).[46] But beneath Strepsiades' acute distress is a naive optimism that the old religion, the traditional laws of family obligation, and a bit of shrewd self-interest will see him through. His name signifies his pain – he tosses and turns at night (*strephei* 36) and will twist even more violently as a victim of Socrates' bedbugs (700ff.) – but also his resourceful guile, his determination to find a way out of everything: he will 'twist' opposing lawsuits (*strepsodikēsai* 434); he looks forward to being reviled as a *strophis*, or crook (450).[47] And his hopes rely with childlike confidence on the protection of the gods (or at least those he does not blame for his misfortunes, cf. 84f.), the sanctity of oaths and the duty of sons to fathers. He cannot conceive of any disruption of these most basic values. The new education seems a safe weapon to use against his creditors (94ff.); he has no idea of its subversive power.

Strepsiades, then, is essentially motivated by personal self-interest, probably of a hedonistic kind (cf. *hēdistos bios* 43), but

46. On the social status and background of the characters see Dover's notes on the opening scene, and V. Ehrenberg, *The People of Aristophanes* (New York 1962), 84ff., 97ff.

47. Cf. Dover, *C*, xxv.

curbed by his habitual obedience to the old morality. He is more or less moral, not because he is good at heart but both because there are some conventions it never occurs to him to question and because he has not been taught the tools of guile. His son has been brought up without the constraints of the old education; in him we see more clearly the Aristophanic picture of human *physis*. Pheidippides is a young aristocrat, linked through his mother with the family of Pericles.[48] But he goes far beyond Periclean morality (as depicted in Thucydides) in his determination to hold nothing sacred, even the commands of parents; with him autonomy has become *hybris*. The play links his way of life with the ways of the new education: in the aristocratic epithets applied to both (*kalos kagathos* 101, 797; cf. 8, 61)[49] and, more clearly, by the description of his hairstyle, shared by urban intellectuals (14, 331ff., 836) and by many members of the audience as well (1098ff.).[50] Thucydides' Pericles, defending Athenians' attachment to freedom and autonomy, argued that an upbringing which allows autonomous choice will produce citizens who 'nobly judge' that they ought to serve the polis.[51] But the behavior of Pheidippides at the beginning of the play bears out the claim of Anti-Right that most men, left to themselves, choose the self-centered pursuit of pleasure. Pheidippides seems to have no social consciousness (even less than his father, who in the map scene manifests some anxiety about Sparta), little religious consciousness (he invokes only the gods of his pleasures, Poseidon Hippios and Dionysus, 83, 91, 108), and only a wavering sense of family loyalty. His first speech is a protest against injustice (25) – but the *adikia* is merely a violation of horse-racing etiquette. He lives entirely for his pleasures (cf.

48. *Ibid.*, 99, xxvii; on his name, xxvi.

49. On *kalos kagathos* see Ehrenberg, 98ff., G. E. M. de Ste Croix, *The Origins of the Peloponnesian War* (London 1972) 359ff.; and the objections of Dover, *GPM*, 41ff., with references. Although Dover offers convincing evidence that the expression is generally commendatory, these passages seem more dubious; they *may* mean no more than the sarcastic use of '*chrēstos*' (see Dover, *GPM*, 45 n. 25); but the effect of Strepsiades' whole portrait is to dissociate both his son and the Socratics from the hard-working 'middle-class' morality of the farmer and to associate them with the lazy and idle aristocrats. Dover's general claims receive strong support from Aristotle's extended discussion of *kalokagathia* and its usage at *Magna Moralia* 1207b22ff. and *EE* 1248b8ff.

50. Cf. Ehrenberg, *People of Aristophanes*, 97.

51. Thuc. 2. 41. 5, cf. Edmunds, *Chance and Intelligence*, ch. 1.

Anti-Right at 1079); morality and religion have their place only relatively to these. He is chronically disobedient in order to go on pursuing the horsey life (73ff.); he even breaks an oath to his father when it turns out that he is being asked to do something that will make him look ridiculous in the eyes of his horse-racing companions (90f., 119f.). He would not, he protests, give up horse-racing for anything – not even if you promised him the best race-horses in the city (108f.). The joke points to the limited range of his objects of desire: only more of the same could make less of the same tolerable. If most men are like this, pursuing pleasure (and not honor or wisdom) when left to make their own choices, it may seem that only a rigid habituation can produce reliably moral citizens; the desires must be trained sternly and suppressed before one can expect the appropriate choice to be made. If the old education was defective in its indifference to reason, the new education may be equally one-sided in its indifference to the training of the passions.

Before father and son encounter Socrates, however, there is still some hope that the old values will see the family through. If there is much that Pheidippides questions, there is more that he has not been intellectually daring enough to question: duties to respect his father's tastes in drama and music, to acknowledge the existence of the gods his father acknowledges, to respect the physical person of his father and of his mother. But Pheidippides, and his father with him, have an underlying respect for cleverness and verbal artifice, characteristic of the times, which makes them dangerously volatile.[52] We suspect that if their remaining values were challenged in a startling and effective way, they would be unlikely to ignore the challenge and retire, like Cephalus, to perform their pious duties. Whether or not they become immoral seems largely a question of what influences they encounter. With the naive expectation of reaping only profit from the venture, Strepsiades puts himself under the tutelage of Socrates.

Socrates is a midwife of ideas (136f.). He begins with the present situation and thoughts of his interlocutor (695) and reduces him to a state of *aporia* (cf. 702–5, 743–5) by teaching him the depth of his own ignorance (842). As Strepsiades says to his son, '(you will learn) as many things as are wise (*sopha*) among men; you will

52. On the fashionable love of verbal artifice see the parabasis and Pl. *Gorg.* 447a, 452e, Thuc. 3. 42. 2ff., etc.

know yourself, how ignorant and thick you are' (841f.). Socrates teaches everyone he encounters; he neither conducts an initial test of the interlocutor to determine whether his moral training has prepared him adequately for questioning and dialectic, nor takes the responsibility for having concluded the educational process in a satisfactory way before discharging the pupil. Although he seems to claim to impart wisdom, his procedure, as we see it, is largely a negative one, an *elenchos* of the pupil's old beliefs. His initial appearance dangling in a basket (223ff.) indicates his remoteness from the interlocutor, his detachment from such 'earthly' matters as moral habituation and the management of the passions. To Strepsiades' description of his predicament (*and* to his offer of money) he replies with a provocative theological question. If this Socrates is teaching human wisdom, he seems to believe that training of the intellect is sufficient for wisdom and all that it implies. His sphere is the air (225), not the gross moral earth of desire and bodily need (228–30).

Socrates, then, is an intellectualist. He indicates that education is a precise matter, a matter for a few initiates, for experts. He has contempt for the old man and the training he has received (cf. 627ff.); it has done nothing if it has not enabled him to argue. Quickness and attention are the necessary prerequisites for wisdom (414ff., cf. 477, 478ff., 627ff.), and this wisdom, which must be imparted by an expert teacher, is implied to be all that is necessary for achieving the satisfaction of one's desires (427ff., 463ff.). Socrates' skill in disputing about recondite matters and his possession of various sorts of out-of-the-way knowledge help to convince Strepsiades that he is an expert of the requisite kind (cf. 165ff., 180ff.). The ordinary man is easily dazzled by an opponent who makes him feel and appear stupid; the idea that experts know how to live better than ordinary men is attractive to someone at a loss to find a way out of a painful situation. After an initial defeat, Strepsiades renounces the religious beliefs of his youth and clings so proudly to his shreds of 'expert' knowledge that he later believes them to justify blatant immorality. The moral he has learned from Socrates, as illustrated in the encounter with his creditors, is that the clever are justified in cheating the ignorant, that ignorance is more to be feared than vice, even that the only real vice *is* ignorance.

We must pause here to ask in what sense we are in fact being offered a portrait of Socrates. For Dover and others believe that this portrait may be a generic portrait of 'the intellectual', a composite figure like the Thales of popular legend.[53] Before we can compare this portrait with the Platonic one, we must try to establish that it is indeed a portrait. This is, I take it, a different job from showing that it is an accurate or good portrait – though it is hard in this case to separate the two. To accomplish the first job is to establish that no member of the audience would fail to recognize the figure they all knew so well, thinking he saw only a type of the intellectual; it is not yet to establish that what the play says about Socrates is right. One is the question whether there is enough here to secure a reference; the other whether what is asserted of the subject is true of him.[54]

We may begin with the physical likeness. First of all, the actor playing the role of Socrates almost certainly wore a portrait mask. Aelian tells us that when foreigners in the audience whispered among themselves, 'Who *is* this man Socrates?' the real Socrates silently stood up and displayed himself to them. The story loses all force if the mask did not create a visual resemblance.[55] (The story also informs us that the non-foreigners in the audience were in no perplexity about who Socrates was, or whether the character on the stage was he.) Bare feet were not customary among sophists in the fifth century. As Dover argues, and as Plato's *Gorgias* and *Protagoras* attest, sophists were represented by their contemporaries as rather opulent gentlemen.[56] To go barefoot was a well-known peculiarity of Socrates (cf. *Smp.* 174, 220); Aristophanes' allusion to the master's habit of going barefoot in the road (362f., cf. 103) would surely be taken as a particular personal allusion. In the same passage the Chorus mentions a habit of casting sidelong glances which is also mentioned by Alcibiades (*Smp.* 220b) as a characteristic Socratic mannerism. The ability to endure pain, cold and discomfort which characterizes Socrates throughout the play, and

53. Dover, *C*, xxxiv ff.

54. It is not clear that Dover really distinguishes these two questions.

55. Aelian *VH* 2. 13, cf. Dover, *C*, xxxiii. Although some of the material I shall bring out here has been well summarized by Dover (*C*, xxxii ff.), it seems necessary to recapitulate, in order to feel the cumulative force of the evidence.

56. Cf. the portraits of Gorgias and Polus in the *Gorgias*; of Prodicus, Hippias and Protagoras in the *Protagoras*; and Dover, *C*, xxxiii f.

which he tries unsuccessfully to impart to his pupil, is, once again, a well-known idiosyncrasy of Socrates, not shared by his other sophist contemporaries (cf. *Smp.* 220b; Xen. *Mem.* 1. 2, 1. 3, 5ff., 6. 2; *Crito* 43b) and the entire death scene in the *Phaedo*, esp. 60a–c, 116a ff.). The Chorus' praise of Socrates at 358–63 sets him apart from Prodicus (typical, here, probably of the other, more 'civilized' sophists)[57] and praises the latter for his urbane wit, Socrates for his squalor and his odd mannerisms. We see the playwright making an effort to *distinguish* Socrates from his contemporaries in such a way as to indicate that a single man, with all his idiosyncrasies, is his target. Dover's hypothesis of the generic intellectual-figure begins to be undercut by some of Dover's own precise observations – for it is obvious that the Socrates of the play does not have the look or manner commonly ascribed to intellectuals or sophists.

To move to more complex matters of character and personal style, we find in this Socrates the same abstraction from worldly life, the same dreamlike remoteness (223) that so impressed observers of Socrates as an unusual and personal habit (esp. *Smp.* 175a–e). This Socrates, like Plato's, is fascinated with his own thought and the conditions for its success (esp. 227ff.); his watchword seems to be the Delphic 'Know Thyself' (842). No sophist depicted for us in the tradition is like this; Protagoras and Gorgias, Hippias and Prodicus, all seem to have been thoroughly urbane men, poised and polished, witty guests in aristocratic households. The angry boorishness of Thrasymachus is even more remote from this gentle self-absorption. In fact, what is particularly striking about all the sophists, as we know them, is their *lack* of self-consciousness and self-inquiry. It is precisely this inattention to the Delphic maxim, which the Socrates of the *Apology* also makes his guiding principle, that is charged to their account as an intellectual and moral blemish by the Socratic *elenchos* of Plato's early dialogues. The only predecessor of Socrates to have made anything of the thought that inquiry must begin with self-examination, that 'the unexamined life is not worth living', was Heraclitus; but he cannot plausibly be said to figure in this play.

57. On this passage see A. Henrichs, 'The Atheism of Prodicus', *Cronache Ercolanesi* 6 (1969) 21 n. 39. Henrichs convincingly assails Dover's claim (*C*, lv) that 358ff. indicate the poet's esteem for Prodicus as an artist; all the text suggests is that Prodicus was 'a more professional sophist' than Socrates.

Again, we see that the Aristophanic Socrates makes much of an analogy between the process of education and initiation into a mystery religion (143, 254ff.). This analogy is characteristic of the Platonic Socrates,[58] and not of his more worldly contemporaries, who treat teaching as available to anyone (for a price) and as imparted by brilliant displays of rhetorical skill. I am not aware that such an analogy for philosophical teaching is used by any predecessor or contemporary of Socrates; the only thing that comes close is Parmenides' proem – but, again, it is out of the question that the Aristophanic figure is an assimilation of Socrates to Parmenides.

We now come to the methods of Socratic teaching. Sophists are characteristically prone to *makrologia*, prefer *epideixis* to dialectic, and have difficulty engaging in Socratic questioning.[59] They teach by precept and example, urging imitation of models of their rhetorical craft or skill. The Socrates of the *Clouds*, by contrast, seems to portray himself as a midwife (137),[60] engaged in bringing forth his pupil's own ideas. He begins with the habits of the pupil

58. The mystery analogy is mentioned lightly in *Tht.* 155e, *Gorg.* 497c, *Meno* 76e, *Euthyd.* 277e; more seriously at *Crito* 54d, *Phaedo* 69c, 81a, and *Rep.* 378a; and developed very fully at *Smp.* 209e–212a and *Phaedrus* 249e ff., esp. 250c–d; cf. Dover, *C*, xli, who, however, cites only a small part of the evidence. A. W. H. Adkins' claim, 'Clouds, Mysteries, Socrates and Plato', *Antichthon* 4 (1970) 13–24, that Plato's early dialogues dissociate Socrates from the controversial use of initiation language has now been effectively criticized by R. S. W. Hawtrey, 'Plato, Socrates and the Mysteries: A Note', *Antichthon* 10 (1976) 22–4; Adkins' discussion of the *Clouds* passages remains valuable.

59. Protagoras and Gorgias have particular trouble, cf. esp. *Gorg.* 465e–466a. The evidence that Protagoras engaged in eristical question-and-answer is tenuous at best and has been appropriately challenged by Sidgwick, 'Sophists', who also offers an attractive, though not fully conclusive, argument that the practise of eristic did not antedate Socrates but was modelled on the Socratic *elenchos*.

60. By itself this passage tells us little, as Dover rightly points out (*C*, xlii ff.). We cannot even be sure that the pregnancy in question is not that of Socrates himself; it is only in the light of the other evidence discussed below that we come to see his procedure as midwife-like and are encouraged to interpret the early passage this way. Certainly it would be unconvincing to press the resemblance to *Tht.* 150e (cf. Schmid, 'Sokratesbild'). The point is rather that both the play and the dialogues treat Socrates' procedure as largely elenctic and as starting from the pupil's own ideas; midwifery then becomes a very natural image for the process, one that might have occurred independently to two writers about Socrates, whether or not he himself made use of it. For a fascinating discussion of the *Theaetetus* image see M. F. Burnyeat, 'Socratic Midwifery, Platonic Inspiration', *BICS* 24 (1977) 7–16.

(478), teaching him by appeals to his own experience and beliefs (cf. esp. 386 *apo sautou 'gō se didaxō*; cf. also 695, 701–3). It was not unparalleled for the pupil to select the topic for instruction (638ff.); this method was probably used by both Hippias and Gorgias.[61] But they used it as an occasion for display of their own extempore rhetorical skill; they did not follow the selection up with brief questions and answers assessing the pupil's own command of the subject. This Socrates is out to strip away his pupil's preconceptions – it is the custom to enter naked into the *phrontistērion* (498) – and to expose the inconsistencies in his current beliefs (cf. esp. 369, 398).[62] He repeatedly insists on the pupil's ignorance and the importance of his becoming aware of it.[63] His faithful follower's first words to Strepsiades in fact are, 'By Zeus, how ignorant you are' (135). (What sophist would so quickly have risked giving offence? And the student's behavior is clearly modelled on his master's.) At a crucial point in the examination Socrates triumphantly points out to the old man how much he did not know (329ff.); Strepsiades' summary of the new learning is that it is a learning about one's own ignorant thickness (842).[64] And, as we have already seen, the play's central display of Socratic technique is the 'shooting down' of traditional moral views – by Socrates' employee onstage, by Socrates himself behind the scenes.

In short, the procedure and its characteristic effects are those of the Socratic *elenchos* as described in the *Sophist*'s contrast between the two ways of education:

> They question a man on these matters where he thinks he is saying something, although he is really saying nothing. And as he is confused, they easily convict his opinions, by bringing them together and putting them side by side, and thus showing that they are contrary to each other at the same time in the same respect about the same things (230b).

61. For Gorgias, cf. Pl. *Gorg.* 447c, *Meno* 70c, Cic. *Fin.* 2.1, Philostr. *Vit. Soph.* 1.1 = *DK* 82 A 1a; cf. Dodds, *Gorg.* on 447c. For Hippias, cf. Pl. *Hipp. Min.* 363d, *Prot.* 315c.

62. On the structure of the Socratic *elenchos* in Plato see Robinson, *Plato's Earlier Dialectic*, ch. 2, n. 1; and Irwin, *PMT*, ch. III. 3.

63. Compare 700ff. with Pl. *Prot.* 352a ff.

64. To these characteristics of the Socratic *elenchos* we might add the use of earthy examples (e.g. 385ff.) and the practice of arguing by illustration and analogy (314, 340, 342). The use of the method of division (742) is probably Socratic but maybe not exclusively so.

The paralyzing effect of the *elenchos*, compared in the *Meno* to the numbing effect of a stingray (84, cf. 80a–b), finds its comic expression in the *Clouds* in the scene in which Strepsiades, enjoined to look into himself and find a solution to his *aporia*, feels himself being bitten by bedbugs that drink his life's blood and torture his genitals (700ff.). The discomfort of the learning process was minimized by the more popular sophists, who gave their listeners a verbal feast (cf. *Gorg.* 447a), flattering their appetites for pleasure and promising easy and rapid progress (cf. also *Prot.* 318a). Talking to Socrates undoubtedly *was* like being bitten and drained; talking to the others was as easy as eating.

The content of Socratic education raises more serious difficulties; but here too deep similarities are to be found. The comic character's emphasis on self-inquiry and self-knowledge, and his apparent goal of achieving and imparting human wisdom (841) are thoroughly Socratic.[65] The emphasis, especially in the debate, on training relevant to moral and political decision-making also marks Socrates off from both the early natural scientists and from many of the sophists, those whose emphasis was on rhetorical style, grammar and language. Protagoras obviously shared Socrates' moral interests (as did Critias, Antiphon and the Anonymus Iamblichi); but none, as far as we can tell, combined this moral interest with an assault on traditional methods of moral education. The emphasis, *within* moral discussion, on achieving real, precise or correct understanding (*eidenai saphōs hatt' estin orthōs* 250f., cf. 228), and on getting in touch directly with the real nature of the subject-matter (the presentation of the *logoi*, cf. above) belongs to Socrates rather than to the relativistic and *nomos*-centered Protagoras. At the same time, there is a conspicuous absence of positive moral advice, or of any substantive account of the human good – with the exception of the hedonism of Anti-Right, not directly endorsed by Socrates. As we shall see, Plato's Socrates also fails to develop a positive account of the good – with the exception of the hedonism of the *Protagoras*, which he may or may not seriously endorse. There are, to be sure, numerous oddities and irrelevancies: digressions into grammatical theory more charac-

65. For further related material see Havelock, 'The Socratic Self', and R. Philippson, 'Sokrates Dialektik in Aristophanes *Wolken*', *RhM* N.F. 81 (1932) 30–8.

teristic of Prodicus, observations about the world of nature quite foreign to the interests of the mature Socrates and associated with earlier natural philosophers.[66] But even the last point – the most serious difficulty – can, I think, be explained as not irrelevant to a penetrating criticism of Socrates. I shall return to this problem below. And in general we may surely allow the comic writer to add humorous material which is not directly pertinent, so long as it does not obscure the fundamentals of the portrait. We have begun to see what those fundamentals are; later I shall argue that the criticisms based on them are valid.

No analysis of the portrait of Socrates in this play would be complete without an examination of his goddesses, the cloud-chorus. For like the Socrates of the *Apology*, this Socrates claims to be not a supreme moral and intellectual authority but merely a servant of powerful deities. He invokes his goddesses, the Clouds, to preside over Strepsiades' training. Here, if nowhere else, we might hope to find some sign of Socrates' positive teaching, insofar as it is separable from the hedonism of Anti-Right – what solid account of *physis* he has to fill the void left by the degradation of *nomos*. As Socrates' first speech ('Why do you address me, O creature of a day?' 223) associates the teacher with the permanent as against the transient or mortal, so his goddesses, in their first words, testify to their eternal character (275). We might expect a dialogue with them to reveal what is behind the many, shifting appearances, what unifies them – hence, to provide us with the reliable moral epistemology we seem to need in order to answer Anti-Right's challenge. But in fact we find no such thing. If the Clouds are anything always, the truth is that they are always in flux (literally *aenaoi*, 'ever-flowing'). They can become anything but can never be grasped in themselves. Even their 'immortal form' (288) can be shaken off. When we look at them, converse with them, we see a form; but it gives us no information about anything beyond ourselves (348ff.): they become like what they see. Insofar as the Clouds are symbolic of Socratic teaching, they display it as elenctic and negative, imparting no insight into anything but the interlocutor's own defects, leaving beyond the structure of the *elenchos* only a formless nebulosity.[67] Vortex, not

66. Cf. Pl. *Phd.* 96a ff.

67. Kierkegaard's discussion of the role of the Chorus seems to me one of the most interesting portions of his analysis (163–6). Though I am clearly indebted

Zeus, is King (379); time-honored tradition has been unseated, but in its place is only the whirlwind, aimless and unknowable. Instead of the old divinities of *nomos*, with their firm moral prescriptions, the intellectual expert offers us a new trinity: Chaos, Clouds and Tongue (424).

The first effect of the Socratic *elenchos* was discomfort. The second, according to the *Meno* and the *Sophist*, should be healing – purification of the soul through purgation of false or unjustified doctrines. In the *Clouds* the effect is different. Strepsiades returns home confident that critical cleverness in argument is a license to act as you please, and that moral claims based on *nomos* rather than on expert knowledge are no longer binding on the initiate into the mysteries of Glotta. 'What right have you to recover your money', he exclaims to his creditor, 'if you have no abstract knowledge?' (1283f.). And he readily concedes even the rightness of father-beating when he feels himself defeated in a contest of words. He still balks at mother-beating; but only in this extreme case is he willing to trust his moral intuitions against the judgments of the intellectual. Pheidippides, however, is young and flexible enough to be willing to use Socratism to overturn *all* traditional values. Using the name of Socrates, he assails traditional artistic taste, the authority of fathers, even the immunity of fathers from beating. In an elenctic argument typical of Anti-Right, he appeals to *physis* to justify the overthrow of *nomos*. An enthusiastic convert to intellectualism, he appears to believe that superior skill in argument not only facilitates, but even justifies, lawbreaking.[68] He takes pleasure in reflecting how, from an inarticulate playboy, he has become an expert in 'new and clever matters' (1399) who can consider himself superior to the established *nomoi* (*hyperphronein* 1400).

The play ends with an abrupt reversal. Strepsiades, prompted by the changeable Chorus (who assume in this case, presumably, the form of his own original moral nature based on *nomos*), reverts to the old values. He embraces Zeus, scorns Vortex, declares his

to it I do not understand all of it. Another suggestive discussion of the function of the Chorus is C. Segal, 'Aristophanes' Cloud-Chorus', *Arethusa* 2 (1969) 143–61, repr. in *Aristophanes und die alte Komödie*, ed. H.-J. Newiger (Darmstadt 1975) 174–97.

68. In this he may be different from the less theoretical Anti-Right, whose interests seem to be much more in getting away with wrongdoing than in justifying it.

immoralism to have been madness. In a climactic finale he burns the school of Socrates, harshly mocking the aetherial posturing of the master. Everything seems to have returned to its initial state; Right is the victor.

But can one call Right back after he has been thoroughly defeated and has deserted to the *euryprōktoi*? Is the process of questioning, once begun, reversible? (Can the Dionysus of the *Frogs* really bring back Aeschylus to save a city corrupted by Euripidean sophisms?) The end of the comedy seems to cast doubt on this. Pheidippides is ominously absent during the finale. After his last denunciation of his father he exited somewhere: 'Probably', suggests Dover, 'into Strepsiades' house.'[69] There is another possibility. The *entautha* of line 1475 suggests the reading, '*You* stay *here* and talk foolishness with yourself' (*entautha sautōi paraphronei kai phlēnapha*); '*I'll* go where I can talk to wise men.' At line 1505 an unnamed student of Socrates shouts that he is dying in the flames. Perhaps comedy does not permit of such a finale – although I shall argue that Aristophanic comedy is less sanguine about human possibilities than has sometimes been suggested. The threat of tragedy remains vague; it is certainly not clearly depicted, as in the similar ending of the comic movie *Joe*. There a reactionary father, enraged at the corruption of his daughter by new *mores*, embarks (with a partner who, in his boorishness and brute selfishness, might well have been drawn after Dicaeopolis or Strepsiades) on a rampage that has an unexpected outcome. The father waits for some of the dirty hippies who have taken his daughter, robbed him, mocked his virility. As they finally emerge from their run-down country refuge, he shoots to kill. The last frame shows us, frozen, the forehead of his own daughter, pierced by mistake, red against the clean snow. The *Clouds* is less melodramatic; we keep wondering whose voice that is from the house and are left in our uneasiness. But even if we can put aside the worst possibility, we must concede that the play ends on a note,

69. Dover, *C*, 265. On equivocal endings in comedy more generally cf. Dover, *C*, xxiv f. For discussion of the two versions of the play and the changed ending, see *C*, lxxx ff., *AC*, 103–5, H. Erbse, 'Über die ersten "Wolken" des Aristophanes', *Opus Nobile* (Wiesbaden 1969) 35–41. On the burning of the *phrontistērion*, see now E. Christian Kopff, '*Nubes* 1493ff.: Was Socrates Murdered?' *GRBS* 18 (1977) 113–22.

not of Hegelian reconciliation and *Grundwohlsein*,[70] but of anguish. A father tries to reassert the lost authority of *nomos* by committing what would be, by any *nomoi*, a horrible crime. And we know that whatever he does he has lost his son. *He* may be able, in his old age, to return to his own nature; the son's more malleable personality has been turned from him by Socratic questioning. To imagine *him* returning to the old paternal ways would be an optimism nowhere justified in the play. As Plato cogently observes in our epigraph, we cannot imagine that the unformed young man, subjected to the confusing force of the *elenchos* with no further positive training, would persist unchanged in his respect for authority. If Strepsiades has Zeus, Pheidippides is left with Chaos and Vortex. And both, as Aristophanes deeply sees, are left, in the wake of education, without the bonds of obligation and family feeling that informed their ignorance.

Socrates the educator[71]

We have by now sketched the rationale of the play's attack on Socrates and pointed to the connection between this attack and some genuine positions taken by the Platonic Socrates. Now we must develop the connections. The play contrasts two forms of moral education, depicting a time of moral upheaval in which the old values have been subjected to challenges they are not equipped to handle. And it accuses Socrates of being one of the challengers of the traditional education – even more dangerous because of his personal courage and magnetism than his overtly immoralist employee, Anti-Right. His use of elenctic questioning and his graphic demonstration of the impotence of *nomos*-virtue in a debate with its adversaries are shown to contribute to the subversion of these values among the young. It is suggested that Socrates' teaching is largely negative: he has no convincing moral principles

70. Hegel, *Vorlesungen über die Aesthetik*, 'Die Poesie', II. C. 3. c. Cf. also the remarks of Schopenhauer in *The World as Will and Idea*, III. 37.

71. For general discussion of Socrates' views and methods, see Robinson, *Plato's Earlier Dialectic*; Irwin, *PMT*, esp. chs. III–IV, and also 'Recollection and Plato's Moral Theory', *Review of Metaphysics* 27 (1974) 152–72; G. Vlastos, *Plato's Protagoras* (Indianapolis 1956) xxiv ff., and 'The Paradox of Socrates', in *The Philosophy of Socrates*, ed. G. Vlastos (Garden City, N.Y. 1971) 1–21; and M. J. O'Brien, *The Socratic Paradoxes and the Greek Mind* (Chapel Hill 1967).

(except possibly hedonism) to substitute for what he ridicules. Even if his aim were not to reject the *content* of Right's enumeration of the virtues, but only to show how urgently it stands in need of reasoned defense, the play shows him offering no defense or justification – or at least none that is understood as such by the pupil. Furthermore, he is shown to be at least culpably negligent in his indifference to the antecedent moral training of the pupil: he mocks habituation without acknowledging that it might be essential in forming a pupil's moral intuitions to a point at which the search for justification can appropriately begin. He entrusts the weapons of argumentation to anyone who will expose himself to teaching, without considering whether he is one of the people who will be likely to put the teaching to good use. He implies that teaching is sufficient and habituation irrelevant. His announcement that he will begin with a pupil's *tropoi* is the prelude not to an examination of moral character but to a test of memory and other intellectual powers.

This intellectualism is what Socrates' pupils retain from his teaching: this insistence that moral teaching is the business of experts, not elders, that a technical training enables you to scoff at ordinary norms. Socrates' teaching, unlike that of Anti-Right, is carefully neutral as to the moral use of clever rhetoric;[72] but his emphasis on argument rather than character encourages the inference that everything is justified if one is clever enough. If hedonism is true as a psychological description of untrammeled human behavior (as the play strongly implies), only long practice in virtue is likely to curb self-serving lawlessness. But Socrates encourages disdain for this laborious work. As Aristotle observes:

> Most people do not *do* these things (sc. virtuous actions); instead, taking refuge in argument, they believe they are being philosophers and that this way they will become respected men. But this is just like sick people who listen carefully to the doctor but do not do anything he prescribes. The latter will not have good bodies by taking care of themselves this way, nor will the former have good souls by doing philosophy this way. (*EN* 1105b12ff.)

72. He predicts that the clever pupil will become shrewd and cagey (260), conversant with all the tricks of rhetoric (874f., 1151), but he never explicitly urges or approves of the use of rhetoric for immoral purposes; it is the Clouds who are the goddesses of rogues and who promise Strepsiades the accomplishment of his dishonest ends (316–18, 331–4).

This is surely a commentary on the influence of Socrates, as well as that of other intellectualists who neglect the training of the character;[73] it is also a correct description of the education of Pheidippides and its results. Aristophanes and Aristotle are in agreement in their censure of an education that ridicules habituation and yet hopes to call itself philosophy.

The *Clouds*, then, attacks Socrates on three counts: (1) his lack of attention to the necessary role, in moral education, of character and the habituation-training of irrational elements; (2) his lack of a positive program to replace what he has criticized; (3) his openness to misunderstanding – his failure to make clear to his students the difference (if there is one) between his aloofness and the immoralism of Anti-Right. (This is connected with the first point, in that his carelessness in selecting students is a large factor in the resulting moral upheaval.) It should by now be emerging that these charges are directly relevant to the Platonic Socrates.

It is clear from Plato's early dialogues that, on the issue of moral education, Socrates stands with the opponents of traditional methods. His elenctic procedure establishes that most men, though they might be able to recognize instances of virtuous action,[74] are unable to provide an adequate account of the virtue. He uses questioning to reveal this lack, and, where he finds it, he concludes that true virtue is absent. He repeatedly asserts (1) that virtue is like an expert craft or skill (and not, for example, a habit or a disposition), and (2) that precise moral knowledge – the sort an expert teacher has and can impart – is by itself sufficient for virtuous action. No further training need precede or follow. Men

73. Aristotle also rejects the Socratic denial of *akrasia* on the grounds that it is plainly at variance with the *phainomena* – ordinary speech and belief about human life (*EN* 1145a22 ff.; cf. G. E. L. Owen, '*Tithenai ta Phainomena*', *Aristote et les problèmes de méthode* (Louvain 1961) 83–103, repr. in *Aristotle*, ed. J. M. E. Moravcsik (London 1968) 166–70, and in *Articles on Aristotle* 1, ed. J. Barnes, M. Schofield and R. Sorabji (London 1975) 113–26). For other Aristotelian criticism of Socrates' intellectualism see *EN* 1116b4, 1144b18; *EE* 1216b3, 1230a7, 1246b34; *MM* 1182a17, 1183b8, 1190b28, 1198a10.

74. It is clear from Socrates' procedure in rejecting proposed definitions that he relies on this ability; the lists of examples proposed by interlocutors are not simply rejected: cf. Irwin, *PMT*, ch. III. 2. 1, ch. II. 8. 2. A different view of Socrates' attitude to examples is in P. Geach, 'Plato's *Euthyphro*', *The Monist* 50 (1966) 369–82.

do wrong only out of ignorance of the good.[75] It follows that in training young people to be good we must not respect the authority of *nomos* as ultimate; we must search out the judgments of the one expert, who knows what virtue is and can give an account of it. In the *Apology* Socrates marvels at the strange priorities of parents, who will carefully seek out an expert trainer for their horses but entrust their sons to someone whose credentials they have not ascertained (20a–c). He calms Crito's worries about how *nomos* will judge him by appealing, again, to the distinction between the many and the expert: just as in physical training only the expert opinion of the doctor or trainer need be heeded, and not the judgment of the general public, so also in morals:

> Ought we to be guided and intimidated by the opinion of the many or by that of the one – assuming that there is someone with expert knowledge? Is it true that we ought to respect and fear this person more than all the rest put together, and that if we do not follow his guidance we shall spoil and mutilate that part of us which, as we used to say, is improved by right conduct and destroyed by wrong? Or is this all nonsense? (*Crito* 47c–d)

The Socratic answer, of course, is that it is true and not nonsense. 'The unexamined life' – the life lived by most men and passed on in this form through teaching to their children – 'is not worth living for a human being' (*Apol.* 38a).

The clearest evidence of the attitude of Plato's Socrates to the old education is, of course, the *Protagoras*, in which he debates a defender of *nomos* on the question of the teachability of virtue.[76] The dialogue opens with another contrast between the judgment of the expert and the opinion of the many: Socrates observes (313a–c) that Hippocrates would exercise a great deal of caution

75. See esp. *Meno* 77b ff., *Prot.* 351b ff.; cf. Irwin, *PMT*, ch. II, esp. 9–11 and n. 43; G. Santas, 'The Socratic Paradoxes', *Phil. Rev.* 73 (1964) 147–64, and 'Plato's *Protagoras* and Explanations of Weakness', *Phil. Rev.* 75 (1966) 3–33, repr. in *Socrates*, ed. G. Vlastos, 264–98; I. M. Crombie, *An Examination of Plato's Doctrines* II (London 1962) 203–5, 225–45; Vlastos, *Protagoras*, Introduction, and 'Socrates on Acrasia', *Phoenix* 23 (1969), 71–88. The best commentary on the *Prot.* argument is C. C. W. Taylor, *Plato Protagoras* (Oxford 1975), and now see also Irwin, *PMT*, ch. IV.

76. See Taylor, *Protagoras*, and Irwin, *PMT*, ch. IV for good accounts (largely in agreement) of the structure and interrelationships of the arguments in the dialogue as a whole.

before trusting his body to an athletic trainer, waiting to find out about him and check his credentials; he marvels that in the case of the soul, so much more precious than the body, he is ready to entrust himself to a man whose expert credentials he cannot possibly have ascertained.

Protagoras gives us an account and defense of traditional education in much the same terms as it was portrayed by Right (cf. esp. 325e–326a). He denies that there is any standard for morality except the time-honored standard of *nomos* and defends the ability of the average Athenian to impart practical wisdom. Socrates' reply culminates in an attempt to demonstrate the central 'Socratic paradox': that knowledge is sufficient for virtuous action. His refutation of Protagoras depends on this argument, which establishes the necessity *and* the sufficiency of a certain type of moral expertise – a skill in measuring pleasure and pain, both present and future – for the good human life. Acculturation is not enough, since without the measuring science we are still confused. It is not even, apparently, a *necessary* part of education: the argument claims that moral error is impossible once one has the expert craft. Socrates concludes:

> Have we not seen that the appearance leads us astray and throws us into confusion, so that in our actions and our choices of both great things and small we frequently affirm and reject the same things, whereas the science of measurement would have cancelled the effect of the appearance, and by revealing the truth would have brought rest to the soul abiding in the truth, thus saving our life? Considering this, would people agree that our salvation lay in the science of measurement, or in some other science?
>
> The science of measurement, he answered. (356d–e)

The important thing in morals, the only thing that can save our lives, is to get to the real nature of things behind the multiplicity of the appearances, the *physis* behind the *nomos*. And it is striking that the subject-matter of the measuring science will be pleasure: we are asked to reckon present and future enjoyings and to see the moral virtues as reducible to a hedonistic calculus. The thesis of hedonism – both as a psychological truth about actual behavior and as a theory of the human good – seems to be seriously endorsed by Socrates here as an answer to the vagueness of the other early dialogues about the nature of the final good which the craft or science he seeks is to pursue.[77]

The *Protagoras* passage indicates why Socrates finds *nomos*-virtue inadequate: (1) it leads to confusion in deliberation and choice, and (2) it is unable to produce a justification of itself when subjected to questioning. The two points are related in that inability to justify may itself contribute to deliberative confusion and moral collapse. Socrates concludes that the ordinary morality is in deep trouble and in need of 'salvation' by a precise science not available to the general public. He hopes, as is evident from all the early dialogues, to preserve most of the *content* of the popular morality, while grounding it in a science which will give, as popular morality cannot, an adequate justification of its principles. Any moral teacher who does less while claiming to teach virtue must, like Gorgias, be held responsible for the sins of his pupils.

But the Socratic assimilation of morality to an expert craft or skill seems questionable.[78] (1) It neglects, as Aristotle points out, the crucial importance of early habituation and the training of the desires; dispositions to behave morally are *not* like capacities to perform. A craft can be separated from the desire to use it well; a good doctor is also a good poisoner.[79] (2) It fails to identify with sufficient precision the aim or end of morals, that of which the expert is an expert producer.[80] In most of the Socratic dialogues we find no positive account of the human good. In the *Protagoras* we have the identification of the good with pleasure. But there is

77. This has often been doubted, largely because commentators have been unwilling to ascribe to Socrates a thesis that they do not admire; see Vlastos, *Protagoras*, Introduction, and J. P. Sullivan, 'The Hedonism in Plato's *Protagoras*', *Phronesis* 6 (1961) 10–28 for two unsuccessful attempts to explain it away. The hedonism is taken seriously by Crombie, Irwin and Taylor. For pertinent philosophical discussions see J. C. B. Gosling's lucid *Pleasure and Desire* (Oxford 1969) and J. Rawls, *A Theory of Justice* (Cambridge, Mass. 1971), ch. IX, esp. sections 83–5 on hedonism as a method of choice.

78. For one account of the craft analogy and a forceful criticism see Irwin, 'Recollection', and *PMT*, esp. ch. III. 9–11.

79. This point is recognized in *Rep.* I. 333e ff., though surrounding arguments still seem to rely on the craft analogy. Cf. also Aristotle, *Metaph.* IX. 2 and 5, *EN* II. 1–5.

80. I do not, however, agree with Irwin that the craft analogy by itself implies that the theorist has in mind some end that can be identified and specified without reference to art- or craft-activities. Gymnastics, flute-playing (cf. Aristotle, *MM* 1211b27 ff., 1197b9 ff.) and many other *technai* have their own activities as their ends. I shall argue this point in detail in a forthcoming study.

no account of pleasure in terms of which we might assess the Socratic thesis.[81] We are, for example, nowhere shown how pleasure can at one and the same time be a single standard of choice and also yield the verdict that the courageous man is better off than the comfortable coward.[82] We find that Protagoras' *nomoi* have been undermined, with no substantial theory to replace them – except a theory about what a theory must look like.

If we now return to the three counts of the Aristophanic indictment, I think we can see that there is a decent case to be made for convicting Plato's Socrates on all three. The first two points have emerged from this analysis of the *Protagoras*.[83] As for the third, we can see from the dialogues that Plato's Socrates, like the comic character, selects his pupils freely, openly, without prior inquiry into their training and beliefs. He talks with Alcibiades as well as with Cephalus. And while he insists that a proper understanding of pleasure would justify conventional courage, he does not clearly distinguish his own position from a cruder sort of bodily hedonism. A reader of the *Protagoras* might very well conclude that Socrates' attack on *nomos* justified shirking his civic duty, despite Socrates' own pious protestations to the contrary.

At this point objections will be raised. What of Socrates' lifelong devotion to virtue? What of his repeated attacks on immoralism and his impassioned defence of virtuous living? Surely no pupil of Socrates could have ignored these interests and commitments. Now one must agree here that Aristophanes omits much that was obviously of central concern to Socrates. But we have seen that Socrates' concern with virtue and its justification, at least as depicted in Plato's early dialogues, leads to no clear or obvious results. In the one place where the theory of the good does become more concrete, it is in a form that invites, rather than prevents, confusion with immoralism. It would not be unfair to say that most

81. Cf. Crombie, *Examination*, 243–5 and Taylor, *Protagoras*, comm. *ad loc.*; Gosling's *Pleasure* gives an excellent account of the difficulties involved in producing an account of pleasure as a single standard – and these difficulties are acknowledged by Plato in the *Philebus*, 12ff.

82. Cf. esp. Crombie, 243–5. It may have been these difficulties, which force their way to the surface in the *Protagoras*, that prompt the abandonment of hedonism in the *Gorgias*, in the context of a very similar discussion of courage.

83. The *Crito* takes a position on *nomoi* and culture which seems problematically different – cf. A. D. Woozley, 'Socrates on Disobeying the Law', in *Socrates*, ed. Vlastos, 299–318.

of Socrates' concern for virtue remains in the realm of personal choice and good intentions for others.[84] Aristophanes' portrait ignores the good intentions while portraying the success of the elenctic attack on *nomos*. This, the play claims, is what Socrates really succeeds in teaching; this is how a pupil really sees and interprets Socratic teaching – especially a pupil of the sort he would carelessly pick, a man more dedicated to pleasure than to virtue. Even a much more substantially elaborated moral position could be misinterpreted; but it seems correct that the peculiarities of Socrates' own teaching make it particularly susceptible to abuse. And one can see the truth of this charge from the history of the play itself. Had Socrates been as clearly different from the immoralists as Dover believes – so different as not to be dangerous – the play's portrait would have been repudiated. But it was, by Socrates' own testimony, widely believed. It simply voiced, he tells us, a pervasive view of his career. This itself tells a great deal about Socrates' effect; the play can be viewed, in a way, as a trial as well as an indictment. If it convinces, this will help show that Socrates' prestige and influence *have* helped to undermine conventional standards, no matter whether or not this is what he set out to do. We might think that anyone whose teaching is so radically critical of tradition had better be more careful not to be misunderstood – especially someone who makes success a criterion of good teaching, misinterpretation a proof of failure (cf. the Gorgias passage cited above, p. 47, and Socrates' ensuing criticism of this view). Even a wonderful teacher can fail with inept pupils. But Socrates' teaching, with its silence about the final good, its subsequent use of hedonistic premises, and its injunction to mistrust and question the teachings of *nomos*, seems particularly open to such problems. And Socrates' neglect of the irrational passions and their training seems to prevent him from asking some crucial questions about who is fit for the challenge of the *elenchos*, and who is likely to be confused without being healed.

Aristophanes was not alone in finding these faults with Socratic teaching. Similar considerations seems to lie behind the sweeping

84. Irwin discusses the way in which Socrates' frequent praise of virtue masks the radical nature of his criticisms (*PMT*, ch. III. 6. 6), and observes that Socrates' philosophical arguments support only his negative criticisms, not his positive convictions (ch. III. 1. 1).

reappraisal of the role of dialectic in the city that we find in Plato's *Republic*. (1) Neglect of habituation was felt by Plato to have been a major defect of the Socratic enterprise. His account of human nature in *Republic* IV opposes itself to Socratic intellectualism by denying that all desires are for the good and conceding the reality of *akrasia*.[85] These views lead him, in his program of education, to separate the training of the non-rational desires from the intellectual teaching of the 'rational part' of the soul. Plato recognizes that this necessitates a return to much that Socrates had discarded. His proposal for the education of the guardians begins: 'What, then, is our education (*paideia*)? Is it not hard to find a better one than that which long time has discovered – which is, I suppose, gymnastics for the body and, for the soul, music?' (376e). The very use of the traditional word *paideia* is unsocratic; Socrates denies that he imparts *paideia* to students (*Apol.* 19d–e). And the system elaborated in what follows has much in common with the old education described by Right; it is even more firmly protected against change and innovation. In short, before any guardian is given a chance to try out dialectic, he has become rigidly habituated, reliably trained to act virtuously. Knowledge may still be necessary for true virtue; it is no longer sufficient.

(2) It is obvious that the *Republic* offers us a substantial positive account of justice and the other virtues; the entire work is an answer to the immoralist demand for their justification. *Republic* I looks like a typical Socratic dialogue and has a typically aporetic conclusion. The interlocutors, confounded by Socrates' challenge to tradition and not satisfied by his admittedly incomplete answer to the immoralist, might have gone off to begin a Pheidippidean life. By writing Book I as a prelude to the positive moral and political work of the *Republic*, Plato indicates to us that Socrates has achieved only a prelude to moral philosophy; the rest of the work shows us what he believes was mistaken in or lacking from Socrates' account.[86]

(3) But it is perhaps in the third area that Plato makes his most radical departure from Socrates. The essence of Socratic

85. Cf. T. Penner, 'Thought and Desire in Plato', in *Plato* II, ed. G. Vlastos (Garden City, New York 1971) 96–118 and Irwin, *PMT*, ch. VII. 6.

86. As I rewrote this paper I discovered very similar remarks in F. E. Sparshott's 'Plato and Thrasymachus', *Univ. Toronto Quart.* 27 (1957) 54–61.

questioning was its openness and publicity. Anyone who encountered Socrates could be subjected to the *elenchos*: he describes himself as the gadfly of the Athenian democracy. Plato, from his perception of the great threat that open dialectic poses to social stability, and his belief that without social stability men cannot live good lives, infers the necessity of restricting dialectic to those who are both initially well trained and outstandingly intelligent. The epigraph to this paper is part of an argument for such a restriction; and the characterization of the practice found dangerous points unambiguously to Socrates. Only he accosted complacent citizens with the 'What is X?' question; it was he who sought for general accounts of the *kalon*, the *dikaion* and the *agathon*; it was he who embarrassed and confused his interlocutors, throwing them into perplexity about the grounding of *nomos*. The double use of the word *elenchos* puts the identification beyond reasonable doubt. Plato charges his teacher (ironically, in his teacher's own *persona*) with contributing to moral decline by not restricting the questioning process to a chosen, well-trained few. Socrates is too optimistic about the potential of the ordinary man for understanding and moral growth. Plato, with Aristophanes, believes that for the ordinary man questioning is destructive without being therapeutic.[87]

87. It might be argued that the restriction of dialectic to the few is applicable only to the ideal state and that Plato would tolerate a more liberal practice in actual states. I do not think this claim could be established. (1) The ideal state is an ideal: that is, we are to approximate as nearly to its practices and institutions as we possibly can in our actual politics (esp. *Rep.* 592a and *Laws* v); since Plato never argues that it will in fact be impossible to restrict dialectic (as he believes, in the *Laws*, it will be to make all property common), we have no reason to think that actual states cannot aim at the ideal with some hope of success; and many actual states have succeeded all too well. (2) The arguments given for the restriction of dialectic to a chosen few appear to be even more applicable to the situation of actual states than to the ideal state; if open dialectic causes civil upheaval it will do so all the more in a city less orderly to begin with, where moral education has been less successful in effecting unanimity of feeling and belief; the question would be whether in a non-ideal state there would be anyone who would have the kind of preparation Plato tells us is a necessity. (3) The passage I have cited is part of an argument about the institutions of the ideal state; but the example of the young man itself does not appear to be set in the ideal state; if the corrupter is Socrates, we are then to think of Athens. With the example Plato indicates that his remarks about the disrupting effects of incautious dialectic are appropriate not just to the ideal state but to any state in which there are well-brought-up young men who still lack full knowledge of the good. There is no sign that he wishes to distinguish the case of Socrates and Athens from the

Moral education: an Aristotelian alternative?

We have seen, then, a criticism of the view that conscious knowledge is both necessary and sufficient for the perfection of the moral life and that in consequence no worthwhile moral understanding is available in the day-to-day life of the polis. The Socratic insistence that morality is a science for experts has been attacked as both unjustified and dangerous. And yet we cannot read the play as advocating a simple return to the old education. Right's program is impotent to deal with the task of justifying morality in a time of social change. And even were a return to his program possible, we have been given reason to be suspicious of his intolerance and irrationality. The play has implied that a disdain for reason may actually be dangerous to some of the fundamental values of democratic *nomos*.

The play presents no positive program; but it leaves us with a challenge. We are shown the need for a form of moral education which combines a Socratic respect for reason with Right's attention to the role of tradition and to the central place of habituation in training the desires. There are two such conceptions of education in the Greek tradition: the Aristotelian and the Platonic. One is compatible with the preservation (to some degree, at any rate) of the democratic values of separateness and autonomy; the other is not.[88] I would like to conclude this paper by briefly examining the Aristotelian program and asking whether the author of the *Clouds* would be able to accept this as a solution to the play's dilemma. This seems to be the best way to determine how deep and how radical the Aristophanic criticism of democratic tradition really is.

The Aristotelian holds, with Socrates, that full adult virtue must

case of the ideal city in these respects. (4) Plato tells us (473c–e) that the founding of the ideal state ruled by philosophers is a necessary condition for happiness both civic and individual. If this is taken seriously then we would not really be asking whether in a non-ideal state there might be a different route to civic happiness; Plato has told us that there is no such route except via the ideal. Even when he appears to concede that rare individuals might reach the good without the ideal city (592a–b) he says that they will do so only by imagining themselves as its citizens and taking part 'in the public affairs of that city only, not of any other'.

88. I discuss these questions in 'Shame, Separateness and Political Unity: Aristotle's Criticism of Plato', in *Mind and the Good: Essays in Aristotle's Moral Psychology*, ed. A. Rorty (Berkeley 1980).

be aware of itself and able to justify itself in argument.[89] And yet he insists that the virtues are neither simply natural capacities nor pieces of learned wisdom, but dispositions, formed by practice in choosing and doing the appropriate actions. The young begin with the natural appetites. By social teaching, in the family and in the polis, they must be trained to find pleasure in the things that reasonable adults agree are right; a pre-rational training must prepare the soul for the full reasoned understanding of virtue.[90]

> Reason and teaching do not have the same force in all circumstances; but the soul of the pupil must be thoroughly worked over beforehand, by habituation, in the direction of taking pleasure and hating nobly, just as earth that is going to be tilled has to be prepared for the seed. The man who lives according to whim will not listen to an argument deterring him, or even understand it (*EN* 1179b23–8).

The good city, ruled by men of practical wisdom who have a clear and explicit picture of their concept of the good, will establish a system of training which makes use of traditional methods – but in the service of the full life of virtue to come. Many men will attain such a life; for those who cannot it will be necessary to follow the advice of others.[91]

The standard of virtue and of teaching is relative, then, to the deliberations of men of practical wisdom.[92] But this standard is not simply the standard of Right's irrationally held *nomos*. The explicit picture of the good and the just held by a virtuous man should be the result of a thorough weighing of 'the appearances' – the manifold data of human life that bear on moral choice. A rational system of norms will be based on a thorough working-through of all the major moral possibilities offered us in the thought and

89. It should be emphasized, however, that the justification need not, for Aristotle, take the form of fitting the action in question into a closed deductive system; on this see my *De Motu*, Essay 4.

90. I have profited, on these issues, from Myles Burnyeat's 'Aristotle on Learning to be Good', in *Mind and the Good*, ed. A. Rorty. Another valuable discussion is Richard Sorabji's 'Aristotle on the Role of the Intellect in Virtue', *Proc. Arist. Soc.* (1973–4); cf. also my *De Motu*, IV (Commentary) on 700b22.

91. Cf. *EN* 1095b10 ff., a passage that Burnyeat's discussion has helped me to appreciate.

92. Cf. esp. *EN* 1106b36 ff. and V. 10; and the discussion of these in my *De Motu*, Essay 4.

speech of the many and the wise.[93] Aristotelian justice is not simply conventional, as is that of Right – the wise man can give reasons for preferring his ways to others; nor is it natural in the sense of being based on some extra-human standard. It is the 'mutable' natural justice of the theory which best saves the phenomena of human action, within the forms of human life as we know them (cf. esp. *EN* 1134b18ff.). The average citizen within a polis should submit his pre-reflective judgments – even those learned within the polis itself – to the arbitration of practical reason, which will adjudicate among the contributions of all. The 'expert' will be special not because he knows something we do not know,[94] but because he sees better and more clearly what we all, collectively, know. Thus moral argument and moral change will take place within a climate of reasoned debate, and will represent an attempt to reach the best possible ordered articulation of our moral intuitions.

Suppose we have in such a city Devlin's man on the Clapham omnibus, with his English attachment to a tradition of political liberty and his irrational prejudice against homosexuals. The job of the man of practical wisdom will not be, as Socrates seems to urge, simply to discard or ignore his views in forming public policy. It will be to take his moral convictions most seriously as part of the legislator's evidence, but to sort out, among these convictions, the more basic and more prevalent from the less important – those he might be willing to discard were they shown to be in conflict with the others. In this case we might try to get the man to see that there is a real conflict between his fundamental attachment to equal liberty and his desire to deny basic liberties to people who offend him. We might also point out that he cannot consistently insist, in most of his life, on the importance of distinctions between prejudice and argument, between well and badly grounded empirical generalizations, while refusing to subject his own views

93. On the *phainomena*, and the crucial passage 1145b2–6 (cf. also 1216b26 ff.), see Owen, '*Tithenai Ta Phainomena*'. A similar picture is more elaborately developed in Rawls, *Theory of Justice*, 20ff., 48–51.

94. Cf. *EN* 1095b3 ff.; Burnyeat's paper contains a valuable discussion of Aristotle's contrast between knowing the that (*hoti*) and knowing the why (*dioti*); it is difficult to understand how the former sort of awareness can consistently be called *epistēmē*.

to this same scrutiny.[95] If he rejects all our attempts to argue with him, we will be entitled ultimately to discount him as a competent moral judge.[96] Again, if he does admit defeat in argument he must give up either his prejudice (or at least his identification with it as a basis of action) or his claim to be regarded as a rational man. (Thus what Lord Devlin refers to as the 'power of common sense' would be expected to complete itself in dialogue with the 'power of reason'; the good public morality would be a harmonious adjustment of the former in accordance with the demands of the latter.)

What is problematic about all this, as Aristotle very clearly saw, is that it is an ideal picture, not easily applicable to political reality. 'The many obey necessity rather than reason...A man who is fair-minded and lives with an eye to the noble will submit to reason, but the mediocre man (*phaulon*) who reaches out for pleasure will have to be chastened by pain like a beast of burden (*hypozygion*)' (*EN* 1180a4–12). The Aristotelian, who believes in the reflective dialogue of principle and intuition, must also concede that in most real situations confidence in reason is insufficient for 'the philosophy which deals with human things' (1181b16). An Aristotelian system of early education will go a long way towards imparting to all citizens a shared concept of the good; but when conflicts and disputes arise, the many – even a relatively well trained many – will be unlikely to moderate their behavior because of argument alone. At the opening of the *Republic* Polemarchus and his friends, reminding Socrates of their superior numbers, offer him only two choices: do as we say, or resist by force. When Socrates reminds them that there is a third alternative, namely persuasion, these good democrats laugh and reply, 'Can you persuade men who do not listen?' (*Rep.* 327c).

Aristotle's own proposed remedy for the political problem of reason has three parts. First he insists on a public system of laws summarizing the decisions of men of practical wisdom, provided with sanctions which would chasten the hedonistic many.[97] Second, to protect legislative activity itself, he extends citizenship only to those whose occupations allow them leisure to have a long

95. This is one of the main objections raised by Dworkin, 'Lord Devlin', to Devlin's arguments.

96. This may not, however, make much difference to him if we are not in a position of political authority over him: see below, pp. 91–2.

97. On the status of these laws see my *De Motu*, Essay 4.

and thorough early training and, later, to reflect philosophically about the good life. Finally, and perhaps most importantly, he enjoins on the ruler(s) the task of fostering friendship among men in the polis *qua* citizens, so that, even if a law seems repugnant to an individual or a group, these men will be inclined to obey it out of good will to the regime itself and to their fellow citizens who are benefited by it.[98]

Thus if the man on the omnibus persists, despite our public education and despite later reasoned argument, in prejudices held by men of practical wisdom to be inconsistent with the society's more basic values, the Aristotelian legislator will be entitled to enact a law protecting the rights of homosexuals from his intolerance, and providing sanctions, should his opposition show itself in harmful action. Towards the success of this attempt the system of public education is once again crucial. First, if it is not successful enough to create moral unanimity and to make rationality prevail throughout the city, it must succeed at least to the point of ensuring that the many will select or acquiesce in the selection of their rational superiors as legislators. Legislation cannot protect reason if the hedonistic *phauloi* tyrannize politically over practical wisdom. Next, the legislator will have to hope, as he acts to protect the rights of a minority, that the opposition will at least have been trained in a very basic attachment to the regime's constitution and to one another as citizens of the regime. If he cannot be brought to feel well diposed to the homosexual minority as men and women (much less as homosexuals) we must hope that he will at least feel a more attenuated, but still binding, friendship with them as citizens subject to the same laws, and thus refrain from outrage even when the law turns its back. At the very, very least the legislator must hope that the people disadvantaged by a law will have some general attachment to the existence of the regime and to the idea of obeying its laws, which will prevail where argument and more immediate friendly feelings do not. The part of Right's program that was a training in patriotism and in love of the symbols, songs and festivals connected with the Athenian regime

98. Civic friendship is a complicated and important issue in Aristotle's political philosophy. The best discussion I know is Janet Hook's 'Friendship and Politics in Aristotle's Ethical and Political Thought' (Senior Honors Thesis in Philosophy and Government, Harvard University 1977).

would have a very important place in maintaining the stability of an Aristotelian state. For patriotism is the indispensable minimum of civic friendship. And 'friendship seems to hold cities together, and legislators seem to work harder over it than over justice' (*EN* 1155a22–5).

The *Clouds* casts doubt on the possibility of this Aristotelian polis precisely by casting doubt on the capacity of the ordinary man for civic friendship and public patriotism when his own interests are threatened. The *Clouds* is probably Aristophanes' least public-spirited play; it evinces none of the passion for reform, none of the delight in civic festivals, that characterize works such as the *Wasps* and the *Acharnians*. Pheidippides prays only to the gods of his private pleasures; Strepsiades calls on Zeus the King to get out of a personal mess. When shown a map he asks only to see his own deme (210); the nearness of Sparta is occasion for personal worry, not public concern. The key question is always *ti kerdanō;*, 'what shall I gain?' (257, cf. 1064, 1115, 1202); the key psychological principle is egoistic hedonism. Even the parabasis is in the first person,[99] preoccupied not with public issues (as is the poet's more common practice) but with the poet's own personal grievances and merits. And his solemn invocation of Athena, Guardian of the City, serves only to underwrite this claim to a private victory (602).

In other plays of Aristophanes there appears to be some possibility, however tenuous, of transforming the hedonism of the ordinary man into a broader concern for the polis as a whole. But even in the *Acharnians*, whose hero is a reformer named Just City, Dicaeopolis' concern for his own personal satisfaction grows more and more solipsistic until it entirely eclipses questions of justice, and an appeal to sympathy is answered with the brusque, 'See to your own business' (1019, cf. *Clouds* 1263). As the Chorus concludes, 'The man has found something pleasant (*hēdy*) in the truce and it looks as if he is not going to give a share of it to anyone' (1036–9).[100] In the *Knights* Demos emerges rejuvenated; but he is a hedonistic character too, lured by vulgarity, roughness and lack of education. Being *kalos kagathos* (185), having a good character (192), having a good moral education (189f., 334) – all are

99. The only known case of this in Old Comedy.

100. On the character of Dicaeopolis see Dover, *AC*, 87f. and *Maia* 15 (1963) 21f. Lowell Edmunds (in this volume) proposes a different interpretation.

disadvantages in securing his favor.[101] The *Clouds*, even more unambiguously than these other plays, presents us with a picture of private hedonism impervious to reason and even to sympathy. These men simply do not *care* about anything but their own satisfactions when it comes to a choice. And lest we too quickly feel ourselves superior to them, the *Clouds* insists that we members of the audience are no different. We are all just *euryprōktoi* waiting passively for pleasure.

Thus none of the necessary conditions for an Aristotelian program is satisfied in Aristophanic democracy. In choice of leaders, in the act of legislating, and in the average man's attitude toward law, irrationality and egoism prevail. The striking affinities we have already noticed between the Aristophanic and the Platonic criticisms of Socrates seem to be part of a deeper similarity in their assessments of what untrammeled human *physis* can be, and how inadequate democratic institutions are to turn it towards virtue. In Plato's democracy and in Aristophanes', legislation itself is ruled by partisanship and prejudice, and the rule of reason is nowhere to be seen.[102] The triumph of the hero is not the triumph of sympathy over egoism, or reason over unreason; it is that of one unselfcritical, self-absorbed ego over other egos.

Northrup Frye tells us that comedy usually ends with a wedding.[103] This is not even literally true of the *Clouds*, or of most other Aristophanic comedies. And I am tempted to think that it is *never* deeply true of them – if, by marriage, we understand (as Frye seems to) any real commitment of two persons to one another, forming a bond of sympathy that will override personal egoism and

101. Here *kalos kagathos* seems to be more generally commendatory than class-linked; cf. above, n. 47.

102. The Assembly in the *Acharnians*, the portrait of lawcourts in the *Wasps* and the description of democratic judgment in the parabasis of the *Frogs* are good examples of this. A full study of Aristophanes' views on the potential for rationality in legislation would, however, have to include a close study of the *Ecclesiazusae* and the *Peace* as well.

103. Northrup Frye, *Anatomy of Criticism* (Princeton 1957) 163ff., esp. 169: 'The society emerging at the conclusion of comedy represents, by contrast, a kind of moral norm, or pragmatically free society. . . We are simply given to understand that the newly-married couple will live happily ever after, or that at any rate they will get along in a relatively unhumorous and clear-sighted manner.' Frye's subsequent claim that the movement of comedy is from *pistis* to *gnōsis*, illusion to truth, seems equally questionable for Aristophanes, if we think of the growing solipsism of Dicaeopolis or of Strepsiades' return to defective and rigid ways.

lay a foundation for community. Aristophanic comedy usually shows us eating and drinking without any sacrifice so that others may eat. (The Megarian Farmer in the *Acharnians* who sells his daughters into prostitution for a little salt is no anomaly in his work.) It shows us moral training where the voice of Right is, if we hear it correctly, as egoistic as the voice of his opposition. It shows us marriage where lust is unaccompanied by sentiment, where the ideal bride (in the *Birds*, one of Frye's chosen examples) is a girl with the happy name of Sovereign Power (*Basileia*), who can both give you pleasure and get you anything you want from the gods. (Peisetaerus won her by eating the creatures who gave him a home and whom he praised as deities.)

I played the role of Basileia once, opposite the late Bert Lahr. The way he played the wedding procession was to hand me up into his golden chariot and then give me a big kiss – prefaced by his characteristic hungry 'ngah-ngah-ngah'. Deliberately, day after day, he did not powder his clown makeup; the result was that unless I cleverly dodged my face emerged splotched with red grease paint, and I too became an object of laughter. I did not much like that. After all, I had at most three minutes onstage; I could not say a word; and once I got into the chariot they could not even see my legs. But Lahr understood a lot about this play. He used to say that the *Birds* was darker to him even than *Godot* – and that, at least, got good reviews. Still, he intuitively knew what that wedding was about. Whether he thought he was, as Lahr, having some fun at the expense of a vain bit-player, or, as Peisetaerus, showing Basileia that power too can be mocked and made ridiculous, he knew and showed somehow the spirit of vanity, greed and self-absorbed gloating that makes an Aristophanic wedding far from a triumph of *Grundwohlsein*. So, of course, did I – without knowing half so well what I was doing.[104]

If I am right to say that the *Clouds* points to the need for an alternative both to the traditional ways and to Socratism, it is also clear that it presents a picture of human nature that casts serious

104. Paul Woodruff has argued, in 'Rousseau, Molière and the Ethics of Laughter', *Philosophy and Literature* I. 3 (1976–7) 325–35, that 'we' consider it unhealthy to laugh at ourselves in a way that involves taking ourselves seriously as characters of a certain sort, with ongoing stable traits. I would argue against him that the healthy laughter inspired by this comedy *requires* taking one's character seriously, and being actively engaged in self-critical deliberation.

doubt on the plausibility of the type of solution that we might like most to put forward. It is closer to Plato than to Aristotle in its portrait of the soul of the democratic man, and in its implications about how far the rule of reason is compatible with political freedom. How far we can say this was Aristophanes' own view of man, and how far in consequence we can speak of *his* critique of democracy or *his* Platonism will of course remain a tough question. What we can conclude from the play is that he thought this a picture worth showing us – one from which, perhaps, something essential to the health of the polis might be learned. If he did not in the end find liberal Aristotelianism impossible, still he thought it vital to point out the difficulties in its way, difficulties that its defenders, then and now, might too quickly dismiss. At the end of the *Wasps* the Chorus observes, 'It is difficult to stand aside from one's ongoing nature' (1457f.). This difficulty, and the selfishness of *physis*, Aristotelian political theory may well have underestimated.

Plato argues that the things that matter to us are too precious to be left (as they are left in democracy) to chance and to the selfish passions. The liberal 'freedoms' and liberal education are bought at the price of the stability and the rational dignity that are constitutive of *true* freedom. The *Clouds*, by showing us the potential violence of the democratic man, and his monumental indifference to the rights, the dignity, even the lives of his fellow citizens, seems to bolster Plato's argument. And by making us laugh at, even sympathize with, this behavior, it shows us (as indeed it also tells us) that we are not exempt from the play's critique. Aristotle is right that comedy shows men as worse than they are – but because it shows only a part of what they are, not because it lies. If, like the comic poet and his audience, we are people who value the right to 'speak the truth without constraint', we can hardly afford not to laugh at this image of ourselves – or to take our laughter lightly.[105]

105. I am grateful to Jeffrey Henderson, Janet Hook, Terence Irwin and Zeph Stewart for their thorough and searching criticisms of earlier drafts. I am sure that I have not answered all of their questions or, indeed, all of my own.

Aristophanes as a lyric poet

MICHAEL SILK

Of the many extraordinary features of Aristophanic comedy, none is more extraordinary than its lyrics – especially, I am tempted to add, if one includes under that heading some of the comments that the lyrics themselves have engendered. The present essay has three main objects: to oppose what seems to be a general notion of Aristophanes as a writer of 'serious' lyric poetry; to clarify the conceptual basis of this notion; and to offer a reinterpretation of his actual achievement as a lyric poet.[1]

I

The general view is easily stated. In the first place, Aristophanes is 'a master of lyric poetry in every vein, humorous, solemn, or delicate' (Dover).[2] And in particular, his lyrics 'frequently rise to the level of authentic high poetry' (Rau).[3] The fact is that he has an 'enchanting, airy manner, which is among the glories of Greek lyric poetry' (Bowra).[4] Hence his lyrics can be spoken of in the same breath as the poems of Pindar and Keats (Stanford);[5] or, not to mince words, 'some of the finest Greek lyrics – and that is to say some of the finest lyrics produced by the human genius – are found in his plays' (Harsh).[6] Such statements tend to be supported by disappointingly little in the way of analysis or comparison or

1. Note: (i) Unless otherwise stated, the text of A used is the Oxford Text of Hall and Geldart (1906–7). (ii) Unless otherwise stated, the translations (which do not, on the whole, have any literary pretensions) are mine. (iii) In the footnotes 'Aristophanes' is generally abbreviated as 'A'.

2. *OCD*² 113 (s.v. 'Aristophanes').

3. '...erhebt sich...nicht selten zu echter hoher Poesie' (P. Rau, *Paratragodia: Untersuchung einer komischen Form des Aristophanes* (München 1967) 13).

4. *AJPh* (1958) 378.

5. Commentary on *Frogs* (1963), xli.

6. P. W. Harsh, *A Handbook of Classical Drama* (Stanford 1944), 264f.

indeed argument of any kind, but their authors indicate sufficiently clearly their agreement on which particular lyrics and which kinds of lyric in general they have in mind. '...especially in *Clouds* and *Birds*...', adds Rau, to general assent. The hoopoe's song to the nightingale (*Birds* 209ff.) and the parodos in *Clouds* (275ff., 298ff.) are most frequently cited. The chorus of initiates in *Frogs* often figure on the list ('their hymn of invocation to Iacchus is a pearl of Aristophanic poetry', Lesky);[7] and from time to time one or two other instances are remarked on, such as the lyrics towards the end of *Lysistrata*.[8] I can see every reason to applaud Aristophanes' mastery of what Dover calls 'humorous' lyric. What I do not see is that the claim for Aristophanes as a master of high 'serious' lyric is in any way justified. Let us first look at the examples – not, in fact, so many examples: the few so often referred to and the comparatively few others that would seem to belong with them as candidates for the title of 'serious' lyric poetry: all those lyrical passages, that is, which, without any sign of deflationary humour or incongruity, consistently recall the serious lyrical tradition – its idioms, its diction, its rhythms, its distinctive features of all kinds.

Birds 209–22, those 'charming lines' (Richards)[9] in which the hoopoe invokes the nightingale, comprising one of 'the finest lyrics produced by the human genius' (Harsh):[10]

ἄγε σύννομέ μοι παῦσαι μὲν ὕπνου,
λῦσον δὲ νόμους ἱερῶν ὕμνων,
οὓς διὰ θείου στόματος θρηνεῖς
τὸν ἐμὸν καὶ σὸν πολύδακρυν Ἴτυν,
ἐλελιζομένη διεροῖς μέλεσιν
   γένυος ξουθῆς.
καθαρὰ χωρεῖ διὰ φυλλοκόμου
μίλακος ἠχὼ πρὸς Διὸς ἕδρας,
ἵν' ὁ χρυσοκόμας Φοῖβος ἀκούων
τοῖς σοῖς ἐλέγοις ἀντιψάλλων
ἐλεφαντόδετον φόρμιγγα θεῶν
ἵστησι χορούς· διὰ δ' ἀθανάτων
στομάτων χωρεῖ ξύμφωνος ὁμοῦ
   θεία μακάρων ὀλολυγή.

7. *Hist. Gr. Lit.*², trans. Willis and de Heer (London 1966) 443.
8. E.g. by Bowra, *loc. cit.*
9. H. Richards, *Aristophanes and Others* (London 1909) 120.
10. *Op. cit.* 265.

Awake, my mate! | Shake off thy slumbers, and clear and strong | Let loose the floods of thy glorious song, | The sacred dirge of thy mouth divine | For sore-wept Itys, thy child and mine; | Thy tender trillings his name prolong | With the liquid note of thy tawny throat; | Through the leafy curls of the woodbine sweet | The pure sound mounts to the heavenly seat. | And Phoebus, lord of the golden hair, | As he lists to thy wild plaint echoing there, | Draws answering strains from his ivoried lyre, | Till he stirs the dance of the heavenly choir, | And calls from the blessed lips on high | Of immortal Gods, a divine reply | To the tones of thy witching melody.[11]

'Charm', yes; 'finest lyrics' etc., no. The song, in anapaests,[12] bears a marked resemblance in part to Euripides, *Helen* 1107–13, a play written two years later. In particular one notes the following pairs:

Av. 213f.	ἐλελιζομένη διεροῖς μέλεσιν γένυος ξουθῆς
Hel. 1111f.	διὰ ξουθᾶν γενύων ἐλελιζομένα
Av. 209–11	σύννομέ μοι...θρηνεῖς
Hel. 1112	θρήνων ἐμοὶ ξυνεργός
Av. 215	διὰ φυλλοκόμου
Hel. 1107	ὑπὸ δενδροκόμοις,

this last pair having identical rhythmical shape (⏑⏑–⏑⏑–), despite participation in two very different metrical contexts (the Euripidean being 'a kind of near-dactylo-epitrite').[13] One can infer that the two passages have a common, presumably lyric, source[14] or alternatively that Aristophanes is actually a direct source for the tragedian.[15] Either way, there is no occasion here to invoke Aristophanes the parodist and every reason, *prima facie*, to take his lyric seriously.[16] It is certainly not conspicuously *funny*, notwithstanding the wider comic context – jokey dialogue, bizarre situation, amazing costumes (as one supposes) and all. But the presumed *seriousness* of the lyric does not in itself make it *good*.

11. Tr. Rogers. Text as codd. (see Fraenkel, *Eranos* (1950) 75–7).
12. Presumably song, not 'recitative' (cf. n. 57 below): v. 226 implies that this is a μέλος and the rhythmical quirk in 214 would seem to point the same way.
13. Dale, *ad loc.*
14. So e.g. Rau, *Paratragodia* 195; van Leeuwen on *Av.* 749–51.
15. So, apparently, Kannicht on *Helen*, *ad loc.* and K. J. Dover, *Aristophanic Comedy* (London 1972) 148f.
16. Rau, *Paratragodia* 195: 'echte, nicht parodische Lyrik'.

The lyric is in fact a piece of hyper-conventional high-lyrical pastiche, written in a very relaxed style devoid of any pressure or pointedness. Its simple theme – the nightingale is to sing and Apollo and the gods in general will answer – is distended to fill up fourteen verses without wit or invention, let alone intellectual point. The distension is achieved in the first place by elevated cliché. Apollo is predictably χρυσοκόμας[17] (note the Doric colouring as guarantor of high poetry); the nightingale, or its throat, ξουθή;[18] Itys gets an inevitable mention; and so on. Convention, of course, plays a very important role in Greek poetry, but the best Greek poetry is much more than conventional. Even more significant – and more unwelcome if one has expectations derived from Pindar or Keats – is a string of pointless repetitions, echoes, and prolixities:

209f. σύννομε ~ νόμους
210f. ἱερῶν ~ θείου[19]
211 διὰ θείου στόματος ~ 220f. διὰ δ' ἀθανάτων στομάτων
215 χωρεῖ διὰ φυλλοκόμου ~ 217–21 χρυσοκόμας...διὰ...χωρεῖ
219–22 θεῶν ~ ἀθανάτων ~ θεία μακάρων,

not to mention a bizarre superfluity of different names for one and the same bird-song: νόμους ὕμνων (210), θρηνεῖς (211), μέλεσιν (213), ἐλέγοις (218). Nor can one honestly say that the phrasing, for all its general conventionality, is always even conventionally adequate. For any conceivable bird-song νόμους ὕμνων is somewhat infelicitous ('hymn-tunes'),[20] and there is also the remarkable expression ἐλελιζομένη διεροῖς μέλεσιν (213), which seems to be, or to aspire to be, a high lyric ξενικόν. The participle is apparently used as portmanteau of LSJ's ἐλελίζω A, which would yield 'quivering' (ἐλελίχθη γυῖα *Il.* 22. 448), and B, which would give 'crying' (ἐλελίζει...ὄρνις Eur. *Pho.* 1514f.). The throat is

17. See my *Interaction in Poetic Imagery* (Cambridge 1974) 159f.

18. An epithet hardly used in the classical period except of flying creatures, a fact obscured by the presentation in LSJ and the argument about whether the word meant colour or movement.

19. If Meineke's popular conjecture δ' ἱεροῖς (for διεροῖς) were right, there would be a third item in this set.

20. Alcman, conceivably A's source for the phrase (by comprehensible association of ideas), more reasonably wrote ὀρνίχων νόμως ('bird-tunes'), *fr.* 40 *PMG.*

'quivering' and the bird is 'crying'.[21] This is not infelicitous in itself; the offence is in the collocations produced. διεροῖς ('wet'), used as a γλῶττα, was perhaps suggested by an unconscious metaleptic pun. Homer wrote διερῷ ποδί (usually translated 'nimble foot', *Od.* 9. 43); a πούς is almost a μέλος (in the first sense of the latter noun); therefore. . . . It is a critical commonplace that a piece of literature prescribes its own level of response. The new collocations would be a little disquieting (moist songs? wet vibes??), but for the fact that we have already been conditioned to respond to the song without too much attention; in context, then, they come across as faintly dithyrambic ornament. Our inattention is indeed required to be pervasive. It perhaps escapes notice, in this mélange of cliché and highly coloured prolixity, that the hoopoe, like us, is totally unaffected by his beloved nightingale's suffering that he invokes so readily. 'Serious' feeling, that we might expect to match the serious idiom of the song, is not simply conventionalized, but non-existent.

One can agree that this lyric has a certain charm – of a strictly literary kind, be it noted: there is nothing in it to evoke the genuine simplicity of folk-song (although a *source* in folk-song might be postulated). Besides which, there is a conventional competence, and not much else. If this lyric *was* one of the glories of Greek lyric, we would do better to switch to tragedy and epic. Let us remind ourselves how glorious true Greek lyric is. At the risk of using sledgehammers to crack walnuts, take Pindar, *Pythian* 8. 81–97:

τέτρασι δ' ἔμπετες ὑψόθεν
σωμάτεσσι κακὰ φρονέων,
τοῖς οὔτε νόστος ὁμῶς
ἔπαλπνος ἐν Πυθιάδι κρίθη,
οὐδὲ μολόντων πὰρ ματέρ' ἀμφὶ γέλως γλυκύς
ὦρσεν χάριν· κατὰ λαύρας δ' ἐχθρῶν ἀπάοροι
πτώσσοντι, συμφορᾷ δεδαγμένοι.
ὁ δὲ καλόν τι νέον λαχών
ἁβρότατος ἔπι μεγάλας
ἐξ ἐλπίδος πέταται
ὑποπτέροις ἀνορέαις, ἔχων
κρέσσονα πλούτου μέριμναν. ἐν δ' ὀλίγῳ βροτῶν
τὸ τερπνὸν αὔξεται· οὕτω δὲ καὶ πίτνει χαμαί,
ἀποτρόπῳ γνώμᾳ σεσεισμένον.

21. Middle, i.e. crying to itself.

ἐπάμεροι· τί δέ τις; τί δ' οὔ τις; σκιᾶς ὄναρ
ἄνθρωπος. ἀλλ' ὅταν αἴγλα διόσδοτος ἔλθῃ,
λαμπρὸν φέγγος ἔπεστιν ἀνδρῶν καὶ μείλιχος αἰών.

Four bodies you threw yourself down on [sc. in the wrestling bouts at Delphi], meaning them harm. Fate at the games denied them a glad home-coming like yours: when they went back to their mothers, there was no sweet laughter round them to arouse goodwill. They slunk along the backstreets, out of their enemies' way, bitten by their misfortune. But one who has found fresh glory – in his moment of splendour his hope is great and he flies on the wings of his manhood with thoughts beyond wealth. But joy is a short time growing, and when some malign purpose shakes it, it falls to earth as quickly. Our life is a day. What are we? What are we not? Man is a shadow in a dream. But when god sends a gleam, there is a brilliant light on us and life is kind.

In about the same length of time as it took the hoopoe to wake up the nightingale, Pindar gives us a masterpiece of taut writing: a formal statement of specific triumphs in the past, vignettes of defeat and victory, and the marvellous 'criticism of life' arising naturally out of them. In detail, we move from the menacing concreteness of ἔμπετες ὑψόθεν σωμάτεσσι to the more unexpected realism of κατὰ λαύρας... πτώσσοντι; then from the more leisurely described delights of victory to the swiftly growing storm that succeeds it (πίτνει χαμαὶ...σεσεισμένον, the image growing out of the 'pivotal' αὔξεται);[22] finally to the syntactic arrest of 95f., where in a majestic three-word sentence Pindar sums up centuries of Greek pessimism and in the next breath adds to it his own inimitable qualification, the λαμπρὸν φέγγος.

One might recall at this point that in his 'serious' lyrics Aristophanes makes no attempt at the metaphysical – as opposed to merely religious – seriousness that is characteristic of Pindar and the choral lyrics of tragedy. (There is, *inter alia*, a marked shortage of what Dover unsympathetically calls the gnomic 'banalities' that figure so prominently in tragic choruses.[23]) And no more does he offer the richness of language or suggestion that one associates with older tragedy and with Pindar. Bacchylides on his dullest days he might be a match for, or Euripides at his most perfunctory – except that he lacks any counterpart to the nervous operatic energy that pervades Euripidean lyrics. Not that his pastiche is necessarily

22. Silk, *Interaction in Poetic Imagery* 90.
23. *Aristophanic Comedy* 184.

imitative of Euripides, let alone of Bacchylides. It is essentially imitative not of the work of any single poet, but of the external features common to lyric poetry in general, especially those features that figure in the lyrical portions of the great sister art, tragedy. The lyrics of Aristophanes may, of course, like those of tragedy, have additional dramatic virtues, irrelevant to his status as lyric poet. They may – and do – evince real poetic gifts of other kinds which we can examine when bogus claims have been disposed of. What we nowhere find is evidence of substantial lyrical gifts of any conventionally 'serious' kind.[24]

Birds 1731–42, though part of a wider whole (a finale complex), can reasonably be taken on its own. It is, after all, a 'true marriage-song worthy of a high occasion',[25] and provides another chance of a look at a fully 'serious' lyric in a play famous for Aristophanes' 'most delicate poetry'.[26]

Ἥρᾳ ποτ' Ὀλυμπίᾳ
τῶν ἠλιβάτων θρόνων
ἄρχοντα θεοῖς μέγαν
Μοῖραι ξυνεκοίμισαν
ἐν τοιῷδ' ὑμεναίῳ.
Ὑμὴν ὦ Ὑμέναι' ὦ,
Ὑμὴν ὦ Ὑμέναι' ὦ.

ὁ δ' ἀμφιθαλὴς Ἔρως
χρυσόπτερος ἡνίας
ηὔθυνε παλιντόνους,
Ζηνὸς πάροχος γάμων
τῆς τ' εὐδαίμονος Ἥρας.
Ὑμὴν ὦ Ὑμέναι' ὦ,
Ὑμὴν ὦ Ὑμέναι' ὦ.

With just such a wedding-song the fates once joined to Olympian Hera the gods' great lord of the steep throne. *Hymen*... Propitious Eros, golden-winged, drove Zeus' and blessèd Hera's wedding car and kept the reins taut back. *Hymen*....

As paradigm for, and comparison with, the wedding of Peisetaerus and Basileia, Aristophanes gives us the story of the wedding of Zeus

24. What I have said of *Av.* 209ff. could largely be said of the rather similar 676ff. (ὦ φίλη...), until the very end of that little *commation* (...ἄρχου τῶν ἀναπαίστων). But since that song has not been singled out as a pearl to set beside ἄγε σύννομέ μοι, while its end makes it, overall, a different kind of case, I leave it for later.

25. Bowra, *AJPh* (1958) 379.

26. Lesky, *Hist. Gr. Lit.*² 438.

and Hera in two matching aeolic stanzas. The form of the lyric, it should be said, is extremely graceful. That apart, the writing, as before, is conventional and unimpressive. Notable signs of weakness are the pointlessly contorted cast of the first sentence (note the double dative)[27] and a plethora of high-style ornate epithets: ἠλιβάτων, ἀμφιθαλής, χρυσόπτερος and παλιντόνους, the first of which, in particular, is (*more dithyrambico*) more notable for its size than its sense.[28]

The parodos of *Clouds* (vv. 275–90, 298–313), strophe first:

> ἀέναοι Νεφέλαι
> ἀρθῶμεν φανεραὶ δροσερὰν φύσιν εὐάγητον,
> πατρὸς ἀπ' Ὠκεανοῦ βαρυαχέος
> ὑψηλῶν ὀρέων κορυφὰς ἔπι
> δενδροκόμους, ἵνα
> τηλεφανεῖς σκοπιὰς ἀφορώμεθα,
> καρπούς τ' ἀρδομέναν ἱερὰν χθόνα,
> καὶ ποταμῶν ζαθέων κελαδήματα,
> καὶ πόντον κελάδοντα βαρύβρομον·
> ὄμμα γὰρ αἰθέρος ἀκάματον σελαγεῖται
> μαρμαρέαις ἐν αὐγαῖς.
> ἀλλ' ἀποσεισάμεναι νέφος ὄμβριον
> ἀθανάτας ἰδέας ἐπιδώμεθα
> τηλεσκόπῳ ὄμματι γαῖαν.

O ever-flowing clouds, let us raise to view our dewy, radiant shapes: let us leave deep-sounding father ocean for the leaf-tressed peaks of the lofty mountains, where we can look out at the far heights and the sacred earth with her watered crops and the roar of holy rivers and the deep-booming roaring sea. The unresting eye of heaven flashes forth in gleaming rays. Let us shake off the watery mist of our immortal guise and with far-glancing eye gaze upon the world.[29]

'The lovely dactylic chorus in which the Clouds appear', with its 'flowing and stately rhythms', is 'one of the most beautiful lyrical passages of Attic literature' (C. Segal).[30] Dover, with more reason, praises the overall *dramatic* point of the chorus and its tone here. A cloud-chorus aptly symbolizes 'unworldly' thought and insub-

27. θεοῖς is ethic dative; cf. Schroeder, *ad loc.*, who compares Pi. *Ol.* 13. 7, τάμι' ἀνδράσι πλούτου.

28. 'Steep' throne (cf. the material in LSJ s.v.); is it supposed to be hard to climb?

29. Tr. based on Starkie.

30. *Arethusa* (1969) 148: 'eins der schönsten Gebilde griechischer Lyrik', Ed. Fraenkel, *Beobachtungen zu Aristophanes* (Roma 1962) 198.

stantial philosophy, while clouds, though easily personifiable as agents of Zeus, are not 'real' deities, hence are 'suitable objects of worship for a man devoted to καινὰ δαιμόνια'. Regarding the dramatic function of the parodos: 'we hear the chorus singing before it appears in the theatre and it drifts into our sight with the slow majesty of clouds which have gathered on the mountains and are spreading over the land. Their opening song is formally much closer to tragedy than to comedy and this befits their status as deities responding to Socrates' invocation'[31] – and, one might add, as elaborately grand figures calculated to make it plausible that both the sophisticated (like Socrates) and the unsophisticated (like Strepsiades) should be able to find them impressive. This one can readily accept as a strength of the passage. One can also give credit for Aristophanes' inventiveness in metamorphosing 'clouds' into the world of religious lyricism and indeed in specifically depicting them at all (which is more than most Greek lyric poets usually do).

But those strengths all involve the organization or conception of the lyric as a whole,[32] and serve, if anything, to show up the fact that in its detail it epitomizes Aristophanes' worst lyrical tendencies: triteness, inflation, and pervasive lack of point. As with the 'serious' lyrics in *Birds*, diction and dialect immediately advertise its high pretensions: βαρυαχέος in the third verse, elevated compound complete with Doric alpha, conveniently embodies both. A string of predictable epithets enforces an overpowering sense of *genre*: Ocean is πατρός, the mountains are ὑψηλῶν, the peaks are δενδροκόμους, and everything is business as usual. The writer also offers us, in unusually inflationary mood, κορυφάς *and* σκοπιάς (279–81), ἱεράν *and* ζαθέων (282f.), τηλεφανεῖς *and* τηλεσκόπῳ (281–90), κελαδήματα *and* κελάδοντα (283f.), ὄμμα αἰθέρος *and* the clouds' ὄμματι (285–90). μαρμαρέαις, the statutory γλῶττα, completes the picture (286). It isn't (to restate) that successful lyric poetry never includes such items. Of course it does, but they are the hallmarks of its lyricism, not of its success. It uses them, but not in such thick quantity, all at once, and so inertly.

31. Dover, *ed. maior* (1968), lxvii–lxix.

32. The same goes for some interesting comments by Segal (*Arethusa* (1969) 143–61) on the cloud-chorus as embodiment of 'natural vitality' and also as user of 'traditional poetic words, not the new abstractions'. It does not follow, nor does it need to, that the poeticisms are effective *per se*.

For instance, one might look back to the Pindar passage and note how sparingly epithets are used there and how strict their local function is.

It might be asked: could a passage like the *Clouds* lyric be parody? – not parody of any specific passage, but burlesque of high lyric as a whole. After all, one might think that the Aristophanes who in *Frogs* and elsewhere shows such sensitivity to Aeschylean grandiloquence and Euripidean opera-style would hardly be unwittingly guilty of something open to comparable criticism himself. Among the objections to this view is the consideration that Aristophanes is not exactly a *balanced* critic of the tragedians' excesses (he gives us very little sense of the positive merits of their writing, of which the excesses are outgrowths); and again that their sins are the sins of defiant innovation, whereas his are the exact opposite. The only substantial reason for appealing to parody would be the comic context of the piece. Socrates and Strepsiades, who are there to greet the chorus, are, in their different ways, equally laughable figures, and the strophe and antistrophe are actually separated by a representative sample of their dialogue (291–7):

Σω. ὦ μέγα σεμναὶ Νεφέλαι φανερῶς ἠκούσατέ μου καλέσαντος.
ᾔσθου φωνῆς ἅμα καὶ βροντῆς μυκησαμένης θεοσέπτου;
Στ. καὶ σέβομαί γ' ὦ πολυτίμητοι καὶ βούλομαι ἀνταποπαρδεῖν
πρὸς τὰς βροντάς· οὕτως αὐτὰς τετρεμαίνω καὶ πεφόβημαι·
κεἰ θέμις ἐστίν, νυνί γ' ἤδη, κεἰ μὴ θέμις ἐστί, χεσείω.
Σω. οὐ μὴ σκώψει μηδὲ ποιήσεις ἅπερ οἱ τρυγοδαίμονες οὗτοι,
ἀλλ' εὐφήμει· μέγα γάρ τι θεῶν κινεῖται σμῆνος ἀοιδαῖς.

'O clouds august, in visible shape you have hearkened to my invocation. Did you hear their voice and withal the awful thunder's roar?' 'I'm in awe, all right, holy ones, and I need to match your thunder with a fart. I'm so dithering with terror, like it or not, I can't help it – I'm taken short.' 'Stop playing the fool: you're behaving like those frightful comedians. Keep a respectful silence: a great swarm of goddesses is moving in song.'[33]

The rustic's coarse χεσείω and the philosopher's pretentious θεῶν σμῆνος are certainly not calculated to keep up any tone of solemnity. On the other hand, there is no specifiable incongruity *within* the lyrics themselves,[34] and all one can say is that if

33. Tr. based on Starkie and Dickinson.

34. One could say the same of e.g. *Ran.* 323–53, where the lyrics are unaffected by the intervening buffoonery of 337–9.

Aristophanes meant to parody the high style here, he has not been successful in a writer's first duty to himself, translating his intention into effect; while, of course, if this passage *is* to count as parody, it immediately drops out of sight as a candidate for 'serious' literature. Parody may have dramatic or, as it were, literary-critical value, but it is not – any more than pastiche – a breeding-ground for creative poetry.

Turning to the antistrophe, we encounter a praise of Athens. Here we definitely find no sign of humour at all, nor, given the subject, need we be surprised at that. Lyrical praise of Athens is inevitably religious praise (and not only praise of Attic religiosity) and the comic drama regularly shies away from any belittling of Athens in this aspect.[35] Verses 298–313:

παρθένοι ὀμβροφόροι
ἔλθωμεν λιπαρὰν χθόνα Παλλάδος, εὔανδρον γᾶν
Κέκροπος ὀψόμεναι πολυήρατον·
οὗ σέβας ἀρρήτων ἱερῶν, ἵνα
μυστοδόκος δόμος
ἐν τελεταῖς ἁγίαις ἀναδείκνυται,
οὐρανίοις τε θεοῖς δωρήματα,
ναοί θ' ὑψερεφεῖς καὶ ἀγάλματα,
καὶ πρόσοδοι μακάρων ἱερώταται,
εὐστέφανοί τε θεῶν θυσίαι θαλίαι τε,
παντοδαπαῖς ἐν ὥραις,
ἦρί τ' ἐπερχομένῳ Βρομία χάρις,
εὐκελάδων τε χορῶν ἐρεθίσματα,
καὶ μοῦσα βαρύβρομος αὐλῶν.

Rain-bearing maidens, let us go to the fruitful land of Pallas, and look on the dear soil of Cecrops, the home of heroes, where the holy mysteries are celebrated that hush the lips in awe; where the Holy of Holies opens its doors during the sacred rites; where the heavenly gods have their gifts and high-roofed shrines and images; and there are holy processions for the blest, and garlanded sacrifices for the gods, and feasts throughout the varying seasons; and as spring draws near, Bromius has his joy and there are the challenges of sweet-voiced dancers and the deep music of the pipes.[36]

The antistrophe, then, gives us our first specimen of a serious

35. Theseus, the Attic hero, and Athene, the Attic goddess, are among the few higher beings to remain unscathed: cf. V. Ehrenberg, *The People of Aristophanes*² (Oxford 1951) 264.

36. Tr. based on Starkie.

Aristophanic religious lyric[37] – but, in other respects, no change. Lyrical elevation is at its most extreme, cliché is pervasive[38] and inflation seems more evident than ever, when in 302–4, for instance, we encounter five different words out of seven meaning 'sacred' or 'sacredness' or 'sacred rite' clustered round the less predictable, but equally sacred-ful, phrase μυστοδόκος δόμος. The compound adjective in that phrase is apparently a coinage on the model of such elevated predecessors as Aeschylus' ἱκεταδόκος (*Supp.* 713) and πρεσβυτοδόκος (*Supp.* 667) and the more established πανδόκος (δόμοι πανδόκοι *Cho.* 662). But, as ever, elevation *per se* is no guarantee of quality.

Compare the antistrophe with Euripides, *Trojan Women* 205ff. The captive women are guessing their ultimate destinations:

— ἢ Πειρήνας ὑδρευσομένα
πρόσπολος οἰκτρὰ σεμνῶν ὑδάτων.
— τὰν κλεινὰν εἴθ' ἔλθοιμεν
Θησέως εὐδαίμονα χώραν.
— μὴ γὰρ δὴ δίναν γ' Εὐρώτα,
τὰν ἐχθίσταν θεράπναν Ἑλένας...

'...or kept as a slave woman to draw water from holy Pirene'. 'May I come to Theseus' land, the glorious, the blessed.' 'Never, never, I pray, to the swirling Eurotas, the cursed abode of Helen...'[39]

Not a particularly startling piece of Euripidean verse, but chosen to suggest, simply, one of the ways in which good lyric poetry makes something of conventions. The epithets σεμνῶν and εὐδαίμονα are complimentary – and banal. Their inertia conveys, with faint irony, just how little a human chattel has to hope for. Their opposition, in turn, to the totally unwelcome δίναν suggests the value to the slave, nevertheless, of even the most pious hope. The passage offers, then, a poignantly effective use of the stock items, compared with which Aristophanes' uncomplicated generic charm – which his 'straight' lyrics tend, despite all else, to retain – is a very slight thing indeed.[40] If παρθένοι ὀμβροφόροι is

37. I note that Starkie (on vv. 275ff.) detects a 'comic effect' in the strophe, but (on v. 303) finds the antistrophe 'very religious'. Apart from anything else, such an interpretation makes it impossible to explain the parallelism of the two stanzas (see Dover on 275–90, p. 137, and note also the echo of κελαδήματα... κελάδοντα βαρύβρομον, 283f. in εὐκελάδων...βαρύβρομος, 312f.).

38. See e.g. Dover on 299f.

39. Tr. Hadas.

40. Any reader who thinks my earlier comparison with Pindar unfair might like to compare instead A's praise of Athens with Pi. *fr.* 33c and the extraordinary

great poetry, so are a dozen of the lesser 'Homeric' hymns, and Pindar and the tragedians might be pardoned for protesting from Elysium that their paths to immortality were needlessly hard.

The other relevant passages in *Clouds* are both, again, religious: the ode and antode of the first parabasis (563ff. and 595ff.), which Bowra, including them among his 'glories of Greek lyric poetry', calls 'an authentic hymn'.[41] It would be superfluous to quote the passages in full. The ode is an invocation to Zeus and other deities, including Aether, aptly personified for the purpose. It begins

ὑψιμέδοντα μὲν θεῶν
Ζῆνα

and ends

μέγας ἐν θεοῖς
ἐν θνητοῖσί τε δαίμων.

The style is elevated and, as usual, largely conventional, although there are one or two unpredictable touches. Poseidon is τριαίνης ταμίαν ('master of the trident', 566) and (curious expression) μοχλευτήν, 'wrencher', of land and sea (567f.). For the rest, there is nothing to suggest the need for any modification of our provisional conclusion. The hymn may be 'authentic', as Bowra says, but his praise of it is absurd. The antode, to Apollo *et al.*,

ἀμφί μοι αὖτε Φοῖβ' ἄναξ
Δήλιε...,

is very similar, with a single odd phrase, αἰγίδος ἡνίοχος ('aegis-driver', 602), in an otherwise highly commonplace stanza. The writing in this instance is pleasingly uncluttered, but frankly unmemorable.

Richards, nearly seventy years ago, offered a pertinent criticism of Aristophanes' pieces of this type – albeit immediately after the

inventiveness (in ideas *and* words) that Pindar shows there in praising Delos. Note especially the felicity of the conjoined 'etymological' plays on Δᾶλον (cf. δῆλος) and 'Asteria' (hidden behind ἄστρον) and the paradox (aptly unearthly for μάκαρες ἐν 'Ολύμπῳ) at the climax of the fragment, χθονὸς ἄστρον. (One might usefully compare that metaphor with A's purely ornamental ὄμμα αἰθέρος, v. 285 in the strophe. The only conceivable point in saying 'eye of heaven' here rather than 'sun' is to get in an extra drop of *color poeticus*.) Any such reader might also like to remember that the comparison with Pindar was not mine, but, implicitly or explicitly, received opinion's.

41. *AJPh* (1958) 378.

customary eulogy of his 'pure lyrical poetry' such as (needless to say) 'the stanzas in which the Clouds make their coming known'. He commented: 'other lyrical passages are less beautiful and some are *a little conventional and perfunctory in their devotional character*' (my italics).[42] Even though the criticism is rather mildly phrased, it is pleasant to find a properly critical response of any kind. Richards gives no examples, but further examples of Aristophanes' elevated devotions are to hand from *Thesmophoriazusae*, vv. 312–30

δεχόμεθα καὶ θεῶν γένος
λιτόμεθα...

and 1136–59

Παλλάδα τὴν φιλόχορον ἐμοὶ
δεῦρο καλεῖν νόμος ἐς χορόν...[43]

The hymns of the initiates in *Frogs* (occupying most of vv. 323–459) are essentially of the same type and subject to the same limitations. 'They reflect with unfailing grace', Bowra assures us, 'another aspect of Greek religion'.[44] They are, actually, in some ways distinctly more impressive than most of Aristophanes' other high-style religious lyrics. That is, while there are unremarkable, if inoffensive, little pieces like (vv. 386ff.):

Δήμητερ ἁγνῶν ὀργίων
ἄνασσα συμπαραστάτει...

there is also a good deal to commend in the form and, intermittently, the phrasing. Take, for instance, 449ff.:

χωρῶμεν ἐς πολυρρόδους
λειμῶνας ἀνθεμώδεις,
τὸν ἡμέτερον τρόπον
τὸν καλλιχορώτατον
παίζοντες, ὃν ὄλβιαι
Μοῖραι ξυνάγουσιν.

μόνοις γὰρ ἡμῖν ἥλιος
καὶ φέγγος ἱερόν ἐστιν,
ὅσοι μεμυήμεθ'...

42. *Aristophanes and Others*, 120.
43. There is also *Thesm.* 947–1000, a mixture of elevated hymnody and rather flat comments on the proceedings.
44. *AJPh* (1958) 379.

Let us go to the rose-rich meadows, full of flowers, in our own way, playing in the lovely dance which the blessed Fates arrange. For the sun's holy light shines only on us, the initiates,[45]

in a very pleasingly coherent iambic-aeolic stanza form, with reizianum as 'natural' cadence to the telesillean (× – ∪ ∪ – ∪ – /– – ∪ ∪ – –), and with deftly parallel – albeit, no doubt, traditional – images, λειμῶνας and ἥλιος, at the start of each stanza. On the other hand, even as we pause to admire, our eye – or ear – registers a familiar sign of weakness, the pleonasm of ἀνθεμώδεις after πολυρρόδους. And further inspection reveals a much wider set of repetitions within the lyrics in this scene, to which our particular lyric contributes its share. The λειμῶνας have already figured, with or without flowers: ἀνὰ λειμῶνα χορεύσων (326), φέγγεται δὲ λειμών (344), εὐανθεῖς κόλπους λειμώνων (373f.). And the collocation καλλιχορώτατον παίζοντες reminds us that 'playing and —ing' (usually 'dancing') has been the stock-in-trade of these lyrics for some eighty lines now: καὶ παίζων καὶ χλευάζων (376), παῖσαί τε καὶ χορεῦσαι (390), παίσαντα καὶ σκώψαντα (394), παίζειν τε καὶ χορεύειν (409), παίζων χορεύειν (419). Harmless enough – but not quite Pindar and Keats.

And yet the scene also contains taut writing like this (vv. 344–50):

φλογὶ φέγγεται δὲ λειμών·
γόνυ πάλλεται γερόντων·
ἀποσείονται δὲ λύπας
χρονίους τ' ἐτῶν παλαιῶν ἐνιαυτοὺς
ἱερᾶς ὑπὸ τιμᾶς,

The meadow is ablaze with fire; the old men's knee leaps; they shake off their cares and their long weary years through the sacred rite,

where successive images are allowed an individual distinctness, smothered neither by each other nor by undue ornament, while the rhythm, which so often has to carry – or palliate – verbal weakness, combines with assonance to enforce the sense of their separateness and their coordination:

φλογὶ φέγγεται...
γόνυ πάλλεται...

45. For the text of 456 see Stanford, *ad loc.*: ἱερόν is confirmed by a first-century B.C. Rhodian inscription. The lyric (or rather vv. 454–9) was engraved, complete with ascription to Aristophanes, by (it must be supposed) initiates, who evidently found no difficulty in taking it seriously. One's assumption of the 'seriousness' of this and other such lyrics is incidentally thereby confirmed.

And for once pleonasm is put to work: the laborious phrase χρονίους...ἐνιαυτούς[46] gives the feeling of overwhelming senescence, which the mystae can yet shake off (ἀποσείονται) so easily, ἱερᾶς ὑπὸ τιμᾶς.

Command of rhythm is the greatest strength of these *Frogs* lyrics. Rhythmically, they are not only elegant, but varied and variously apt. The initiates enter to 'exotic'[47] ionics (324ff.):

Ἴακχ' ὦ πολυτίμητ' ἐν ἕδραις ἐνθάδε ναίων...,

and summon themselves to the procession in solemn[48] 'long anapaests' (372ff.):[49]

χώρει νυν πᾶς ἀνδρείως
ἐς τοὺς εὐανθεῖς κόλπους...,

while a few minutes later they are calling on Iacchus in an exuberant iambic skip (399f.):

Ἴακχε πολυτίμητε, μέλος ἑορτῆς
ἥδιστον εὑρών, δεῦρο συνακολούθει...

It may be noted in passing that the lyric to which the last instance belongs has other elements which put our discussion on to a different footing. The stanza beginning Ἴακχε πολυτίμητε... ends (404)

Ἴακχε φιλοχορευτὰ συμπρόπεμπέ με,

and the two responding stanzas (405ff. and 411ff.) end with the same verse as a refrain. We have so far been measuring Aristophanes against a high lyric tradition. Such refrains are not, on the whole, a feature of that tradition.[50] The refrain, in fact, points to something altogether 'lower', and confirmation of this lower generic affinity is provided by the diction of the second stanza (405ff.):

σὺ γὰρ κατεσχίσω μὲν ἐπὶ γέλωτι
κἀπ' εὐτελείᾳ τόδε τὸ σανδαλίσκον
καὶ τὸ ῥάκος,

46. Radermacher *ad loc.* establishes the textual soundness of this verse, albeit without reference to literary-critical considerations.

47. See A. M. Dale, *The Lyric Metres of Greek Drama*² (Cambridge 1968) 124f.; Dodds on Eur. *Bacch.* 64ff. (ed. 2, p. 72).

48. See Dale, *op. cit.* 55; C. Prato, *I Canti di Aristofane* (Roma 1962) 295.

49. To which they have fluently 'modulated' (so to speak) from the recitative anapaestic tetrameters immediately preceding.

50. See n. 89 below.

It's you who tore our sandals and old clothes for a laugh – and for economy,

and the diction – and content – of the third, with its μειρακίσκη and her τιτθίον προκύψαν (411–15). A slighter, but ultimately comparable, descent from the heights is visible at the end of

χωρῶμεν ἐς πολυρρόδους
λειμῶνας...(449ff.),

involving, in that instance, a drop to the prosaic (457ff.):

εὐ-
σεβῆ τε διήγομεν
τρόπον περὶ τοὺς ξένους
καὶ τοὺς ἰδιώτας.

We live in piety towards outsiders and our own folk.[51]

We may note, for future reference, how elevation can melt away in the course of a single lyric.

Lysistrata is the only other play to provide complete specimens of Aristophanes' elevated style. The play concludes with three odes, one Athenian (1279ff.) and two Spartan (1247ff. and 1296ff.), by way of celebrating the newly agreed peace. All are more or less religious in character and accordingly – and notwithstanding their presence in Bowra's short list of Aristophanic contributions to the glories of Greek lyric poetry – tend towards what Richards called the conventional and the perfunctory. This is obvious in the case of the Athenian song:

πρόσαγε χορόν, ἔπαγε δὲ Χάριτας,
ἐπὶ δὲ κάλεσον Ἄρτεμιν,
ἐπὶ δὲ δίδυμον ἀγέχορον
Ἰήιον
εὔφρον', ἐπὶ δὲ Νύσιον,
ὅς...   (1279–84)

On with the dance and bring the Graces with you. Call on Artemis; on her gracious brother, Apollo, patron of the dance; on the lord of Nysa, who...

and only less obvious in the other cases, one is tempted to say, because of the impenetrable Laconian dialect with which the versatile poet has cloaked them:

51. The scene also contains the ritualistic *gephyrismoi* (*vel sim.*, 420–43), which, by definition, are 'low' throughout.

κλέωα τὸν ᾽Αμύκλαις σιὸν
καὶ χαλκίοικον ᾽Ασάναν... (1299f.).

...praising the god of Amyclae and Athene of the brazen temple.

This would actually be unfair. The earlier of the Spartan songs differs in one important respect from the other two songs in the group and from Aristophanes' other high lyrics as a whole. These others deal with gods and goddesses and, in general, *timeless* entities. The divinities of 1279ff., that is, ultimately belong in the same timeless world as the sorrowing nightingale in *Birds* and the ἀέναοι Νεφέλαι in *Clouds*. This lyric, in contrast, has an active concern with the historic past: the Persian wars, when Sparta and Athens fought a common enemy. What is striking here is how muscular the writing becomes in evocation of that specific occasion, when:

ἐπ᾽ ᾽Αρταμιτίῳ
πρῴκροον σιοείκελοι
ποττὰ κᾶλα...(1251ff.).

...at Artemisium they struck god-like against the boats.[52]

Leonidas it was who led the Spartans at Thermopylae, 'like boars, whetting their teeth':

πολὺς δ᾽ ἀμφὶ τὰς γένυας ἀφρὸς ἤνσει,
πολὺς δ᾽ ἀμᾷ καττῶν σκελῶν ἀφρὸς ἵετο (1257ff.).

And the sweat from our jaws ran slavering, | We were blood to the knees...[53]

'Boars' (κάπρως) symbolizes not only ferocity, but (via Homeric simile) the world of martial epic, and with particular aptness evokes heroic resilience in defeat, a common situation of the wild beast in that Homeric context, roaring inwardly as it gathers itself, panting and slavering:

52. κᾶλα as native Doric equivalent for πλοῖα (cf. Xen. *HG* 1. 1. 23; see Bechtel, *Gr. Dial.* II. 375), evokes the Spartan presence with particular directness. My distinction between a single event within living memory and the 'timeless entities' is not invalidated by the truism that for Classical Greece history and myth were not yet entirely distinct categories. They were distinct enough (the differences between Herodotus and Sophocles are not purely formal!); and in any case I am more concerned with the difference between fable and *experience*.

53. Tr. Dickinson. ἀφρός probably does suggest blood (or a mixture of blood and slaver) the second time round; for the usage, cf. Aesch. *Eum.* 183, Soph. *Trach.* 702, Hippocr. *Aph.* 5. 13 (αἷμα ἀφρῶδες, so Arist. *HA* 512b. 10, cf. Diog. Apoll. 6).

ἐάλη τε χανών, περί τ' ἀφρὸς ὀδόντας
γίγνεται, ἐν δέ τέ οἱ κραδίῃ στένει ἄλκιμον ἦτορ
(*Iliad* 20. 168f.).

This is a far cry from the flowery sweetness of *Clouds* and *Birds*. The intensity is not sustained for long, but long enough to help to suggest – again, for future reference – one reason for Aristophanes' comparative lack of distinction in high lyric verse. Traditional Greek lyric, and, specifically, traditional choral lyric, tends towards the general, the world of myth and timeless truths. Aristophanes' most fundamental instincts go the other way, towards the particular.

Besides the passages so far discussed, there are one or two fragments in the high style, such as:

ὦ πόλι φίλη Κέκροπος... (fr. 110).

In the extant plays, there may be other lyrics of a partly 'religious' character,[54] and of course there are also the parodies of or in the high style (usually paratragic):

ὦ πάτερ, ὦ πάτερ, ἆρ' ἔτυμός γε
δώμασιν ἡμετέροις φάτις ἥκει,
ὡς σὺ μετ' ὀρνίθων προλιπὼν ἐμὲ
ἐς κόρακας βαδιεῖ μεταμώνιος;

Father, father, is this true, | This rumour that's round the house, | That you're leaving me, *you*, father, | To fly in the face of fortune?[55]

– recognizable as parodies, usually, by internal incongruity (as here the joke on ἐς κόρακας). But none of these passages can offer anything to modify the negative conclusion, which can now, I hope, count as established.

II

Modern interpreters of Aristophanes' elevated lyrics have tended to see them as embodiments of the perfect form to which all his

54. I am not counting as properly 'religious' those passages with a marked parodic element, such as *Thesm.* 101–29 (on which see Rau, *Paratragodia* 104–8; W. Horn, *Gebet und Gebetsparodie in den Komödien des Aristophanes* (Nürnberg 1970) 94–106, especially 105; and Prato, *Canti di A* 243), or *Pax* 385–99 (Horn 81–3). There is also the slightly aberrant *Eq.* 551–64 ~ 581–94 (see below, n. 138).

55. *Pax* 114ff.: tr. based on Dickinson. On this passage see Platnauer *ad loc.* and Rau, *Paratragodia* 92f.

lyrics do, or should, aspire, however far most of them may fall short of the ideal. Hence the familiar stance whereby the citations of his 'pure lyrical poetry' are accompanied by a wistful note to the effect that 'we may regret that chance or the poet has not given us more examples of his powers in this way...Other lyrical passages are less beautiful...'[56] But if we can no longer regard his pure lyrical poetry as any kind of real achievement, we can no longer see it as the *telos* of his lyrics as a whole, and our interpretation of his status as lyric poet is necessarily altered. In search of a new interpretation, we would do well to examine the terms of reference or principles of classification that underlie discussions of his lyric verse.

Aristophanes' lyrics are, by any standard, extremely varied and permit a good many classifications from different points of view. One can classify, most straightforwardly, by metre. 'Lyric metres' means sung metres. We distinguish these first from the various 'stichic' spoken metres of the dialogue and also from the intermediate types collectively known as 'recitative' (παρακαταλογή),[57] the usual manifestations of which are dimeters or tetrameters in iambic, trochaic and anapaestic rhythms. We can then distinguish the different types within lyric metres proper. According to a convenient recent survey, Aristophanes' lyric verse falls into nine metrical groups, of which three – iambo-trochaic, aeolic, and 'mixed' – cover almost three-quarters of his output.[58] Pursuing the metrical classification on to a structural plane, we can sort out individual odes: some are polymetric, others metrically 'homogeneous';[59] some are strophic, others astrophic; and the formal structural properties of the odes can be classified from these and other standpoints.

Again, one can classify the lyrics in terms of their context within the drama as a whole. Most of them are sung by the chorus, as

56. Richards, *Aristophanes and Others* 120.

57. I.e. involving some kind of musical accompaniment, but still spoken rather than sung. There remains great uncertainty among the experts about the exact nature of its delivery and also, sometimes, about what is recitative and what is song proper (see e.g. Dale, *Lyric Metres* 77 and cf. n. 12 above). In general see A. W. Pickard-Cambridge, *The Dramatic Festivals of Athens*² (rev. J. Gould and D. M. Lewis) (Oxford 1968) 156ff.

58 T. McEvilley, *AJPh* 1970, 264–7.

59. Dale's terminology (*Collected Papers* (Cambridge 1969) 252).

at one time all of them would have been; some are monodies or duets. A majority of lyrical passages (especially choral lyrics) occur in 'conventional' contexts, such as the agon or the parabasis or the exodos; a minority (increasing as time goes by) in others.[60] Dramatic function is obviously another possible criterion, that would serve to distinguish, for instance, lyrics that provide new information or promote new action from more static expressions of the mood of the moment – and also to distinguish those two kinds from the 'irrelevant' set-piece that lacks any really organic connection with its drama. More obviously still, to take account of the difference between the rich variety of lyrics in *Acharnians* and their near-extinction in *Plutus*, and the many developments *en route*, we need the historical classification.[61]

All of these classifications have their value, but none of them, nor any combination of them, unaided, can provide an answer to the central question: what kind of lyric poet is Aristophanes? – meaning, where do his strengths and his weaknesses lie? That question is not, in fact, usually posed, apparently because the answer to it – the answer that I hope to have discredited – has been assumed. To answer it better, we can start by looking more closely at the wrong answer and, specifically, at the classification that its concern with 'elevated' poetry presupposes.

That classification derives from the ancient theory of literary types – or 'styles', as we more commonly render it; but 'style' in this context has rather limiting implications. The theory was by no means monolithic. In its prevalent form, it involved a classification into three types, according to the degree of elevation involved. Various names were used; let us use the names closest to the root meaning of 'elevation' and call them 'high', 'middle' and 'low'. The triadic scheme was applied primarily to *oratory* – by rhetoricians – and was, on the whole, purely descriptive: each type had its place and none was *per se* superior to any other. The scheme had originally been normative, with the *middle* χαρακτήρ regarded as supreme – as, in fact, the golden mean. But if we look at those ancient theorists most interested in *poetry*, we find a distinct

60. McEvilley, *op. cit.* 258ff.

61. See McEvilley, *op. cit.* 257–76 *passim*. On the prehistory of Old Comic lyrics note also G. M. Sifakis, *Parabasis and Animal Choruses* (London 1971), *passim*, though cf. n. 111 below.

tendency for the high to be credited with the greatest value, and by corollary, explicit or implicit, the low with the least. So it is with 'Longinus', who approximates his new category, the 'sublime', so far as possible to the high style;[62] so it is with Horace,[63] however much his irony serves to mask the fact; and so it is, incipiently, with Aristotle in his preference for tragedy over comedy and, if it comes to that, with Aristophanes himself in *his* preference for Aeschylus over Euripides – notwithstanding the fact that the full triadic scheme is only formulated after Aristophanes' and Aristotle's death.[64]

Among his other dicta, Aristotle suggested that the ideal of poetic *lexis* is to be clear without being ordinary.[65] We may say that where poetry is concerned, antiquity tended tacitly to reverse his emphasis: the best poetry is elevated without being obscure. Whether in fact it *is* inherently more meritorious to be elevated may be questioned (as it has been questioned by and ever since Wordsworth). What is not in doubt is that serious Greek poetry was customarily elevated in varying degrees, not by whim, but by traditions associated with each genre. This elevation, let us stress, is not in itself a matter of *heightening* – that is, of intensified poetic expression – but chiefly of *dignity*.[66] The basis of the doctrine is the principle of *decorum*, according to which each genre, with its own characteristic subject areas, has its own appropriate expression: each genre, except for a composite form, without any consistent seriousness or consistent anything, like Old Comedy. The tradition of predictable stability that held good for Greek literature in general did not hold good for Aristophanes' own genre, whose *raison d'être* was, precisely, freedom from predictable decorous restraint, freedom to move at will over the whole expressive range.

Remarkably enough, very little explicit reference is made to the

62. Cf. D. A. Russell, introduction to '*Longinus*' *On the Sublime* (Oxford 1964) xxxviff.

63. Most obviously in *Sat.* 1. 4. 39–63. See C. O. Brink, *Horace on Poetry, Prolegomena to the Literary Epistles* (Cambridge 1963) 161–4, 203f.

64. The formulation is usually ascribed to Theophrastus. See Russell, *op. cit.* xxxiv.

65. *Poetics* §22.

66. What I call 'elevation' and 'heightening' are sometimes confused – thanks partly to the fact that the ancients often used the same words (e.g. *ornatus*) for both.

theory of types in discussions of Aristophanes,[67] for all its influence on modern interpretation of his writing. Richards' discussion, published in 1909 and dealing specifically with the limited area of diction, remains exceptional. For his Aristophanic purposes, Richards somewhat refines the theory, although its main presuppositions are evidently preserved. According to his formulation, Aristophanes' work as a whole ranges over 'four or five different levels', each of which correlates fairly constantly with a particular metrical type. The lowest type is the iambic trimeters, the highest the lyrics, which, however, we find 'varying infinitely among themselves in subject and language, character and elevation, some still humorous and common, some purely poetical'.[68] He adds that 'we do not pass at one bound from the prosaic level of iambics to the poetic diction of song. We have the gradations between, mainly trochaics and anapaests.'[69]

Richards' formula is open to various objections. In the first place, although there are certain tendencies, there is no fixed correlation between level and metrical form, especially where the lyrics are concerned. Not only do they 'vary infinitely among themselves'; the level may also change, as we have seen, within individual stanzas. Secondly, Richards' 'four or five' imports a specious precision[70] into an area where the traditional magic number of three is distinctly preferable. Two extremes and a middle ground – this is probably as far as one can reasonably take the subdivision.[71] A third objection is the most important. Richards

67. Dover's recent article 'Lo stile di Aristofane', *Quad. Urb. Cult. Class.* 1970, 7ff. (reprinted in German in *Aristophanes und die alte Komödie*, ed. H.-J. Newiger (Darmstadt 1975)), offers a five-fold schema, loosely based on the traditional formula, but is not immediately concerned with *lyrical* 'style'.

68. *Aristophanes and Others*, 119. Note that 'purity' apparently excludes humour. With Richards, as indeed with others, it is evident that a sub-Romantic conception of 'the poetic' sometimes colours the traditional terms of reference.

69. *Op. cit.* 124.

70. I am not here concerned with the very proper attempts to distinguish what Dover calls 'specialised vocabularies', such as those of medicine etc. (in M. Platnauer, ed., *Fifty Years (and Twelve) of Classical Scholarship* (Oxford 1968), 126, and similarly in his article cited in n. 67).

71. It also seems natural, though perhaps misleadingly tidy, to have a number coinciding with the division into dialogue, recitative, and song. Cf. P. Maas' discussion (*Greek Metre*, tr. H. Lloyd-Jones (Oxford 1962) 53f.) of the relation in tragic solo utterance between the character's social standing and the metres

writes of the various 'levels' as if each was somehow autonomous, equally natural, and there by rights. But this is surely perverse, theoretically possible only if we shut our eyes to all the presuppositions of the comic form. Aristophanic comedy, as much as any artistic form imaginable, refers us to a contemporary public, from the point of view of whom the comic drama can only be analysed as a norm and intermittent deviations from it or (it would be better to say) superimpositions on it. And that norm must inevitably be the 'level' closest to the audience's own socio-linguistic experience and the level that predominates, above all, in the iambic trimeters which are the staple of all the plays: that is, the *low*, *colloquial*, level. (Richards' 'prosaic' is ill-chosen.) In practise, the most closeted modern reader can testify to this. After all, even admirers of Aristophanes' high lyrics speak of his verse as 'rising' to that level: rising from *what*, if not from the norm? But since the implication of autonomous natural orders threatens to mislead, let us stop thinking in terms of 'levels'. Let us say that Aristophanic verse has an underlying *substrate*, which is a low colloquial substrate;[72] and that this substrate equally underlies dialogue and lyrics (and recitative). We can add that the precise character of this substrate remains to be determined, and that it need not be entirely a matter of language narrowly conceived; that whereas dialogue may stay recognizably close to this substrate, lyric has an extra range superimposed; and that the characteristic distance between the two extremes of comic expression consists in this.

Richards' category of *diction*, referring, as it does, primarily to words' social or socio-literary affiliations, is too narrow a category for our purposes. Among other things, we must attend to the way words are used in context and their mode of meaning: are they, for instance, abstract or concrete? generic or specific? timeless (like the names of myth and legend) or topical (like the famous or infamous names of the moment)? There seems to me to be an important connection between this last set of distinctions and – what would overtly appear to be a quite separate matter – the

he or she is allowed – these being classified in the three groups 'dialogue metres', 'out-and-out lyric metres' and 'semi-lyric metres'. On this see further L. D. J. Henderson, *Maia* (1976) 19ff.

72. Cf. Dover, *loc. cit.* n. 70 above, 'the substratum of Aristophanic language is presumably colloquial', and *Quad. Urb.* (1970) 7.

traditional preference for the high. Some theoretical authority for the link is provided, once again, by Aristotle. For the author of the *Poetics*, poetry falls into two groups, according to whether its representation of life involves what is 'serious' (σπουδαῖον) or 'trivial' (φαῦλον).[73] But in addition to this, poetry as a whole is a more serious thing (φιλοσοφώτερον καὶ σπουδαιότερον) than, for instance, history, because poetry tends to express the universal and history the particular.[74] It is further apparent, though Aristotle is not as explicit here as he might have been, that within Greek poetry as a whole, one particular poetic tradition, which in his time was all but defunct, must by this criterion be less 'serious' than the rest: the tradition that begins, for us, with Archilochus in the early archaic age and reaches its zenith in Aristophanic Old Comedy. It is this tradition with its particular satirical targets that stands apart from most Greek poetry, including those types of comedy that replaced the Old with typical, 'universal', names, events and concerns: not Socrates and Euripides and the day-to-day politics of Athens, but Chremes and Sostrata and the (almost) timeless questions of manners and characters and family relationships.[75]

There is relatively little literature that consists exclusively of *either* the universal *or* the particular; and, *pace* Aristotle, the most completely successful works, or moments, of literature tend to be those that give scope to the expression of *both*. The famous passage from Pindar's *Pythian* VIII with its specific, historical, victories and its general truths related to them is one such; and that author's characteristic reassertion, or reinterpretation, of the links between *polis* or noble family and the realm of the timeless divine would be another, very pertinent, instance on a larger scale. High lyric overall, however, especially the choral lyric of tragedy, tends towards the universal, just as Aristophanic comedy does towards the particular. Aristophanes, as a master of his genre, has his roots in the particular, and this is one reason why, as I have suggested

73. *Poetics* §§2–5. Tragedy, as opposed to comedy, is μίμησις πράξεως σπουδαίας at 1449b24.

74. 1451b5f.

75. See *Poetics* §9. New Comedy proper was, of course, post-Aristotelian, but it is clear from 1449b7–9 and 1451b11–15 that 'comedy' for Aristotle meant the late 'Middle Comedy' of his day, whose lack of topicality (etc.) must have brought it very close to New Comedy proper. (A's *Plutus* is close enough already.)

earlier, his high lyrics, with their almost obligatory universalizing, are not all that they might be. But if, as so many have assumed, high is superior to low, in lyrics or elsewhere, and if (by Greek tradition, reinforced by Aristotelian theory) high tends towards the universal, it follows that any self-respecting lyric *ought* to be universal too. I suggest that this syllogism, operating, no doubt, unconsciously (and the more irresistibly for that), is one cause of the prevalent indulgence towards the limited competence and charm of Aristophanes' universalized high lyrics and of the accompanying reluctance to do justice to his *other* lyrics.

It is true that no one eager for universality in the high lyrics can have failed to notice the absence there of its most typical Greek manifestation: metaphysical seriousness. It may be, however, that this loss has been surreptitiously made good by the imaginary transference to these lyrics of the 'serious' purpose visible as Aristophanic *doctrina* in particular passages or whole plays elsewhere. 'For even comedy has its moral purpose',[76] expressed in satire or some other comic means. 'Serious' – so conveniently opposed to 'trivial', 'frivolous', *and* 'comic' – can be a very slippery word; and the Greek σπουδαῖος was, if anything, still worse: opposite to φαῦλος, 'trivial', 'inferior', *and* γέλοιος, 'funny', 'absurd', *and* πονηρός, morally 'bad'. If Old Comedy aspires to be topical, and comically topical, and yet also in some sense serious (καὶ πολλὰ μὲν γέλοιά μ' εἰπεῖν, πολλὰ δὲ σπουδαῖα),[77] it is hardly surprising that it should be resistant to any categorization in, or derived from, ancient terms. According to all such categorizations, Old Comedy is inherently contradictory and its very existence becomes a problem. Could it be that the creators of such a form themselves sensed a problem and felt for a way round it? Aristophanes' high lyric venture[78] could perhaps be, not an original manifestation of the problem, but one of its less acceptable solutions.

III

The substrate of Aristophanic expression is colloquial; where other, more literary, modes of Greek make their presence felt, they are

76. τὸ γὰρ δίκαιον οἶδε καὶ τρυγῳδία *Ach.* 500.

77. *Ran.* 391f.

78. Not necessarily meaning that A himself was the first in the field; cf. n. 97 below.

superimpositions on it. The lyrics of Aristophanic comedy have the same basis. That is, Aristophanes the lyric poet does not belong to the line that runs from Alcman and Stesichorus to Simonides, Pindar and the authors of the magnificent choruses of tragedy. His lyrics may be more or less affected by that line, but he does not belong to it. His affinities[79] are rather with the tradition of low lyric that descends from folk song and Archilochus – or, presumably, from folk song *to* Archilochus – and is drawn on variously by Hipponax and, underneath the aristocratic accent, by Anacreon:[80] a tradition that, by comparison with the 'serious' line, kept recognizable links with folk elements. The *gephyrismoi* of *Frogs*, already mentioned,[81] represent one example of the connection.

All this is to say that the ultimate affiliations of Aristophanic lyric, no less than those of Aristophanic comedy in general, are, for better or for worse, with popular culture. *Hence* its topical satirical element (which is as proper here as in any department of the drama): popular culture lives in the topical present. *Birds* 1470ff.:

πολλὰ δὴ καὶ καινὰ καὶ θαυ-
μάστ' ἐπεπτόμεσθα καὶ
δεινὰ πράγματ' εἴδομεν.
ἔστι γὰρ δένδρον πεφυκὸς
ἔκτοπόν τι Καρδίας ἀ-
πωτέρω Κλεώνυμος...

In our flights we've seen many strange, new, fantastic things. There's an extraordinary tree growing a safe distance from *Hert*ford called *Cleonymus*...

Topical satire: the birds have been and seen, and report back with a minimum of high colouring.[82] Despite the punning (καρδία,

79. I am not here speaking of the historical origins of the comic forms themselves, but rather (like Aristotle in *Poetics* §4, 1448b24–1449a6) of spiritual ancestry, albeit without prejudice to historical origins proper.

80. The low tradition, then, includes, but is wider than, *iamboi* (however broadly conceived), on the ethos of which M. L. West has some pertinent remarks in *Studies in Greek Elegy and Iambus* (Berlin 1974), 22–39, especially 23–5, 35–7.

81. See n. 51 above.

82. There is the -μεσθα of 1471, usually regarded as an epic/poetic form and certainly alien to prose (Kühner–Blass II. 61, Schwyzer, *Griech. Gramm.* I. 670), but perhaps not so purely poetic: the form is surprisingly common in A himself (nine citations in G. Curtius, *Das Verbum der griechischen Sprache* I² (Leipzig 1877) 94, including such very 'unpoetic' verses as *Plut.* 1160) and reappears in the Koine (Schwyzer, *loc. cit.*, n. 3).

'heart', as symbol of courage, and Cardia, one of the chief towns in the Thracian Chersonese), the strength of such a passage is not in verbal finesse, let alone in any lapidary verbal poise, but in the immediate play of ideas, whose vigour is the vigour of the passing moment.

Hence too the tonal range of Aristophanic lyric, down (with the same vigorous relish) to the juiciest obscenity, which once again (and *pace* Richards) is as proper here as elsewhere in Aristophanes. *Lysistrata* 821ff., a brief duet between old woman militant and old man truculent but wary:

— τὴν γνάθον βούλει θένω;
— μηδαμῶς· ἔδεισα γάρ.
— ἀλλὰ κρούσω τῷ σκέλει;
— τὸν σάκανδρον ἐκφανεῖς.

'Want a crack on the jaw?' 'I'm scared stiff; no thanks.' 'A bang from my leg?' 'You'll show your —.'[83]

Hence various of its formal chracteristics, such as the fairly extensive use in comedy (as compared with tragedy) of the simple 'systematic' grouping of rhythmical cola and the short stanza-unit, which one associates with Archilochus, Anacreon and the Lesbians, rather than the 'periodic' groupings favoured in serious choral lyric.[84] And hence in general the simpler coherence of the rhythmic constituents of Aristophanes' odes compared with those of tragic lyrics: 'the lyrics of comedy were in general more homogeneous metrically than those of tragedy, and the effect of this in certain metres was to make the song go with a swing'.[85] Again: 'in its search for the sort of metre which could be expressed in vigorous dance...comedy evolved certain kinds of patter rhythm with quick resolutions; such are the cretic–paeonic...'[86] – from which it follows that, quite apart from possible external associations, rhythms and rhythmic combinations are to some extent low or

83. Text as Coulon (Budé). On σάκανδρος see J. Henderson, *The Maculate Muse: Obscene Language in Attic Comedy* (Yale 1975), 133.

84. See Dale, *Lyric Metres* 196. The distinction seems originally to have been related to dialectal traditions, with the long 'periodic' strophe a feature of the Doric lyric tradition (cf. M. L. West, *CR* (1973) 181f.), at a time when serious choral lyric meant Doric lyric. From a late-fifth-century standpoint, however, such correlations are all but defunct.

85. Dale, *Collected Papers* 253.

86. *Ibid.*

high *per se*: 'rhythm might be φορτικός or τραγικός by its inherent properties'.[87] And one can add to the list certain unliterary elements in the rhythmical basis of the songs, notably the occasional appearance of 'syllabic', rather than quantitative, rhythm, and of 'approximate responsion' between strophe and antistrophe.[88]

Hence, finally, the marked prevalence in Aristophanes' lyrics of refrains and, more generally, of parallelisms of a kind not associated with (say) Homer or Pindar or Sophocles.[89] I have already commented on the refrain in *Frogs* (vv. 404, 410, 416):

Ἴακχε φιλοχορευτὰ συμπρόπεμπέ με.

Beside that, note, for instance, the iambic rhyme in *Acharnians* 1015–17:

ἤκουσας ὡς μαγειρικῶς
κομψῶς τε καὶ δειπνητικῶς
αὑτῷ διακονεῖται;

metrically responding to another in 1044–6:

ἀποκτενεῖς λιμῷ 'μὲ καὶ
τοὺς γείτονας κνίσῃ τε καὶ
φωνῇ τοιαῦτα λάσκων.

Or, from the same play, the cry and counter-cry of Lamachus and Dicaeopolis (1218–21):

— εἰλιγγιῶ κάρα λίθῳ πεπληγμένος
καὶ σκοτοδινιῶ.
— κἀγὼ καθεύδειν βούλομαι καὶ στύομαι
καὶ σκοτοβινιῶ

(with an agonistic element particularly familiar in Aristophanic recitative, as with Cleon and the sausage-seller at *Knights* 294f.:

— διαφορήσω σ' εἴ τι γρύξει.
— κοπροφορήσω σ' εἰ λαλήσεις).

87. *Ibid.*, 256 (cf. Demetrius, *Eloc.* 5 etc.). For various relevant instances, see Dale, *Lyric Metres* 54–7, 113, 147.

88. See Dale, *Lyric Metres* 56f., 62–6, 78f., 86, 89–91, 207; Ussher on *Eccl.* 952a–975; Wilamowitz, *Griech. Versk.* 470–86. Not all authorities rush to call syllabic rhythm popular (cf. Dale, *Lyric Metres* 78), though it is hard to think what else it could be, despite its exceptional occurrences in high poetry proper.

89. Though certainly found more frequently in Aeschylus (see W. B. Stanford, *Aeschylus in His Style* (Dublin 1942) 83–5). As Stanford, following Kranz, remarks, Aeschylus' source for such features as refrains was probably magico-religious ritual, which tends to confirm, rather than belie, their 'popular' character.

Or the intricate structure of sound echoes in *Lysistrata* 1189–93:

> στρωμάτων δὲ ποικίλων καὶ
> χλανιδίων καὶ ξυστίδων καὶ
> χρυσίων, ὅσ' ἐστί μοι,
> οὐ φθόνος ἔνεστί μοι πᾶσι παρέχειν φέρειν
> τοῖς παισίν...

In each case the context is clearly low.

It is, of course, true that authentic high poetry made use of various forms of symmetry.[90] Aristophanes himself parodies one at *Clouds* 717–19:

> ὅτε μου
> φροῦδα τὰ χρήματα, φρούδη χροιά,
> φρούδη ψυχή, φρούδη δ' ἐμβάς,[91]

with which compare (e.g.) Euripides, *Hecuba* 159–61,

> τίς ἀμύνει μοι; ποία γέννα,
> ποία δὲ πόλις; φροῦδος πρέσβυς,
> φροῦδοι παῖδες.

But equally there can be no doubt that, except in such special cases, the comic poet's refrains and his other parallel structures are usually of popular provenance,[92] to be paralleled from the Greek proverbial collections:

> ἄλλοισι μὲν γλῶττα, ἄλλοισι δὲ γομφίοι,

or from magico-ritual contexts, like the refrain in Theocritus II:

> ἶυγξ, ἕλκε τὺ τῆνον ἐμὸν ποτὶ δῶμα τὸν ἄνδρα,

or from the extant folk-songs:

> ἦλθ' ἦλθε χελιδὼν
> καλὰς ὥρας ἄγουσα,
> καλοὺς ἐνιαυτούς,
> ἐπὶ γαστέρα λευκά,
> ἐπὶ νῶτα μέλαινα.
> παλάθαν σὺ προκύκλει
> ἐκ πίονος οἴκου
> οἴνου τε δέπαστρον
> τυροῦ τε κάνυστρον.[93]

90. See e.g. W. Kranz, *Stasimon*, 1933, 127ff. and Dover, comm. on *Clouds*, p. 137, but cf. nn. 89 above and 94 below.
91. Contrast the 'low' parallelisms at 711ff. (cf. Dover *ad loc.*).
92. See Silk, *Interaction in Poetic Imagery* 224f.
93. Zen. *Paroem.* I. 73; Theocr. II. 17, 22 etc.; *Carm Pop.* 2 (Page *PMG*).

Such structures are not much in evidence in Aristophanes' 'serious' high lyrics, which reinforces the presumption that a striking assonance like the one at *Frogs* 344f., already cited,

> φλογὶ φέγγεται δὲ λειμών·
> γονὺ πάλλεται γερόντων,

is not to be thought of as an Aristophanic instance of some established resource of elevated poetry, but as an infusion of 'popular' vigour into an otherwise more genteel construct – or rather, in conformity with our notion of the substrate, as a welcome surfacing of native strength at a moment when upper-class manners might have smothered it altogether.[94]

Low lyric, then, is Aristophanes' *primary* idiom. From which it does not follow, however, that low lyric represents, in his case, an ideal type any more than its genteel cousin. It is the low lyrics in which (as Dover reminds us) we sometimes find the most 'tediously unsophisticated aspects of Greek comedy'. He makes the comment apropos the rival choruses of old men and old women in *Lysistrata*, and adds: 'while the two choruses are at odds, their abusive words and threats of violence go on longer than (to our taste) humorous invention can be sustained, and when they are united they devote no less than four whole stanzas to the primitive joke, "if anyone wants to borrow anything from me, let him come to my house at once – and he'll get nothing"'.[95] This is popular vigour at its most restrictive and trivial; entertainment arising out of the immediate dramatic moment, and playing, perhaps, on some current resonance outside the drama – but not, to use the modern dichotomy, art; no more, and probably less, of an achievement than the high lyrical pastiche. And though, as we have seen, both the high and the low lyrics have their points and their moments, Aristophanes' substantial achievement as a lyric poet lies elsewhere.

Specifically, it lies in a creative combination of low with high. The product is a new compound, not a mere *mixture*, which has the vigour and various attributes of the low together with the formal grace and discipline of the high and an enlarged tonal and expressive range all round. Several of the momentary felicities that

94. This parallelism might well, given its context, have a cult flavour, which would take it out of the truly *literary* sphere. The same goes for the items listed by Kranz (n. 90 above); cf. Silk, *Interaction* 224.

95. *Aristophanic Comedy* 154 on *Lys.* 1043–71 and 1189–1215.

I have noted in the high lyrics are in fact (I have already implied) traceable to the low substrate and so exemplify the fusion in miniature. Thus it is with the verbal organization of φλογὶ φέγγεται... (*Frogs* 344f.) and even perhaps with the immediacy and (almost) topical reality of *Lysistrata* 1251ff., ἐπ' Ἀρταμιτίῳ.[96] What I am now suggesting is that such compounding constitutes a *central* Aristophanic achievement,[97] not some occasional, freakish, *tour de force*; and I would add that the impressiveness of the achievement consists partly in the very fact that the compounding involves such a drastic violation of traditional norms.

Knights 973–84 provides a good example of Aristophanes in command of his new medium:[98]

ἥδιστον φάος ἡμέρας
ἔσται τοῖσι παροῦσι καὶ
τοῖσι δεῦρ' ἀφικνουμένοις,
ἢν Κλέων ἀπόληται.
καίτοι πρεσβυτέρων τινῶν
οἵων ἀργαλεωτάτων
ἐν τῷ δείγματι τῶν δικῶν
ἤκουσ' ἀντιλεγόντων,
ὡς εἰ μὴ 'γένεθ' οὗτος ἐν
τῇ πόλει μέγας, οὐκ ἂν ἤ-
στην σκεύη δύο χρησίμω,
δοῖδυξ οὐδὲ τορύνη.

Sweetest light of day to us | And our children's children, | Day of Cleon's downfall! | But some cynical old brokers | On 'change are putting forward | A counter-theory – | That were he not in power, the State | Would lack two useful tools: | A pestle and a ladle.[99]

A paradigm of topicality given permanent form and expression. We begin with a 'timeless' line in the high style (and a phrase reminiscent of Euripides)[100] and move swiftly to more down-to-

96. Even though the immediacy is, in part, Homeric; and even though, as it might be said, A is only doing here what (say) Aeschylus, in a different tradition, does in *Persae*.

97. It is hard to avoid implying that A had no precursors, even though an argument to that effect would be little more than *ex silentio*. One should be prepared to interpret 'A' as 'Old Comedy' here and elsewhere. See further n. 135 below.

98. The antistrophe 985–96 provides another, rather less good.

99. Tr. Dickinson.

100. See Rau, *Paratragodia*, 188.

earth Greek and the specifics of Cleon and contemporary Athens. The stanza form, three finely controlled aeolic quatrains (three glyconics and a pherecratean), creates a presumption of a resolution or climax on the pherecratean at the end of each four. The first instance (ἦν..., 976) satisfies expectation with an almost brutal directness;[101] the second (ἤκουσ'..., 980), a resolution neither in form (with the run-on of lines) nor sense, acts as a foil to the final climax (δοῖδυξ..., 984), which rounds off the last, witty,[102] quatrain and the whole stanza with a vigorous ironic image to match the earlier dismissive phrase δείγματι τῶν δικῶν ('suit-shop').[103]

Acharnians 263–79, the famous ode to Phales, god of the phallus, is an altogether superb example of the new mode, a lyric of extraordinary richness and verve:

> Φαλῆς ἑταῖρε Βακχίου
> ξύγκωμε νυκτοπεριπλάνη-
> τε μοιχὲ παιδεραστά,
> ἕκτῳ σ' ἔτει προσεῖπον ἐς
> τὸν δῆμον ἐλθὼν ἄσμενος,
> σπονδὰς ποιησάμενος ἐμαυ-
> τῷ, πραγμάτων τε καὶ μαχῶν
> καὶ Λαμάχων ἀπαλλαγείς.
> πολλῷ γάρ ἐσθ' ἥδιον, ὦ Φαλῆς Φαλῆς,
> κλέπτουσαν εὑρόνθ' ὡρικὴν ὑληφόρον
> τὴν Στρυμοδώρου Θρᾷτταν ἐκ τοῦ Φελλέως
> μέσην λαβόντ' ἄραντα κατα-
> βαλόντα καταγιγαρτίσ' ὦ
> Φαλῆς Φαλῆς.
> ἐὰν μεθ' ἡμῶν ξυμπίῃς, ἐκ κραιπάλης
> ἕωθεν εἰρήνης ῥοφήσει τρύβλιον·
> ἡ δ' ἀσπὶς ἐν τῷ φεψάλῳ κρεμήσεται.

O Phales, friend and fellow reveller of Bacchus, night-wanderer, paramour, pederast, glad I am to return to my people and greet you after six years. I have made my own treaty and freed myself from fighting and

101. Especially as this is the first – and only – time that Cleon is mentioned by name in the whole play. (The *character* Cleon is referred to as Παφλαγών throughout the play.)

102. 'Even his old partisans of the Philocleon type defend him only as a necessary evil' (Neil on v. 977). καίτοι (977), is bland understatement.

103. On δεῖγμα, see Neil *ad loc.* The phrase shows metaphor enforced by alliteration in a way I discuss in *Interaction in Poetic Imagery* 179–81 and 226f., under the heading 'genitival link'.

fussing and Lamachusing. Much sweeter it is, O Phales, Phales, to catch Strymodorus' pretty Thratta pilfering wood from the fells, and take her by the hip and lift her up and lay her down and crush *her* grape, Phales, Phales. Drink with us now, and the morning after the party you'll have Peace to drink in cupfuls; and the shield shall be hung up in the sparks of the fire.

The ode, sung by Dicaeopolis, the Athenian Everyman in search of peace, is tied to the plot (προσεῖπον κτλ.), and in no way the worse for that. We start high with a formal invocation marked by asyndeton between florid compound epithets (which nevertheless offer a pertinent characterization of the relationship between Phales and the god of wine), only to be propelled with disarming abruptness to the low μοιχὲ παιδεραστά and thence to the specifics, Lamachus and all that: specifics, though, that issue in a universal celebration of life. Throughout, the lyric moves at a remarkable speed and yet allows the symbols of peace, in particular, to be given a firm delineation. It is in fact a masterpiece of concrete expression all round: φελλέως,[104] καταγιγαρτίσαι, ῥοφήσει, τρύβλιον, φεψάλῳ κρεμήσεται. Formally and rhythmically, it is a joy. The iambics conform perfectly to the exuberant mood and to the rapidity of the thought (there is no pleonasm here), the tribrachic resolutions on νυκτοπεριπλάνητε and καταβαλόντα καταγιγαρτίσ' being particularly expressive. The ode is structured to a triumphant climax on 269f. (πραγμάτων...), with its 'low' word-play and parallelism, and a second climax (in both senses of the word) on 274–6, with an intensifying assonantal series (λαβόντα κτλ.) resolved on, and so preparing, the unexpected καταγιγαρτίσαι.[105] That metaphor (aptly, in the setting of Bacchus and the drinking-bowl) comes from grapes.

There will be those for whom the moral ethos of the song, although or because typically Aristophanic, leaves something to be desired; and it might be said that, quite apart from the sexual amorality, the song is unashamedly male-chauvinist and in some ways undisguisedly wish-fulfilling. (Note that the girl is conveniently caught *in flagrante delicto*, which gives the male a pretext, and

104. See Dover on *Nub.* 71.

105. On which word see Starkie *ad loc.*; J. Taillardat, *Les Images d'Aristophane* (revised ed. Paris 1965), 100 (with whom I incline to agree); and Henderson, *The Maculate Muse* 166.

that she is conveniently a slave,[106] which allows him to get away with it.) Against that, one could say that such heartfelt exuberance is a persuasive counsel for its own guilt-free standpoint; particularly so, when one notes that the song is in no sense an individual's private self-glorification: for Dicaeopolis' wife and daughter are both present and, indeed, given supporting roles in the celebration, and the celebration itself is a religious celebration, and *therefore* (and even though the religion is low religion) of universal significance. The ode in this, as in other ways, is not immature. Overall, with its effortless and enviable unity of art and entertainment, sacred and profane, it sums up the richness of the rich culture it has grown out of.[107]

How are we to characterize such lyrics? In terms of level, they are, so to speak, low lyrics *plus* – but not (to restate) a co-presence of high and low on equal terms. For this reason it would be misleading to relate the new mode to the rhetoricians' middle χαρακτήρ: that is, to that ancient notion of the middle way that made it the golden mean, the perfect, harmonious compromise between two extremes. The relation between high and low in Aristophanes' new compound is anything but that. The essential inequality of the relationship is symptomatized by an interesting feature of the two passages just discussed, which is in fact a characteristic feature of the new mode. The lyrics start high, then dip low, and usually end low. The *Knights* passage began ἥδιστον φάος ἡμέρας..., then dipped to plain 'topical' Greek and ended quite aggressively the same way – δοῖδυξ οὐδὲ τορύνη – with diction, and to a lesser extent idiom,[108] alien to high poetry. Likewise Dicaeopolis' monody, with its ornate opening and sudden

106. Indicated by the name Θρᾷττα: see Headlam–Knox on Herodas I. I.

107. Horn, *Gebet und Gebetsparodie* 57–9, contrives to classify the lyric (with *Ran.* 420–34) as 'serious pastiche' of a popular form. That τὸ φαλλικόν was a popular form is not in doubt, and some features of A's song must be conventional (e.g. the ὦ Φαλῆς Φαλῆς refrain?), but its predominant peace/war theme obviously could not be and it is gratuitous (although flattering to the popular form in question) to suppose that much else is. *Pastiche* means something other than 'based on'.

108. 'The metaphorical identification of persons with inanimate objects' (Stanford, *Aeschylus in His Style* 94, instancing *Pers.* 51 λόγχης ἄκμονες, said of the Persians, as a rare instance in Aeschylus), being akin to one of those 'Plautinities in Plautus' which are in fact paralleled in *Greek* popular usage: see H. W. Prescott, *TAPA* (1932) 112f.

drop to μοιχὲ παιδεραστά, at which level it stays, more or less,[109] until the end. And likewise most other comparable lyrics besides.[110] In some of the nominally high lyrics there is, as we have seen, a momentary – nothing more than a momentary – appearance of the low. In the composite mode, the low is predominant, predictable, and therefore, for a time, dispensable with; whereas the high (the new *plus*), having no such status, requires a formal introduction at the outset if it is to be allowed to take part in the proceedings at all; its survival thereafter remains in doubt, whereas the reassertion of the low is inevitable. There is also a certain mischievous comic logic behind the pattern, a conjuring trick with δόξα and ἐπιστήμη: you purport to stake a claim to high lyrical status, only to subvert your own pretension at the next stroke. This is, obviously, a psychological, rather than a historical, explanation. In historical terms, one would ask: low lyric *plus*? how did the 'plus' get there in the first place? – and answer, presumably: under the influence of tragedy, the parallel dramatic form that influenced comedy in so many of its aspects, thanks to its huge preeminence within the Athenian culture that Old Comedy fed on and, in its turn, enriched. It is tragedy, above all, that supplies the comic poet's need for elevation in his lyrics: tragedy that provides most of the specific models for high parody and high pastiche alike; and tragedy that helps to engender the new, irregular compound as well.[111]

109. There is a touch of elevation about σε...προσεῖπον...ἄσμενος 266f. (cf. *Pax* 582 and the passages assembled by Rau, *Paratragodia* 144–8), though hardly about ὡρικήν (272), *pace* Starkie. Note the 'low' metric in the trimeters at the end: 278 violates Porson's canon and 279 has no main caesura. (I presume that these trimeters were *sung*, like those at 271–3; cf. Dale, *Lyric Metres* 76f., 198.)

110. See n. 136 below.

111. It is evident that, by comparison with tragedy, other serious poetry had only a minor influence on A's lyrics. One tiny, but revealing, instance is provided by the metre of *Eq.* 1264–73 ~ 1290–9. The passage is dactylo-epitrite, but with an ithyphallic element. Dale, *Lyric metres* 180, remarks: 'the strophe is a parody of a Pindaric προσόδιον, but the ithyphallic is not found in any of Pindar's extant dactylo-epitrite' – whereas it *is* found there in tragic lyrics. It is unusual enough for A to parody Pindar at all, and even when he looks that way, he keeps one eye on tragedy the whole time. N.B. that Sifakis (*Parabasis and Animal Choruses* 17–21, 56, 68f.) would have us believe that the hymnic lyrics of Old Comedy are relics of a *Kultlyrik* (presumably high, not low, lyric) which existed in its own right in primitive comedy, and that to this extent at least the influence of tragedy is not apparent. But apart from anything else, it is procedurally suspect to explain

At this point in our investigation of the new mode, let us take stock. We can start by reminding ourselves what we are *not* talking about. We are not talking about uncompounded low lyric: *that*, unlike the 'low lyric plus', is purely homogeneous. Nor about high lyrical pastiche, which is again homogeneous and is also inherently unoriginal: it confines itself to what *could* be done elsewhere, whereas the essence of our mode is that it presents what could *not*. In this respect, the new mode is like parody: both involve violations of norms. The difference is that in parody the violation directs us *either* to the real literature whose normal features have been satirized, or whose normal context has been replaced by something incongruous, *or* to the incongruous relationship between the parody and its real original.[112] Either way, it does not do what our mode does: turn the attention to that open-ended reality we call 'life'. When Aristophanes has Aeschylus parody Euripides' verse, we think of Euripides and his verse. When Trygaeus is up on his beetle, and his daughter runs out to him in tragic distress (*Peace* 114ff.),

ὦ πάτερ, ὦ πάτερ, ἆρ' ἔτυμός γε...,

we are mainly occupied in savouring the incongruity between this situation and mood and those of the Euripidean original (which concerns Aeolus and his children).[113] But when Dicaeopolis sings of the phallic god and an Athenian general and a girl carrying wood, we think about a phallic god and an Athenian general and a girl carrying wood.

However, when we think about the god and the general and the girl, we do not think of them quite as we would if they were represented separately in whichever genres each might be separately represented, and we were thinking about them separately. The strangeness of their co-existence in the given tonal context means that we see them to a greater or lesser extent in a new perspective: the mode carries with it the germ of a new comic vision. Such a comment, of course, is liable to sound pretentious or, simply, vacuous; but in this instance it has, I think, a peculiar

the problematic (high lyric in comedy) by reference to the hypothetical with unknown properties (*Kultlyrik* in proto-comedy), rather than to the known (tragedy) – especially when the known is known to have influenced comedy in other respects anyway.

112. Cf. Dover, *Aristophanic Comedy* 73.

113. See Platnauer *ad loc.* and (in more detail) Rau, *Paratragodia*, 92f.

justice. Greek culture was not only a rich culture, but, axiomatically, a *whole* culture, the culture from which envious later ages derived their notion of the 'whole man'. And yet, the Greek view of life, as articulated and developed by Homer and his successors, was highly stratified. To put the matter in the simplest relevant way: things were seen as *either* serious and valuable *or* trivial and less valuable; and the serious deserved a high treatment in a high context, which would reinforce its value, and the trivial the opposite. Hence the theory of *decorum*: τῶν πραγμάτων πρέποι ἂν καὶ τὰς φωνὰς ἔχειν ἀξίας ('we ought to use words worthy of things').[114] The new mode challenges this vision and offers another – more anarchic? or merely more realistic? – in which the correlations, and therefore the values, make way, however momentarily, for a more open view of life. Aristophanic parody, of course, recombines 'serious' and 'trivial' elements as well. But with parody we hardly see living reality at all; the preexisting view is therefore unchallenged.

From the conventional standpoint, there is clearly something fantastic about the comic vision; and fantasy is an important characteristic of the new mode in its own right. There are in fact some lyrics where fantasy simply takes over. *Frogs* 209–23, the chorus of frogs and the suffering Dionysus:

— βρεκεκεκὲξ κοὰξ κοάξ,
βρεκεκεκὲξ κοὰξ κοάξ.
λιμναῖα κρηνῶν τέκνα,
ξύναυλον ὕμνων βοὰν
φθεγξώμεθ', εὔγηρυν ἐμὰν ἀοιδάν,
κοὰξ κοάξ,
ἣν ἀμφὶ Νυσήιον
Διὸς Διόνυσον ἐν
Λίμναισιν ἰαχήσαμεν,
ἡνίχ' ὁ κραιπαλόκωμος
τοῖς ἱεροῖσι Χύτροισι
χωρεῖ κατ' ἐμὸν τέμενος λαῶν ὄχλος.
βρεκεκεκὲξ κοὰξ κοάξ.
— ἐγὼ δέ γ' ἀλγεῖν ἄρχομαι
τὸν ὄρρον ὦ κοὰξ κοάξ.

'*Brekekekex coax coax.* | Spawn of marsh and spring | Sing loud and sweet on a splendid | Theme set to the flute | *coax coax.* | That anthem for the sake | Of the son of Zeus, | Dionysus of Nysa, | We shrieked round the

114. 'Longinus', *Subl.* 43–5.

lake | At the Pitcher Wake | And the old soaks went rocking | Round our sacred acre. | *Brekekekex coax coax.*' | 'My arse aches *coax*...'[115]

We have our extraordinary combinations here: high (εὔγηρυν ἐμὰν ἀοιδάν, Doric alpha and all) and low (τὸν ὄρρον); the matter-of-fact and 'topical' Χύτροισι[116] alongside the timeless Νυσήιον Διὸς Διόνυσον,[117] in the context, needless to say, of the 'real' – and distinctly ungodlike – god himself; and in addition a scatter of bizarre onomatopoeic sound effects and fancifully misapplied appellations (ὕμνων? εὔγηρυν??), all within the framework of a most unequal duet in an extraordinary setting.

This kind of comic fantasy[118] and the greater realism of the song to Phales represent the two poles of the new mode. Such labels as 'fantasy' and 'realism' may require a certain amount of qualification to be acceptable, but the differences between them are distinct enough. In pragmatic terms, the difference is that the realistic lyric invites us to look at the 'real' world that it so aberrantly depicts. With the fantastic lyric, we stop *seeing* any reality and, probably, can do no more than gaze in astonishment at the fantasy itself; we are offered not a new vision of life, but almost a new kind of life, hardly relatable to our own. In terms of our formula, 'low lyric *plus*', one could say that the fantastic type exaggerates the inherent tension between 'low' and 'plus' (which in parody remains mere incongruity) into an object of interest in its own right. This, as much as anything in Aristophanes, is an extraordinary and truly anarchic achievement, but as a

115. Tr. Dickinson.

116. χύτρος, Χύτροι, and if it comes to that, χύτρα are prose/comedy words (see LSJ s. vv.), though perfectly decent. χύτρα occurs in low lyric: *Carm. Pop.* 29 (Page, *PMG*). κραιπαλόκωμος nearby is more straightforwardly low.

117. πόθι Νύσας...θυρσοφορεῖς θιάσους, ὦ Διόνυσε...; ...αὐδῶ, ὁ Σεμέλας ὁ Διὸς παῖς (Eur. *Bacch.* 556ff., 580f.).

118. This expression is used in a comparable connection by Rau. During a discussion (*Paratragodia* 13) of what constitutes parody in A, and immediately after his remark about A's serious lyrics (n. 3 above), he notes: Aristophanic comedy [sc. in its lyrics] frequently rises to authentic high poetry...'*oder aber sie mischt*, wie in der Arie des Wiedehopfs (*Av.* 227ff.), dem Preis der Vogelgötter (*Av.* 1058ff. = 1088ff.) und dem köstlich prahlerischen Autoelegium der Frösche (*Ran.* 209ff.), *in so phantasticher Weise' Trivialität mit hoher Poesie, dass man lieber von autonomer komischer Lyrik als von Parodie sprechen möchte*' (my italics). Elsewhere he writes summarily of 'komisch-phantastische Lyrik' (e.g. of *Av.* 227ff., p. 195). But it is apparent that he means something more restricted by the phrase than I do.

constructive achievement it falls some way behind that represented by the more realistic type.[119]

Within these two extremes it is possible to place other instances of the new mode. Near the realistic end comes *Peace* 582–600. The chorus greet the incoming goddess, Peace:

χαῖρε χαῖρ', ὡς ἀσμένοισιν ἦλθες, ὦ φιλτάτη.
σῷ γὰρ ἐδάμην πόθῳ, δαιμόνια βουλόμενος εἰς ἀγρὸν ἀνερπύσαι.
. . . .
ἦσθα γὰρ μέγιστον ἡμῖν κέρδος ὦ ποθουμένη
πᾶσιν ὁπόσοι γεωργὸν βίον ἐτρίβομεν.
μόνη γὰρ ἡμᾶς ὠφέλεις.
πολλὰ γὰρ ἐπάσχομεν πρίν ποτ' ἐπὶ σοῦ γλυκέα κἀδάπανα καὶ φίλα.
τοῖς ἀγροίκοισιν γὰρ ἦσθα χῖδρα καὶ σωτηρία.
ὥστε σὲ τά τ' ἀμπέλια καὶ τὰ νέα συκίδια
τἄλλα θ' ὁπόσ' ἔστι φυτὰ προσγελάσεται λαβόντ' ἄσμενα.

Welcome, welcome, darling – and now you've come | You can understand | How terribly we yearned for | You and our return to farm our land. | Most beloved, you were our greatest benefactress; | To all of us who make a living farming | There was none but you | To give a helping hand. | In the days before the war, | All the precious and delicious | Perquisites there were! | You were our groats and our salvation, | And so the vine and fig-shoot | And the other plants | Laugh with delight to see you![120]

There is not much that could be called fantasy here – apart, that is, from the fundamental incongruity of a chorus of farmers singing in elevated rapture (albeit in essentially low cretic-paeonic rhythms) like the romantic lead in a Euripidean recognition duet:

ὦ φίλτατ' ἀνδρῶν Μενέλεως...
ἔλαβον ἀσμένα πόσιν ἐμόν...
(Euripides, *Helen* 625–7).

Dearest of men, Menelaus...with delight I greet my husband.[121]

The passage in fact combines the specifics of the countryside (so often a stimulus to Aristophanes' inventiveness) with this most familiar of romantic–tragic moments into an unpredictably

119. Mindful of the ancient antitheses between σπουδαῖος and its various opposites, one might be tempted to relate the realistic (in contradistinction to the fantastic) to the category of the *spoudogeloion*; but for us the relevant opposite of σπουδαῖος is not so much γέλοιος as φαῦλος, and *spoudogeloion* carries with it particular associations of Menippean satire.

120. Tr. based on Dickinson.

121. For a full list of parallels, see Rau, *Paratragodia* 144–8.

poignant whole, whereby the ordinary (low) facts of rural life on which our eyes are kept – are revalued upwards. One detail deserves special mention. The phrase χῖδρα καὶ σωτηρία (595, 'groats and salvation') epitomizes Aristophanes' new compound: the specific that points outwards to 'life' conjoined with the general that evokes the high-poetic context again:

ὦ φίλατον φῶς, ὦ μόνος σωτὴρ δόμων
'Αγαμέμνονος, πῶς ἦλθες;

O dearest light, O sole saviour of Agamemnon's house, have you really come?[122]

Right at the realistic end, *Acharnians* 692–702, the lament of the Μαραθωνομάχαι:

ταῦτα πῶς εἰκότα, γέροντ' ἀπολέσαι πολιὸν ἄνδρα περὶ κλεψύδραν,
πολλὰ δὴ ξυμπονήσαντα καὶ θερμὸν ἀπομορξάμενον ἀνδρικὸν
ἱδρῶτα δὴ καὶ πολύν,
ἄνδρ' ἀγαθὸν ὄντα Μαραθῶνι περὶ τὴν πόλιν;
εἶτα Μαραθῶνι μὲν ὅτ' ἦμεν ἐδιώκομεν,
νῦν δ' ὑπ' ἀνδρῶν πονηρῶν σφόδρα διωκόμεθα, κᾳτα προσαλισκόμεθα.
πρὸς τάδε τίς ἀντερεῖ Μαρψίας;

How *can* this be fair, to ruin a grizzled ancient, in the clutches of the law, who has often been joint labourer with you, and has wiped away warm streams of manly sweat – a good man and true at Marathon in the clutches of his country's foes? At Marathon we charged the foe; but now base men charge *us* – and convict us too. What Marpsias can answer this?[123]

High colouring is considerably less in evidence here, residing in the cast of the phrasing, rather than in any high-flown vocabulary;[124] but for once 'high' implies *heightened* as much as *elevated*. Once again we have the largely φορτικός cretic-paeonic

122. Soph. *El.* 1354f.

123. Tr. based on Starkie.

124. Besides the points commented on in the discussion, note the double ellipse of τήν with κλεψύδραν (cf. Starkie *ad loc.*) and ἐστί with εἰκότα; γέροντ' as adjective with ἄνδρα (as Thgn. 1351, cf. LSJ s.v. γέρων); and ἱδρῶτα δή, the particle being rare after substantives in prose and comedy. (On this last point see Denniston, *Greek Particles*[2] (Oxford 1954), 213f., who quotes two other passages in A along with eight in prose. I note (i) that most of these eight are in Plato, who is half a poet anyway (Arist. *fr.* 73; Silk, *Interaction* 48, 220f.); and (ii) that four others from the complete list – two in Xenophon and the other two in A (*Th.* 1228, *Ec.* 1163) – involve the phrase ὥρα δή, which is presumably a set expression, without any bearing on the poetic status of the noun + δή idiom as a whole.)

rhythm, this time serving to steady the rising emotion resulting from a series of evocative repetitions. The effect of the piece derives from an accumulation of simple touches. There is, first, a phrase of poetic cast,[125] plangently echoed:

> γέροντ' ἀπολέσαι πολιὸν ἄνδρα...
> θερμὸν ἀπομορξάμενον ἀνδρικὸν ἱδρῶτα...,

jarring against the concrete-prosaic περὶ κλεψύδραν[126] almost ironically – as if the old men's claim to dignity was mocked by the context of their present treatment. Then a 'ring-form' to convey the *scale* of the veterans' efforts, πολλὰ δὴ ξυμπονήσαντα ∼ ἱδρῶτα δὴ καὶ πολύν.... Then another plangent repetion, ὄντα Μαραθῶνι ∼ Μαραθῶνι...ἦμεν, a wry allusion back to περὶ κλεψύδραν in περὶ τὴν πόλιν,[127] and a sardonic pun: ἐδιώκομεν (in war) ∼ διωκόμεθα (in law) ∼ προσαλισκόμεθα (both),[128] the concrete ('war') senses of these verbs being summed up finally by the name Μαρψίας.[129] Meanwhile an overriding series reaches its climax. The chorus speaks for the πολιὸν ἄνδρα, who has expended so much ἀνδρικὸν ἱδρῶτα – not just a case of *man*, then, but of *manliness* and, actually, unqualified manly worth, ἄνδρ' ἀγαθὸν ὄντα – now suffering at the hands of ἀνδρῶν πονηρῶν. The restrained elevation of the lyric intensifies the pathos; the play of wit, along with the rhythm, keeps the focus on the emotive subject, not (operatically) on the emotion itself.

At least one lyric, *Acharnians* 971–99, contrives to offer *both* realism *and* fantasy side by side. The rhythm, cretic-paeonic once again, is one of the more predictable features of this song. After an opening high flurry:

> εἶδες ὦ εἶδες ὦ
> πᾶσα πόλι,

and a rapid descent to ἐμπορικὰ χρήματα (973), we pass on to an elaborate personification of the hated πόλεμος (978ff.) and a praise

125. Adjective (*vel sim.*)–verb–adjective–noun. Cf. e.g. Eur. *Hec.* 445f. ποντοπόρους κομίζεις θοὰς ἀκάτους, *Hipp.* 750f., *Med.* 1263f.

126. 'Water-clock', symbolizing the law-courts.

127. Starkie *ad loc.* notes the repetition, but fails to see its point.

128. I.e. *law* literally ('convict'), *war* metaphorically ('capture').

129. Cf. *Il.* 22. 199–201 ὡς δ' ἐν ὀνείρῳ οὐ δύναται φεύγοντα διώκειν...ὣς ὁ τὸν οὐ δύνατο μάρψαι.... The name is perhaps fabricated *ad hoc* (cf. Starkie on the passage).

of the private-peace-maker, to finish with a remarkable depiction of rustic *eros* (994ff.). Aristophanes gives us a 'series of sexual double entendres based upon agricultural terminology: Dicacopolis' reworking of the land after long years of wartime sterility is seen simultaneously as sexual rejuvenation and procreation'.[130] The combination of private peace and the sexual imagery is fantastic enough, and yet even here the rustic reality is not idealized or distorted, but conveyed more richly than generic propriety would permit.[131]

At the fantastic end of the spectrum, alongside the βρεκεκεκέξ (etc.) of *Frogs*, we have the ἐποποῖ (etc.) and the τιὸ τιό (etc.) of the hoopoe's monody (*Birds* 227–59). The passages are clearly on a par, quite apart from the menagerie sound effects. If the *Birds* situation is not quite so extravagantly impossible, it still offers us an extravagant mélange of tonally hybrid compounds – high formally, low semantically – like κριθοτράγων ('barley-eaters'):[132] the ultra-poetic voice (γῆρυν 233) and the prosaic gnats (ἐμπίδας 245).[133]

Fantasy of a quite different sort is provided by the choric

130. Henderson, *The Maculate Muse* 61 (cf. *ibid.* 118, 125, and Starkie *ad loc.*).

131. I would put into this same (mixed) category two less impressive lyrics. First, *Ach.* 665–75 (the strophe to which the Marathon song, 692–702, is the antistrophe) with its high Acharnian Muse at the start and fried fish to follow. The fish are actually evoked quite forcefully, but not to any particular end, while the Muse pulls the whole stanza out of the orbit of realism. Still, the passage contains one gem of an incongruity: Θασίαν...λιπαράμπυκα (671). The epithet is pure lyric in form (see Starkie *ad loc.* on the -άμπυξ compounds, and cf. Silk, *Interaction* 201f.) and had already been used of Μναμοσύνα by Pindar (*N.* 7. 15), but Θασίαν means 'Thasian pickle' and λιπαρός, besides its elevated sense, 'bright' (LSJ s.v. IV), also means 'oily'. (This passage has, incidentally, engendered strikingly different interpretations of its status: contrast, e.g., Horn, *Gebet und Gebetsparodie* 59, and Ehrenberg, *The People of Aristophanes* 254, with Ed. Fraenkel, *Horace* (Oxford 1957) 198.) Secondly, *Pax* 775–818, another invocation to the Muse, containing *inter alia* some remarkable abuse of A's rivals.

132. τρώγειν and its compounds and derivatives are overwhelmingly prose/comedy words (cf. the distribution in LSJ s.v. τρώγω). Homer uses the verb once, *Od.* 6. 90; low lyric also, Hippon. 26. 5, 66, Sol. 38. 1 (West), *Carm. Pop.* 1 (Page *PMG*). κριθοτράγος and κοτινοτράγος (240) were perhaps formed on the analogy of συκοτράγος, not yet attested in the classical period, but either in fact of earlier use or extracted by back-formation from the low συκοτραγίδης, Arch. 250, Hippon. 167 (West).

133. There are those (including Richards, *Aristophanes and Others* 120) who take this piece as a specimen of 'pure lyrical' verse. This I find almost as fantastic as the monody itself.

introduction to the contest between the tragedians at *Frogs* 814–29, Aeschylus with his fierce roar (ἐριβρεμέτας), Euripides with his quick tongue (ὀξυλάλος). 'This is', writes Stanford *ad loc.*, 'a brilliant piece of pseudo-elevated diction...superbly contrived to make the spectators view the coming contest...as a mock-epic conflict of savage beasts or of heroes in chariots.' And 'subtleties of metre, vocabulary, and imagery contribute to the general effect'. The lyric is by any standard an amazing *tour de force* and embodies important insights – possibly original to Aristophanes, though now familiar enough to us – into the fundamental difference between the representative of traditional Athens and articulate modern man. For instance, as Stanford notes, there is 'a psychological contrast: Aeschylus is maddened by deep-felt passion... (μανίας ὑπὸ δεινῆς ὄμματα στροβήσεται): Euripides is cool and subtle...(ἡ στοματουργὸς ἐπῶν βασανίστρια λίσπη γλῶσσα)'. And yet, powerful as the lyric is, and for all the vividness of its contrasting images, it is not apparent that this power induces us – or, indeed, even allows us – to look for very long at the ostensible target: I return to that simple implication of 'fantasy'. Insights *are* embodied there, but so bizarrely dressed that what one sees is largely the dress. The body comes into view in prose paraphrase – Stanford's or mine. The moral of which is not that prose paraphrase is superior to amazing verse, but that this type of amazing verse is not cut out to achieve exactly what a more 'realistic' version might have.[134]

I have now set out what seem to me to be the main tendencies in Aristophanes' lyrics: high lyrical pastiche, low lyric, parody, and the new composite mode with its realism and its fantasy.[135] As must be evident already, these are not clear-cut types, such that any single Aristophanic lyric is necessarily classifiable under a single heading. They are tendencies, variously in evidence in particular songs. As I have said, most of those in the composite mode start high and dip low; but that is almost a presupposition of the type.[136] Some lyrics simply switch unclassifiably. The

134. The same goes for the weaker piece 1099–1108.

135. Apropos A's own part in the invention of the new mode (cf. n. 97 above), note that there is at least one extant (albeit presumably undatable) fragment of Old Comedy outside A which looks very like an instance of the fantastic, Strattis *fr.* 66 Kock.

136. To avoid any confusion with those high lyrics that contain a trace of the

commation to the nightingale at *Birds* 676–84, for instance, begins as high lyric pastiche:

ὦ φίλη, ὦ ξουθή,
ὦ φίλτατον ὀρνέων
πάντων,

O beloved, O tawny-throated, | Dearest of all birds...[137]

but ends on a note of superb fantasy that destroys the dramatic, as well as the high lyrical, illusion at a stroke:

ἀλλ' ὦ καλλιβόαν κρέκουσ'
αὐλὸν φθέγμασιν ἠρινοῖς,
ἄρχου τῶν ἀναπαίστων.

But O, play the tones of spring on the sweet-voiced flute and start the anapaests.

What is tonally an anticlimactic deflation is simultaneously a comic climax thanks to a masterly use of aeolic rhythm in the final verse. The verses preceding are glyconics (– – – ∪ ∪ – ∪ –), inviting the 'natural' pherecratean clausula, which duly comes in the shape of

ἄρχου τῶν ἀναπαίστων (– – – ∪ ∪ – –).

low, I would define the norm as follows. Lyrics in which there is a substantial low element, along with a high element, tend to start high and end low. This is true of *Ach.* 263–79, 665–75, 971–99; *Eq.* 973–96; *Ran.* 399–416, 449–59 (all discussed already in this connection). Also of *Av.* 539–47 (πολὺ δὴ πολὺ δή – cf. Rau, *Paratragodia* 196 – dipping down to νεοττία); *Pax* 775–95 (Μοῦσα down to Καρκίνος etc.), 1159–71 (ἡνίκ' ἂν δ' ἀχέτας [Lenting] – cf. Hes. *Op.* 582ff. etc. – down to γίγνομαι παχύς); *Ran.* 372–83 (χώρει νυν down to Θωρυκίων), 674–85 (Μοῦσα down to Κλεοφῶντος etc.), 706–17 (εἰ δ' ἐγὼ ὀρθὸς ἰδεῖν – see Rau, *Paratragodia* 202 – down to πίθηκος etc.), 1099–1118 (μέγα τὸ πρᾶγμα – cf. Aesch. *Prom.* 901, Soph. *Ant.* 332 etc. – down to βιβλίον τ' ἔχων ἕκαστος etc.); *Vesp.* 1060–70 (ὦ πάλαι ποτ' ὄντες down to εὐρυπρωκτίαν). A rare exception is *Eq.* 397–408 (rising to ἐπ' ἄνθεσιν ἵζων 403, on which cf. Neil *ad loc.*). Some lyrics (as different as *Ran.* 209ff. and *Ach.* 692ff.) are not so easy to classify, or conform only partially by starting high, dipping, but ending on a more or less high note (thus *Pax* 582–600 and 796–816).

137. The song has special affinities with what Rau (*Paratragodia* 144–8) discusses under the heading of 'paratragodische Begrüssung' (although it is not parody, nor does Rau cite it). After a more general opening resonance (e.g. Eur. *Alc.* 460 ὦ μόνα, ὦ φίλα γυναικῶν [*codd.*], Sapph. 108, Soph. *OC* 1700 etc.), we have the familiar flavour of recognition scenes: ὦ φίλτατ' ἀνδρῶν...Eur. *Hel.* 625 (~ *Av.* 677); ἐμόλετ' ἀρτίως, ἐφηύρετ', ἤλθετ', εἴδεθ'...Soph. *El.* 1234f. (~ *Av.* 680).

That clausula, however, equally 'naturally' prepares for the anapaestic rhythm of the parabasis that now follows (685ff.):

ἄγε δὴ φύσιν ἄνδρες ἀμαυρόβιοι...,

evoking, as it does, the familiar anapaestic *paroemiac*, like the line a little earlier in the same play:

αὐτῶν ὥσπερ κενεβρείων (538) (– – – – ∪ ∪ – –).

But this 'modulation' from aeolic to anapaestic rhythm is also, obviously, an enactment of the explicit instruction in this verse: the clausula, blandly programmatic, is rhythmically *exemplum sui.*[138]

In so far as Aristophanes' impulse as a lyric poet is creative, it expresses itself in fantasy and – especially – in comic realism. His counter-impulse is imitative: it actuates the high lyric pastiche and acquiesces in the ubiquitous, but doubtfully creative, or merely embryonically creative, mode of parody. Parody for Aristophanes, in lyric as elsewhere, becomes second nature. In *Frogs* or *Thesmophoriazusae* it may have dramatic relevance. Often it is there for momentary effect – which is something not surprising in a comic writer, but, equally, something suggestive of a self-indulgence that is bound to militate against permanent literary achievement (however pompously inappropriate that last phrase may seem). There are indeed times when his imitative impulse produces writing that can only be thought of as damagingly, parasitically, dependent on *his own* earlier work. All writers, of course, repeat themselves,[139] but Aristophanes seems at times to do it

138. A different kind of switch is presented by the famous lyric *Eq.* 551–64, which begins like a piece of typical high (religious) lyric, ἵππι' ἄναξ Πόσειδον, ᾧ..., and on the whole proceeds like one, except for a rather unexpectedly concrete touch in χρεμετισμός (553) and a pair of quite unexpected topicality-prosaisms in μισθοφόροι τριήρεις (555) (the noun is not used in elevated verse) and Φορμίωνι (562). The mixture is reminiscent of *Lys.* 1247–72, except that this lyric has more charm and less bite. The antistrophe (581–94, ὦ πολιοῦχε Παλλάς...) is much more orthodox, until the religiosity, and with it the elevation, peters out towards the end. A commoner type of mixture (though hardly a switch) is to be found in some parodic lyrics which convey a certain effect of fantasy of one kind or another, e.g. *Av.* 851–8 (on the parodic aspect, see Rau, *Paratragodia* 197).

139. A classic instance is Shakespeare's persistence in associating *dogs*, *licking*, and *candy* with *flattery*. See C. Spurgeon, *Shakespeare's Imagery* (Cambridge 1935) 194–9.

indiscriminately – even, on occasion, producing weaker evocations of earlier successes. For example, the phallic song in *Acharnians* contains the sequence:

> πολλῷ γάρ ἐσθ' ἥδιον, ὦ Φαλῆς Φαλῆς,
> κλέπτουσαν εὑρόνθ' ὡρικὴν ὑληφόρον
> τὴν Στρυμοδώρου Θρᾷτταν... (271ff.),

which is feebly echoed[140] at a junction of low lyric and recitative in a very similar context ('make love, not war') in *Peace*:

> οὐ γὰρ φιληδῶ μάχαις,
> ἀλλά... (1130f.)
>
> ...τὴν Θρᾷτταν κυνῶν
> τῆς γυναικὸς λουμένης.
> οὐ γὰρ ἔσθ' ἥδιον ἤ... (1138ff.)

I don't enjoy fighting, but...kissing Thratta while the wife's in the bath. For there's nothing sweeter than...[141]

Furthermore, elements of the same *Acharnians* lyric reappear in the second Iacchus song in *Frogs*. That lyric begins Ἴακχε πολυτίμητε (399), which in rhythm, structure and cadence echoes a pair of Phales' epithets, ξύγκωμε νυκτοπεριπλάνητε (*Acharnians* 264f.); other more extensive reminiscences follow.[142] But all this is nothing compared with the dependence of some of the previous *Frogs* lyrics (both the better and the worse) on passages from earlier plays. We are confronted, at times, with little more than a cento.[143]

After pondering on these *Frogs* lyrics and the facts of their ancestry, one might be tempted to think in terms of a decline in

140. Unintentionally, I don't doubt – which makes it no less feeble. Whether the following examples would be in any way conscious must be harder to decide.

141. Cf. pp. 131–3 above.

142. Notably the reduction of *Ach.* 271–6 (πολλῷ γάρ...) to *Ran.* 411–16 (καὶ γάρ...). The two sequences are metrically alike (lyric iambics), share the same structure (first-person erotic incident followed by refrain), and have identical rhythm (resolution and all) to close (*Ach.* 276 ~ *Ran.* 416).

143. *Ran.* 324–36 and 340–53 depend heavily on *Nub.* 275–90 and 299–313 and on *Av.* 1088–1100; *Ran.* 372–83 equally on *Av.* 1058–68, 1088–98. The reminiscences are not simply verbal, like *Av.* 1098–1100 ξυμπαίζων...μύρτα χαρίτων ~ *Ran.* 330–5 μύρτων...φιλοπαίγμονα...χαρίτων; or like *Nub.* 287 ἀλλ' ἀποσεισάμεναι ~ *Ran.* 346 ἀποσείονται δέ (both in the context of bright light). Sometimes, and more significantly, they are rhythmic and verbal together. Thus *Av.* 1093f. ἀλλ' ἀνθηρῶν λειμώνων / φύλλων τ' ἐν κόλποις ναίω engenders *Ran.* 374f. ἐς τοὺς εὐανθεῖς κόλπους / λειμώνων ἐγκρούων with a similar ('spondaic') anapaestic rhythm.

Aristophanes' imaginative powers – except that *Frogs* overall shows as much invention as any of his earlier plays, in which, in any case, the self-imitative tendency is already visible.[144] At all events, the phenomenon suggests that he was faced with temptations, easy solutions, that he was not always strong enough to resist. We can point to evidence of this kind of weakness in various aspects of his dramaturgy. For instance – to confine ourselves to matters directly relevant to his lyrics – the author of the ode to Phales and the Knights' satire on Cleon is willing to give *Wasps* a lyrical finale in which the words give every appearance of being (in the words of their latest commentator) 'mere accompaniment' to the dance.[145] This is one example of a tendency that appears in other comedies as well, namely to relax the pressure of the writing in the last, lyrical, scene. There is nothing very wrong with that in itself, perhaps, but in the present context it is symptomatic. Aristophanes is destroying his own marvellous balance between 'art' and 'entertainment', and the loser is art.[146]

The weakness under discussion, as much as any of Aristophanes' strengths, can be related to his ultimate status as a popular writer of, essentially, low literature. Such a writer is rooted in his time and its experience – tied to *its* strengths and *its* weaknesses, albeit weaknesses (and strengths) which only a coterie or an alienated individual artist can altogether escape. The experience of fifth-century Athens was rich; and Aristophanes reflects that richness, in his lyrics as elsewhere. The last quarter of the century, when all of his extant plays, up to and including *Frogs*, were written, was also a time of rapid cultural change. One focus of change, among

144. It may be no coincidence that in A's composite mode the best examples of realism are in the earlier plays (up to and including *Peace*), while the purest examples of fantasy are in the two later plays *Birds* and *Frogs* – but, again, such fantasy hardly shows less *invention* than the realism.

145. MacDowell on vv. 1516–37. I choose an instance from one of the *earlier* comedies advisedly.

146. The criticism, incidentally, has nothing to do with modern distaste for alien ancient conventions. I have in mind Dover's comment (*Aristophanic Comedy* 155): 'we are brought up in a theatrical tradition which makes it hard for us to adjust ourselves to the principle of ending...on the note "now that that's settled, let's have a song and dance"'. On the contrary: few dramatic patterns have been more familiar in our own century than that of (say) the Astaire–Rogers–Irving Berlin film musical *Top Hat* (1935), which ends precisely thus (even down to the irrelevance of its final set-piece, 'The Piccolino').

many others, was the New Music, to which, as to an established fashion, a popular writer of lyric verse would naturally attune his work – in Aristophanes' case, probably via the mediation of Euripides. It is this influence that has been plausibly offered as explanation for several technical features of his compositions: his increasing use of polymetric lyrics and lyrics outside the 'conventional' positions, and his mixtures of choral and monodic song.[147] For our purposes the most crucial innovation of the New Music was its intensification of music at the expense of the word, resulting, in extreme cases, in a tasteless 'dithyrambic' verbal style. This style Aristophanes largely ignored, perhaps because his favourite opponent, Euripides, ignored it too. Nevertheless, that tragedian was himself willing to sacrifice the word for more than one kind of musico-emotional effect, as Aristophanes' satire in *Frogs* reminds us:

ἄτρακτον
εἱειειειλίσσουσα χεροῖν
. . . . . .
ἐμοὶ δ' ἄχε' ἄχεα κατέλιπε,
δάκρυα δάκρυά τ' ἀπ' ὀμμάτων
ἔβαλον ἔβαλον ἁ τλάμων.

Wi-i-inding the spindle with my hands... To me he left woe, woe; and tears, tears from my eyes I shed, shed, unhappy one.[148]

And though the writer Aristophanes shows no more taste than Aristophanes the critic for these particular operatic tics, we can recall that he has his own brand of verbal weakness in his high lyrics. It is worth considering whether the glossy prolixity and relaxation so evident there might be relatable to another aspect of the same *Zeitgeist*,[149] to which a writer of his type could hardly be immune.

The comic poet's rootedness in his own time is a *datum* of special relevance when we contemplate, with the lyrical component in mind, the changes in the nature of Old Comedy after *Frogs*. As far as Attic poetry as a whole was concerned (and for decades now, most of the Greek poetry that mattered had been Attic poetry), the cultural change of the early fourth century meant largely fragmentation and diminution. An epoch in which poetry, espe-

147. T. McEvilley, *AJPh* (1970) 269–76.
148. *Ran.* 1348–55. On the satirical targets, see Stanford on 1314, 1335f., 1349.
149. Contrast, therefore, my position with McEvilley's (n. 147 above).

cially dramatic poetry, was at the heart of the city's political and intellectual life gave way to one in which *politics* became the special province of oratory, *thought* of philosophy, and (partly as corollary of the latter development) the traditional mytho-religious basis of serious verse became impossible for the best minds to take seriously. Euripides, in the van of change, may have found such a problematic basis a stimulus to invention. The limited evidence suggests that for his fourth-century successors in all fields of poetry – and in all parts of the Greek world – the problem was a dead weight, eventually soluble only by the Alexandrian expedient of treating such matters as part of a sophisticated literary game. For such reasons, high poetry, as the handbooks say, 'declined', not in bulk, but in prestige and (to the best of our knowledge) in quality; and tragedy along with the rest. Serious lyric poetry, in all its contexts, suffered a particular decline, thanks to the cumulative effects of the New Music and its subversion of the word.[150] The well-known diminution of the role of lyric in late fifth-and fourth-century tragedy is one particular consequence of these developments.

Aristophanic comedy, as a popular form, accommodated itself to the new climate. The most important outcome for our purposes is that its lyrics, choral and monodic, were reduced in extent, in range of interests and in dramatic role, until eventually nothing was left but mere ἐμβόλιμα, choral interludes[151] punctuating the acts of a drama, which would gradually, *en route* to Menander, confine itself to the world of apolitical, amythical domesticity – particularly congenial, no doubt, to a city defeated in a long war and unable to recover the intensity of its earlier collective energy. The drift of this development is already apparent in *Ecclesiazusae* (392) where, symptomatically, the parabasis, traditional occasion

150. In the case of non-dramatic lyric, there are also socio-cultural factors to be considered relating to the changing position of the traditional aristocracy (one facet of what F. M. Heichelheim, *An Ancient Economic History* II, tr. J. Stevens (Leyden 1964) 121, calls 'the levelling of the ancient Hellenic class distinctions'), with which, or with whose *ambience*, some types of lyric had been closely associated. In the case of choral lyric, there may also have been socio-economic factors associated with the increasingly unwelcome expense of equipping a chorus at all. (Cf. e.g. Ehrenberg, *The People of Aristophanes* 22f.)

151. Not necessarily even written by the playwright: cf. K. J. Maidment, *CQ* (1935) 1ff., and Dover's brief comments in *Aristophanic Comedy* 194.

for public concern with the topical diversities of life and one of the traditional occasions for choral lyric, has disappeared. The cultural range that this play represents is still, by most standards, generously large, but has begun to shrink, and the range of the lyrics that are left has shrunk with it – range not only of subject, but of tone. Topicality is less welcome in the low lyrics and, even more drastically, elevation is hardly welcome anywhere. Along with its newly concentrated vision, comedy was beginning to evolve a greater homogeneity. That being so, it had less use for its high lyrical element; and, in any case, if high lyric was now an intractable medium for tragedy, where it belonged, it must be so *a fortiori* for comedy.

The upshot is that in *Ecclesiazusae* and *Plutus*, the last two extant plays, which are conventionally regarded as the beginnings of 'Middle Comedy', the remaining songs are largely confined to the low lyrical range (but stripped of most of their topical reference), at the expense not only of high lyrical pastiche, but also of the high 'plus' through which Aristophanes made low lyric a vehicle for his most creative lyrical effects. And that is to say that as a literary achievement, and by comparison with his own earlier achievement, the lyrics of *Ecclesiazusae* and, even more, of *Plutus* are negligible. It seems symbolic that of the few elevated touches in the lyrical parts of *Ecclesiazusae*, most are concentrated into the tasteless love-duet (952ff.):

δεῦρο δή, δεῦρο δή,
φίλον ἐμόν...,

which adds them like squirts of synthetic colouring to a not very appealing dish, apparently by way of parody, or simply imitation, of some hybridized low lyric form:[152]

ἐν τῷ σῷ
βούλομαι κόλπῳ πληκτίζεσθαι
μετὰ τῆς σῆς πυγῆς.
Κύπρι, τί μ' ἐκμαίνεις ἐπὶ ταύτῃ;
μέθες, ἱκνοῦμαί σ', Ἔρως... (963ff.)

. . .

ὦ χρυσοδαίδαλτον ἐμὸν μέλημα, Κύπριδος ἔρνος,
μέλιττα Μούσης, Χαρίτων θρέμμα, Τρυφῆς πρόσωπον,
ἄνοιξον, ἀσπάζου με·
διά τοι σὲ πόνους ἔχω. (972ff.)

152. See Bowra, *AJPh* (1958) 376–91.

I am burning to yield myself to voluptuous sport, lying on your bosom, to let my hands play with your bottom. Aphrodite, why dost thou drive me so mad for her? Oh! Eros, I beseech thee, have mercy...Oh! my jewel, my idol, child of Aphrodite, foster-child of the Graces, honey-bee of the Muses, you living picture of voluptuousness, oh! open for me, press me to your heart, 'tis for you that I am suffering.[153]

as if to demonstrate the irreconcilability of mytho-religious and secular in the new dispensation by trivializing both in one go.

Plutus goes one stage further. The only lyric in the play with any pretensions (290–321) is a duet between the slave Carion and the chorus of farmers, a song with, again, popular connections:

> καὶ μὴν ἐγὼ βουλήσομαι θρεττανελὸ τὸν Κύκλωπα
> μιμούμενος... (290f.)

And I too, *threttanelo*, want to imitate the Cyclops...

albeit partly a parody of Philoxenus and his New Dithyramb.[154] Its most striking feature is the presence of such gems of artless humour as

> τῶν ὄρχεων κρεμῶμεν,
> μινθώσομέν θ' ὥσπερ τράγου
> τὴν ῥῖνα... (312ff.).

We'll hang you up by your balls and rub your nose in the muck, like a goat.

Looking at the comic chorus, original source of all comic lyric, in a long perspective from its subliterary prehistory to its merely nominal survival in Menander, Maidment commented that 'the comic chorus begins as κῶμος and ends as κῶμος'.[155] Let us add that the high literary element in choral and other comic lyric is a temporary phenomenon due, partly, to the cultural preeminence of lyrical tragedy in the fifth century; and that in *Plutus* the chorus, without which comic lyric could not survive for long, has returned to its low lyric base – at its coarsest and without its topical satire – in preparation for the final withdrawal into a subliterary existence.[156] Over the next generations, the new domesticity

153. Tr. based on Oates and O'Neill. On the precise implications of 964f., see Henderson, *The Maculate Muse* 140f.

154. See Holzinger's commentary on the play, pp. 110ff.

155. *CQ* (1935) 24.

156. A's late *Aeolosicon* apparently had no choral lyrics at all: see *Schol. in Aristoph.* ed. Koster, I. IA, p. 4, 22f. (Platonius).

became synonymous with domestic restraint, a climate in which low lyric, stripped of all its gentility, had no chance of survival. A truly middle-range lyric, if Old Comedy had ever evolved one, might have had a future here; the actual ranges, even had they been persevered with, must have been either too high or too low, or both at once.

One need not assume that as far as Aristophanes' part in these developments is concerned, he felt the loss as keenly as we may. As Dover reminds us, 'all the evidence suggests that Aristophanes was a leader, not a follower, in the changes undergone by comedy in the early fourth century B.C.'[157] But this does not mean that he was innovating out of strength. It is, rather, to say that a writer in a popular form, rooted in his age, must sometimes (if that age is no longer all it was) connive at the attenuation of his own best instincts.

T. S. Eliot wrote: 'Sensibility alters from generation to generation in everybody, whether we will or no, but expression is only altered by a man of genius.' The realistic–fantastic lyric is Aristophanes' great achievement as a lyric poet and it represents, precisely, an alteration of expression from any previous poetic norm, serious or (so far as we know) comic. That this achievement has barely been acknowledged seems to me to be due partly to critical preoccupation with red herrings, but partly, also, to its own lack of influence: the new expression was stillborn. The pity of the situation is not only that it should have been so, but that it should have been Aristophanes himself who, by his later innovations, helped to ensure that in this superb product of his own best instincts he had no successors.

157. *OCD*[2] s.v. 'Aristophanes'. Cf. his remarks in *Aristophanic Comedy* 193–5.

Lysistrate: The Play and its Themes

JEFFREY HENDERSON

Lysistrate has never been the subject of a thoroughgoing critical essay.[1] The commentaries, while they have succeeded in establishing a relatively sound text, do not always offer the kind of interpretive enlightenment that readers require, especially in regard to Aristophanes' management of a complex plot and his development of its themes. Wilamowitz, the most recent commentator (Berlin, 1927), goes the farthest in presenting the play as a work of theater and of literature. One wishes, however, that his commentary were much fuller than it is. Pending the appearance of a badly needed new text and commentary I offer the following observations. First, the theater: what sort of arrangements must have been available to Aristophanes for the production of this play? Then an interpretive summary of the action, focusing on difficulties about which there is still room for argument. I shall use the text of V. Coulon (Paris, 1928), supplementing and correcting it with regard to transmission and previous scholarship when necessary.[2]

Lysistrate was produced at the Lenaia of 411 (early February). Alan Sommerstein has recently reevaluated the evidence (*JHS* 97 (1977) 112ff.) and I refer the reader to his discussion; differences on points of detail will be apparent in what follows. The play best fits a time shortly after the 'first assembly' of Peisander (Th. 8. 53f.) and I ask that the reader bear this in mind.

1. The best treatments are C. H. Whitman, *Aristophanes and the Comic Hero* (Cambridge, Mass. 1964) 200ff.; A. O. Hulton, 'The Women on the Acropolis: A Note on the Structure of the Lysistrata', *G&R* 19 (1972) 32ff.; J. Vaio, 'The Manipulation of Theme and Action in Aristophanes' *Lysistrata*', *GRBS* 14 (1973) 369ff.

2. I shall publish the first complete collations of the mss. of *Lysistrate* in the near future. For a full account of textual work I refer the reader to my repertory in *HSCP* 82 (1978) 87ff.

The theater

Our understanding of *Lysistrate*, a play with an unusual abundance of physical action and an unusually large cast of characters, will often depend upon proper visualization of the theatrical resources available to Aristophanes. Since the remains of the Theater of Dionysos date almost entirely from Hellenistic or Roman times our reconstruction must emerge primarily from an accurate evaluation of passages in this and other comedies that imply or demand specific theatrical conditions. In addition many details concerning the comic theater are still hotly debated; it will therefore be worthwhile to try to determine what light *Lysistrate* might shed on these disputes.

Let us begin with the area in front of the skene, a wooden stage building that faced the audience across the orchestra: was this properly speaking a distinct stage, that is an area separated by height from the orchestra? The answer will help us judge how close the contact was between actors and Chorus, how strong a distinction was made between their performing areas. Some of the action in the first half of *Lysistrate* will be obscure if we do not make up our minds on this question. External evidence suggests but does not prove that the stage was slightly elevated: an Attic vase of *c.* 420[3] depicts a comic actor on a low wooden stage. This kind of stage appears also on South Italian Phlyax vases, which can be shown to reflect Attic theatrical practice,[4] and can be reconstructed for the fourth-century theater at Eretria. Internal evidence also suggests a raised stage. At 254 the Chorus of Men enter with fire and a ram intending to smoke out the women on the Akropolis. The Chorus of Women enter at 319 and after a fight douse the old men with water. The semichoruses' battle is temporarily ended by the arrival of the Proboulos and his police (387), who attempt to enter the Akropolis and are repulsed in a battle with Lysistrate and her stouter allies. At this point the Koryphaios complains to the Proboulos of the earlier dousing and criticizes him for wasting words on the women (467). Obviously they have been following

3. See A. W. Pickard-Cambridge, *The Dramatic Festivals of Athens*² (Oxford 1968), Plate 76.

4. T. B. L. Webster, 'South Italian Vases and Attic Drama', *CQ* 42 (1948) 15ff.

the discomfiture of the Proboulos but have not lifted a hand in his defense. Had the Chorus been in the same acting area as the Proboulos their noninvolvement in the second battle would be awkward. Theatrically it seems more satisfying to enact the two battles in distinct areas: the actors on the raised stage and the Chorus in the orchestra.

Here it might be objected that if Aristophanes did not have a distinct stage at his disposal he would simply have presented the second battle right beside the idle Chorus and that the audience would therefore have accepted the awkwardness as conventional. Of course we cannot prove that this is not what actually happened, but is it likely that Aristophanes would have conceived the scene in quite this way had he not a distinct stage? A bit of comic business at *Wasps* 1341ff. poses the same question much more vividly. There Philokleon returns from a party with a flute girl. As he approaches the stage from the parodos he tells the girl to grab hold of a rope (his phallus) as if she were ascending a ladder or stairway. This action could have been mimed on level ground but it is hard to imagine why the idea should have occurred to Aristophanes in the first place if there were no raised stage to ascend.[5]

A more difficult problem concerns the skene itself: how many doors were available to Aristophanes and how many are needed for *Lysistrate*? Our earliest information comes from Hellenistic representations of a three-door skene; the text of Menander's *Dyskolos* (316 B.C.) explicitly identifies three 'houses': The only fifth-century evidence is negative: no extant tragedy requires more than one door, and since comedies were performed in the same theater it has been argued that comedy too made do with only one. Dearden (n. 5 above, p. 20) stresses the fact that tragedy was introduced to the Dionysian festival *c.* 534, whereas comedy was not introduced for another fifty years, and asks why writers of comedy would have written plays requiring more than one door even though the theater in which they were to be performed provided only one. But theatrical ideas change with time and there

5. C. W. Dearden, *The Stage of Aristophanes* (London 1976) 14 remarks that '*Wasps* 1341 can be interpreted in an obscene sense and cannot therefore be used independently as evidence.' Why not? See K. J. Dover, *Aristophanic Comedy* (Berkeley/Los Angeles 1972) 18f.

is no reason to think that the advent of plays requiring more than one door would not have led to changes in the skene. The addition of one or more extra doors to a wooden structure would have been quite easy.

It seems to me that the evidence of the comedies is decisive in favor of two or three doors. The most productive line of argument follows from a hypothetical question of Dover's:[6] '*If* Aristophanes had only one door available, would he have written this passage in quite this way?' That is, Aristophanes could have made do with one door but would not have written passages whose humor or relevance is best explained by assuming two or more doors. Certain scenes in *Clouds*[7] and *Ekklesiazousai*[8] have been discussed in this connection, but the most recent writer, following the lead of A. M. Dale,[9] argues that in fact one door will satisfy the needs of any situation found in our texts.[10]

Let us examine two scenes in *Lysistrate* with Dover's question in mind. At the outset Lysistrate enters (1) and remarks that no woman has yet arrived except her neighbor (κωμῆτις 5) Kalonike[11] who is now coming outside (ἐξέρχεται), that is emerging from a door. We presently learn that the other wives have been told to meet at this spot (13). Lysistrate has summoned the young wives to arrange a sex strike (124ff.) and has also arranged for the oldest women to capture the Akropolis while she and the young wives are conferring (177–9). As first formulated by Lysistrate the sex strike requires the wives to parade before their husbands as provocatively as possible but to withhold sex until the men agree to treat for peace (149ff.); this is to be done at home (ἔνδον 149, οἴκοι 217). After the wives' emotional aversion to this plan has been overcome an oath of solidarity is arranged and Lysistrate orders

6. *Ibid.*, pp. 23f. See also his 'The *skene* in Aristophanes', *PCPhS* 192 (1966) 2ff. = *Aristophanes und die alte Komödie*, ed. H.-J. Newiger (Wege der Forschung CCLXV, Darmstadt 1975) 99ff. Further arguments in Newiger, *Dioniso* 48 (1977) 319ff.

7. Dover (n. 5 above) 24, 208.

8. R. G. Ussher, 'The Staging of the *Ecclesiazusae*', *Hermes* 97 (1969) 22ff., repr. in Newiger (n. 6 above) 383ff.

9. 'An Interpretation of Aristophanes *Vesp.* 136–210 and its Consequence for the Stage of Aristophanes', *JHS* 77 (1957) 205ff.

10. Dearden (n. 5 above) 20ff.

11. For the name, altered by Wilamowitz and Coulon to Kleonike, see J. D. Beazley, *Arch. Ephem.* 92/93 (1953/54) 204.

a slave to fetch a wine cup and a jar from inside (ἔνδοθεν 199). After the oath-taking ceremony Lysistrate tells her Spartan counterpart Lampito to return to Sparta and tells the other wives: 'But let us go inside (εἰσιοῦσαι)[12] and help the others who are now on the Akropolis to make fast the locks' (245f.). She assures the women that the men have not enough threats or firebrands to force open 'these gates' (τὰς πύλας ταύτας 250f.), that is, the Propylaia. At this point the wives exit, leaving the stage empty. The Chorus of Men enter and announce their intention to force the gates. From now on the action is represented as taking place before the Akropolis and the door (or, a door) of the skene is explicitly designated as the Propylaia.

In a later scene Kinesias comes from his house to the Akropolis and demands to see his wife Myrrhine (845ff.). He asks her to 'come home again' (899). After Myrrhine 'descends from' the Akropolis through the gates (884), Kinesias asks her to sleep with him. Myrrhine asks, where? and Kinesias replies, the Shrine of Pan.[13] 'But how then will I be able to reenter the Akropolis pure?' asks Myrrhine (912). 'Wash in the Klepsydra', replies Kinesias. Here Myrrhine feigns to give in, but in a cruel parody of the dutiful wife keeps putting off her husband by going offstage for various items of bedding and some perfumes. At 953 she is said to have suddenly run off (οἴχεται), having made Kinesias even more desperate than he was before.

Is there anything in these scenes that would be awkard or confusing to the audience on the supposition that there was only one door? Or anything that would make us assume that Aristophanes would have written differently had he in fact had only one door at his disposal? In the opening scene we naturally assume that Lysistrate and Kalonike are conversing in front of a house; Lysistrate later explicitly distinguishes the setting of the sex strike and the oath from the Akropolis, where the older women are carrying out the occupation. The wine cup and jar must obviously be fetched from a house. It is not until 250 that a door

12. The verb can mean simply 'go off' as at *Ach.* 202, where specific locale is ignored. But here Lysistrate specifically identifies the gates and tells the wives to help her fasten them from within. All must therefore exit through a door representing these gates.

13. Here Apollo slept with Kreousa: see Owen at Eur. *Ion.* 17, 287, 938.

is identified as the Propylaia. If there was only one door Lysistrate must enter through the parodos and the door represents Kalonike's house, from which Kalonike enters and from which the oath paraphernalia are fetched. It would be here that Lysistrate has told the others to assemble. This same door will then have become the Propylaia at 250.[14]

It is possible that the audience would have had no trouble with this arrangement and it might be argued that at 250 the explicit designation of the Propylaia was written especially to mark the change in the door's identity. But there is some awkwardness. Lysistrate has plainly been waiting for the women to arrive; but if we see her enter through the parodos and take up a position in front of another woman's house moments before that woman emerges, it must be obvious that she is barely on time herself, not to mention the oddness of Lysistrate's having arranged her meeting at the house of a woman who demonstrates in the ensuing dialogue that she knows nothing of what is afoot. It would surely have been more natural, had there been one door, to show Lysistrate emerging from her own house and Kalonike entering through the parodos. The action here is best explained with two or more doors: one represents Lysistrate's house, one Kalonike's; one of these (or a third) subsequently becomes the Propylaia.[15]

The Kinesias–Myrrhine scene is more telling. Once Myrrhine has come down from the Akropolis and assured her husband that they will sleep together (an act said to require ritual purification for Myrrhine before she can reenter the Akropolis) it would be theatrically most awkward for Myrrhine to keep going back through the Propylaia to fetch pillows, bedding and perfume. The couple are supposed to be away from the Akropolis; they must have strolled across the stage until they come to another door, which becomes the Shrine of Pan (911).[16] At the end of the scene,

14. So Dearden (n. 5 above) 22, 166.

15. Ideally there would be three doors, the central, largest (?) one representing the Propylaia: see Vaio (n. 1 above) 372; T. Gelzer, 'Aristophanes der Komiker', *RE Supplbd.* XII (1972) 1498. 33ff., 1513. 14ff.; E. Simon, *Das griechische Theater* (Heidelberg 1972) 12 n. 17; Newiger (*art. cit.* n. 6 above) 333ff. The only hint of three doors in the fifth century is Eupolis 42 (*Autolykos*), 'here they live in three huts, each with his own dwelling'. Absence of context prevents us from pushing this too far.

16. Vaio (n. 1 above) 377 n. 39 rightly rejects the idea that this grotto was naturalistically represented.

while Kinesias reclines awaiting his wife's embraces, Myrrhine dashes back to the Propylaia and vanishes. The audience sees that she has gone to rejoin her companions but this only gradually dawns on Kinesias, who reacts with horror to find her gone. The comic impact of Myrrhine's departure suffers if she departs through the same door from which she has repeatedly fetched the paraphernalia. How would the audience know that she is not going to return once again? In addition (and most important) the logic of the plot requires that the scene (which represents the sex strike in action) be played out in an area distinct from the Akropolis (scene of the occupation). These two facets of Lysistrate's initiative against the warmakers are developed quite differently in the course of the play.

Some minor details: (1) That the skene had a roof on which action took place is abundantly attested for both tragedy and comedy. The Kinesias–Myrrhine scene tells us in addition that communication between the interior of the skene and the roof was quite easy: at 884 Myrrhine is on the roof (representing the walls of the Akropolis, 829, 873, 883f.) and by 889 she is on stage. (2) The stage is estimated on the archaeological evidence to have been approximately 1·3 metres deep.[17] But this seems rather shallow in view of the battle between the women and the Proboulos' police (437ff.) and of the turbulent crowd-scene at 1216ff. Perhaps this estimate is too conservative, and perhaps the stage area could be extended at need. (3) There were probably windows on the skene front, but since the skene represents the Akropolis for most of the play they are not used. (4) There may well have been a permanent altar situated at some distance from the front of the stage; many tragedies and several scenes in comedy take an altar for granted. During the oath-scene (185ff.) the women momentarily contemplate performing a blood-sacrifice over a shield, but this does not imply that there was no altar: Lysistrate's idea parodies an event reported in Aischylos' *Seven* (42ff.).[18]

17. See Dearden (n. 5 above) 11.

18. For *Peace* 937, where Trygaios seems to imply that an altar must be fetched, see P. Arnott, *Greek Scenic Conventions in the Fifth Century BC* (Oxford 1962) 49f.

The actors and their costumes

How many actors are needed to perform *Lysistrate* and how are they dressed? The traditional view, held in late antiquity and defended by some to this day, that there was a maximum of three for tragedy and comedy alike, has come under heavy attack since the publication of K. Rees' book early in this century.[19] We need not concern ourselves here with all the details of this debate since *Lysistrate* provides our clearest evidence that four (or five) actors are sometimes needed. In the prologue: Lysistrate (1), Kalonike (6), Myrrhine (69), Lampito (77), and a possible fifth at 136 (see below). In the scene of battle between Lysistrate's troops and the Proboulos' police (387–466): Proboulos (387), Lysistrate (430), and three women (439, 443, 447).[20] In the desertion-scene (706–80): Lysistrate and four wives (727, 735, 742, 760). At 1216ff.: two Athenians (1216, 1221), Spartan Ambassador (1242), Spartan Singer (1247). At the beginning of the Kinesias-Myrrhine scene we need four as well. Among the women on the roof (837) are Lysistrate and Myrrhine; onstage is Kinesias. Before Myrrhine recognizes Kinesias (837) Lysistrate talks about him with some other women (829ff.). It is possible to assign the part of Lysistrate's interlocutor here to Myrrhine and give 836b to Lysistrate,[21] thus preserving the three-actor rule. But there is no pressing reason to do so, and in fact the dramatic effect surely suffers if the woman who recognizes her husband at 837 is the same woman who at 830 speaks of him to Lysistrate as a stranger.

The conclusion to be drawn is that although not every play needs more than three actors and although three may have been normal a fourth or even fifth was available if the playwright needed them. The fact that four- or five-actor scenes are uncommon does not mean that they were felt to violate a norm. Given the limited space available on the Attic stage and the difficulty of writing four- or five-way dialogue, it is hardly surprising that we find it only infrequently. In *Lysistrate* the plot as conceived by Aristophanes demands more than three. In the prologue the heroine must have a Spartan counterpart and a sidekick (Kalonike) who takes the

19. *The So-called Rule of Three Actors in Classical Drama* (Chicago 1908).
20. I leave the identification of these women until later: see n. 89 below.
21. Hermann, followed by Dearden (n. 5 above) 90.

role of buffoon to relieve with humor the main character's single-minded determination. Yet another character must represent the ordinary housewife who will eventually enact the sex strike (Myrrhine). Later on a fifth actor was occasionally used in 'crowd-scenes'. Having once decided on a primarily four-actor script Arisotophanes was free to use his fourth performer to enliven other scenes which might otherwise have been written for only three.

It is often argued that when a fourth actor was used his part was kept to a minimum and that in the distribution of roles we must assign the heaviest load to the principal three. Thus Dearden (n. 5 above, p. 99) would assign to the 'extra actor' only Lampito (81–244) and Woman (830–6), a total of about 30 lines. But nothing prevents us from distributing the load more evenly, and it might well be thought surprising if Aristophanes did not use his fourth actor to the fullest. This hypothesis gains support from a scene in *Clouds* (889–1104) where the fourth part is both lengthy and important.[22] It would not be amiss to assign to the fourth actor at least most of the Spartan roles: perhaps this actor was especially good at speaking, singing and dancing in ethnic parts, and *Lysistrate* would have provided ample opportunities for a display of his skills. I also incline toward giving the second actor the roles requiring an expert clown. To the fifth I have assigned only a few minor parts. The following is one of several possible assignments of roles in the play:

I. Lysistrate (1–864, 1112–87), Spartan Ambassador (1241–end).

II. Kalonike (6–253), Proboulos (387–613), wife (727–80), Kinesias (845–1013), Athenian Ambassador (1086–1188, 1216–end).

III. Myrrhine (69–253, 837–951), old woman (439–603), wife (735–80), Athenian (1221–end).

IV. Lampito (81–244), old woman (442–66), wife (742–80), wife (830–6), Spartan Herald (980–1013), Spartan Ambassador (1076–1188), Spartan Dancer (1242–end).

V. Wife (? 136b), old woman (447–66), wife (760–80).

22. See K. J. Dover, *Aristophanes Clouds* (Oxford 1968) lxxviii f. Dearden (n. 5 above) 89 stresses 'some disturbance of the text' as a reason to doubt the value of this scene as evidence; the rebuttal is already in Dover, *ibid.*, n. 3.

Mutes: Athenian wives (65), Boiotian wife (85), Korinthian wife (90), slaves (199, 908, 1216ff.), archers (387ff.), older women (456ff.), child (879), Spartan Ambassadors (1072), Athenian Ambassadors (1082), Diallage (1114), doorkeeper (1216), Athenians (1216ff.), Spartans (1241ff.), husbands and wives (1273ff.). Many of the details implied in these assignments will be argued in the discussion of the plot later.

In envisioning fifth-century comic costuming we must be guided mainly by the texts of the plays, although we must keep in mind Arnott's warning[23] that when the playwright describes something he may do so because it cannot be seen. Our main ancient description of comic costuming (Pollux 4. 115ff.), which must draw on Hellenistic sources but which dates from the second century A.D., provides little help for the student of Old Comedy. Contemporary vases and terracottas are better evidence, but the artists would probably not normally have attempted to execute faithful reproductions of what they saw on the stage; they seem often to have interpreted freely.

As in tragedy male and female roles alike were played by men. Underneath the costume they wore tights that may in the case of male characters have been padded in stomach and rump and to which a large artificial phallus could be attached.[24] The phallus could be visible when the action required, or covered up, and seems to have been capable of display in various states of tensility: it might dangle, be tied back, erected, circumcised.[25] In *Lysistrate* the phallus does not appear on stage until the climactic (if that is the word) arrival of Kinesias, whose monstrous erection is obvious to the women on the Akropolis ramparts (831f.) and which is the object of several jokes. The Spartan and Athenian husbands who make appearances from this point on all sport hefty erections. In this play, for reasons of plot, no one displays a dangling phallus. The men with whom Lysistrate fights and argues during the epirrhematic scenes bridging the prologue and the entry of the deserting wives (706ff.) have no visible phalli, for they play no role

23. See n. 18 above, pp. 91ff.

24. For literature see J. Henderson, *The Maculate Muse: Obscene Language in Attic Comedy* (New Haven/London 1975) xi n. 7.

25. *Ibid.*, pp. 110f.

in the sex strike.[26] The old men of the Chorus will be discussed presently.

There is good reason to believe that the naked women who sometimes appear on the comic stage were played by men wearing female masks and tights bearing exaggerated breasts and genitalia, not by female slaves or prostitutes, as Wilamowtiz (on line 1114) thought.[27] The arguments are: (1) the weather would have been too cold for actual nakedness, and (2) spectators farther from the stage would have had trouble seeing the bodies of actual women.[28] Vaio adds 'the tendency of Old Comedy not to reflect reality but grotesquely to distort it'.[29] The action of such scenes as *Wasps* 1373ff. and *Peace* 891ff., where features of a naked woman's body provide material for jokes and byplay, seems to demand a costume and not flesh. The prologue of *Lysistrate* offers further corroboration. At 83ff. the Athenian women admire Lampito's breasts; as a Spartan she is very skimpily dressed. At 87ff. they remark on the well-kept pubic area of the Boiotian. At 91f. they point to the generous proportions of the Korinthian's genitals and hindquarters.[30] Deictic pronouns show that these physical features are uncovered before they are described. It would be arguable that the Boiotian and Korinthian were played by naked mutes were this not out of the question for Lampito, who has a speaking part. We must conclude that these wives were played by men costumed to represent naked women; there is no reason to assume differently in the case of Diallage (1114) as well. Diallage is commonly imagined as being totally naked, as the surrounding action indeed makes clear. At 1162f. the Spartan, when asked what he wants before he is willing to go along with a peace settlement, replies,

26. The Proboulos' barbarian police may have worn grotesque phalli: see K. J. Dover, *Greek Homosexuality* (London 1978) 129.

27. This view had been argued more thoroughly by A. Willems, *Aristophane* (Paris/Brussels 1919) vol. III, pp. 388ff.

28. See K. Holzinger, 'Erklärungen umstrittener Stellen des Aristophanes', *SB* (Wien) 208. 5 (1928) 37–41.

29. N. 1 above, p. 379.

30. For the ms. τἀντευθενί we should print Bentley's κἀντευθενί, the apparent reading of the scholiast (ἁπτομένη τῶν δύο φύσεων ταῦτά φησι): 'she's clearly most handsomely constructed both here in front and here behind'. For jokes on the Isthmus of Korinth cf. *Peace* 879f., *Thesm.* 647, Henderson (n. 24 above) 137. Genitals are here compared to features of the wives' native landscapes.

'We're certainly ready if someone is willing to return to us this *enkyklon.*' Lysistrate asks, 'What do you mean, good sir?' The Spartan then specifies Pylos. van Leeuwen (*ad loc.*) thinks this refers to an actual item of clothing. But the scholiast is right in thinking that the word here is used metaphorically to mean 'rotundity': the Spartan points to Diallage's rear end (to which the Spartans are especially attracted) and uses a word which, in the absence of any clothing to be seen on the ravishing personification, prompts Lysistrate's question. Pylos is a more explicit double entendre for the hindquarters.

For the costumes our most important evidence comes from the dressing-scenes of *Thesm.* 249ff. and *Ekkl.* 73ff. Study of the references to dress in our texts and in archaeological remains[31] suggests that Old Comic costume was not as stylized as Pollux's list and the texts of New Comedy show it to have become in the fourth century. In the fifth century the costumes appear to have been designed with specific needs in mind and to have followed the fashions of the day. The items of dress mentioned by Kalonike and Lysistrate at 43ff. are meant to sound very fancy; the tenses of the verbs in 51, 52, 53 indicate that the speakers are not now wearing them but can afford to. Perhaps Myrrhine wears them for her scene with Kinesias, which illustrates the seduction now being planned out. The same is true of the (flaxen?) undergarments (*chitonia*) mentioned at 150, which are diaphanous and specially dyed (*amorgina*) and thus not for everyday wear;[32] the saffron-colored undergarment (*krokotos*) at 219, an expensive item worn at festivals (cf. 645); and the Persian slippers at 229. Presumably, then, the Athenian women are wearing everyday clothing of the sort that well-to-do citizen ladies would wear. 640ff., 1125ff. as well as certain details of the prologue to be discussed presently, give us to understand that the women involved in Lysistrate's plans are not to be thought of as run-of-the-mill but as belonging to the highest social class. No slaves take part, but part of the battle against the Proboulos is waged by market women (546ff.), whose clothing will not have been as fancy as the young wives'. The wives probably wore a (woollen?) undergarment (*chiton* or *chitonion*: cf. *Frogs* 1067), probably longer than that worn by men (cf. *Ekkl.*

31. See Pickard-Cambridge (n. 3 above) 210ff.

32. *IG*² 1523. 22 mentions τρύφημα ἀμόργινον as evidence of wealth.

268); and an outer garment variously colored (*himation*) and consisting of a single rectangular piece of woollen cloth draped around the body with the end thrown over the right shoulder (cf. *Birds* 1567). Myrrhine mentions a girdle (*zonion*) at 72 and later loosens a sort of brassière (or headband) (*strophion* 931). The speaker of 113 wears a wrap (*enkyklon*) over her dress and Lysistrate wears a veil (*kalymma* 530). Lampito, as a Spartan, will be dressed in native attire considerably more revealing than that of her Athenian colleagues.[33] The Boiotian and Korinthian will wear clothing that must be either transparent or easily lifted away from the body (87ff.). Note that none of the Athenian wives is subjected to the kind of physical scrutiny that the foreigners suffer.

The men, too, are dressed in everyday clothing, the *chiton* and *himation* (1084, 1093). The Spartan Herald wears a *chlamys* (normal for soldiers and horsemen). Kinesias' clothing must be short enought to reveal his erection (831ff.). Presumably the Proboulos, Ambassadors, Policemen, Slaves and Doorkeeper wore costuming appropriate to their roles.

The dress of the twenty-four members of the Chorus is unlikely to have been much different from that of the actors: they look like very old men and women. Specifically mentioned for the men are skimpy wraps (*himatidia* 470) and the *exomis* (662, 1021), a short *chiton* with a single armhole and girdled around the waist, a garment particularly associated with poor people and slaves. This threadbare appearance of the old men is visible proof of the penury which they complain of at 624f. The women mention wearing the *kothornos*, a thin-soled boot normal for women. At one point the men and women strip down to undergarments or tights to allow more freedom of action (662, 686). There is no particular reason to think that the men wore the phallus:[34] when the women say that the men have unkempt pubic hair (800) and when the men reply in kind (824); and when the women twice remark that the men look ridiculous without clothing (1020, 1024), we are not necessarily to assume that reference is being made to actual features of the costuming. Aristophanes may have equipped the old men with limp phalli but their decrepitude is obvious enough without that. The situation is different in the case of Philokleon,

33. On the immodesty of Spartan women see e.g. Eur. *Andr.* 590ff.
34. *Pace* Vaio (n. 1 above) 372 n. 14.

who wears a limp phallus to underscore the emptiness of his boast that he has been rejuvenated. As for the flute-player who accompanied the Chorus, we have no textual evidence but vases indicate that he wore a long patterned *chiton* with full sleeves.

We are poorly informed about the masks of Old Comedy, which all characters wore (including, probably, mutes). It is possible that some of the masks described by Pollux and visible in monuments illustrating later comedy survived from Aristophanic times, but for the most part we must make our own deductions from the plays. The mask was linen, cork or wood, had apertures at the eyes large enough that the actor could see what he was doing, and a fairly large aperture at the mouth to allow sufficient enunciation. The young wives of the prologue (all are mothers of small children, 17ff.) – Kalonike, Myrrhine and Lampito – will have worn masks with light complexion, snub nose and black hair (a more tanned complexion and lighter hair, perhaps, for Lampito) fashionably styled, such as is worn by Nike on a well-known contemporary vase.[35] Kalonike calls Lysistrate *teknon* (7) but this simply means 'friend' and does not imply that she is older than Lysistrate.

With the exception of Myrrhine these wives appear in speaking parts only in the prologue and in the desertion scene at 727ff.; one of them speaks a few lines at 829ff. The women who stand with Lysistrate against the Proboulos (433ff.) and contribute supportive interjections and byplay during the agon are specifically (457f., 506) referred to as the old women who originally seized the Akropolis (177); the young wives are reserved for the part of Lysistrate's plan having to do with sexual abstinence. Some at least of these old women are market women (456ff.), who had a reputation for loud and abusive behavior (*Wasps* 1388, *Frogs* 857f., Fr. 125). Presumably these women are sufficiently old to be useless in the sex strike but effective as curmudgeonly allies in a fight. Whether they were as old as the women of the Chorus is impossible to determine. Their masks might be similar to those with a mop of unruly hair and straight nose we see first in the early fourth century.[36]

The Proboulos is described by the women as old (599ff.) but their description is abusive and might exaggerate what we actually see.

35. Pickard-Cambridge (n. 3 above) Plate 77a.
36. A. D. Trendall, *Phlyax Vases*, *BICS Suppl.* 8 (1959) 23.

He is certainly older than the husbands against whom the sex strike is aimed; perhaps he wears the embittered-looking mask with full head of hair (sometimes white) and short wedge beard found from the early fourth century onward,[37] but most of the possibilities listed by Webster[38] will serve. All the husbands are young[39] and will have dark hair and beards. The slaves, if they wear masks, will have full hair, short beards and open trumpet mouths.[40] The archers (387ff.) are Skythians, probably clean-shaven with longish hair.[41] The Spartans probably wear exaggeratedly long and unkempt hair and beards (1072, cf. 278ff.). The Chorus of Men, who are τυφογέροντες ἄνδρες (336), are extremely old (they refer to events of their youth which occurred over a century earlier) and wear white hair and beards. The Chorus of Women are white-haired, snub-nosed and wrinkled.[42]

Lysistrate herself is described as having a severe expression (τοξοποιεῖν τὰς ὀφρῦς 8, σκυθρωπός 707), although these references come at points in the action at which she may be expected to be annoyed (the women are late; they attempt to desert) and might therefore have been written to indicate an expression that Lysistrate could not on account of her mask actually assume. In any case Lysistrate must be young enough to be a sympathetic leader of young wives but august enought both to enlist the support of older women and to carry her will against the opposition of the most powerful men in the Greek world. She never mentions her age; whether she is a wife or mother; or any other clue about her status or physical appearance. As we shall discover presently, Aristophanes takes care to differentiate her from all the other women. We must imagine her to be taller than the other women and to wear a mask indicative of high social standing, strength, sobriety and feminine charm (cf. 1108f.), however that might have looked.

The plot

Although Aristophanes, who knew nothing of Aristotle, has often been criticized (particularly in comparison with tragedy and with

37. T. B. L. Webster, *Greek Theatre Production* (London 1956) 57.
38. *Monuments Illustrating Old and Middle Comedy*, *BICS Suppl.* 23 (1969) 7f.
39. I do not see why Dearden (n. 5 above) 137 assumes Kinesias to be a greybeard.
40. Trendall (n. 36 above) 60.
41. *Ibid.*, p. 78.
42. *Ibid.*, p. 78.

Menander) for constructing loose plots and one-dimensional characters,[43] he is generally credited with having constructed in *Lysistrate* a more consistently logical plot, steadier suspense, subtler characterizations and a more imaginative use of traditional comic structures than ever before.[44] It has also been pointed out, however, that certain features of Lysistrate's plan as formulated in the prologue are at variance with what we actually see as the play develops. Such inconsistencies of dramatic logic may frequently be excused as characteristic of the genre: once the poet has exhausted the humor of one idea he will passion to the next with little regard for consequence or logic. But before we apologize for Aristophanes we ought to make sure at any given point that he has no subtler goals in mind. Sometimes inconsistencies are simply inconsistencies, but sometimes they are deliberate mechanisms for the full realization of a play's chief themes.

In a genre where surprising and fantastic ideas are expected of the poet, where ordinary laws of cause and effect are often suspended from the start, we will not be amazed to discover that extravagant themes frequently demand much more from the limited potential of the Attic stage than even the most acrobatic of playwrights could hope to accommodate within the bounds of logic. This is part of the fun, and so it happens in *Lysistrate*: the women of Greece are to end a panhellenic war by employing traditional female attributes in new ways. The feat must be accomplished not only in the traditional female realm, the home, but also in the public realm of the men, both fighting men and politicians, and not only in Athens but in Sparta as well. All Greece is to be recalled from the madness of an ongoing war to those peaceful days when Athens and Sparta jointly led the Greek world. This emphasis on the Good Old Days was a familiar comic stance then as now; the desire for panhellenic unity, on the other hand, has a claim to be a particularly Aristophanic motif, since it is found

43. The best treatment is W. Süss, 'Scheinbare und wirkliche Inkongruenzen in den Dramen des Aristophanes', *RhM* 97 (1954) 115ff., 229ff., 289ff. See further M. Landfester, *Handlungsverlauf und Komik in den frühen Komödien des Aristophanes* (Berlin/New York 1977) 1ff.

44. See D. Grene, 'The Comic Technique of Aristophanes', *Hermathena* 50 (1937) 87ff., 122ff.; W. Schmid, *Griechische Literaturgeschichte* I. 4 (Munich 1946) 319ff.; Gelzer (n. 15 above) 1475. 37ff., 1479. 10ff.

scarcely at all in the fragments of other comic poets[45] and does not appear prominently until the fourth century. All this is a tall order for a playwright who had only four actors, a Chorus, an orchestra, a small stage and a couple of doors on a wooden building. Yet the task is accomplished and in the realization of this complex and ambitious idea Aristophanes offers us a good opportunity to observe a master playwright manipulating his traditional medium to its fullest potential.

Prologue (1–253)

Lysistrate emerges from her house in the middle of a thought (ἀλλά 1). We are not told the time of day but it soon appears that it is no longer early in the morning (60). Lysistrate has been waiting for women to arrive and complains that if the women had been invited to some festival of Dionysos, Pan or Aphrodite Genetyllis the crowd would have been impassable. As it is no one is yet here. These opening words tell us two things. (1) Lysistrate is the organizer of a meeting for women that is not of the usual (i.e. festive) kind. (2) She feels herself to be superior to the others in that she can think of an activity that does not fall into the category of revelry, drinking, sex and childbirth (for these are the activities associated with the deities mentioned and traditionally said by men to be the sole preoccupations of women). Lysistrate assumes a role traditionally assumed to be a male prerogative: calling a meeting, possessing will-power and entertaining ideas rather than physical drives.

The audience is likely to have been surprised to hear this and indeed to see a woman in the first place. Although heroines had long been customary in tragedy (since they were prominent in heroic myth) they were a rarity in comedy. In Aristophanes' earlier plays we have seen nothing like this. The only women who have appeared before were the odd market woman or minor goddess. A dozen or so Old Comedies of which only titles and/or fragments remain can be said to have had female Choruses,[46] but only Pherekrates' *Tyrannis* can be said possibly to have had a

45. See A. Meder, *Der athenische Demos zur Zeit des peloponnesischen Krieges im Licht zeitgenössiger Quellen* (Munich 1938) 113f.

46. See Schmid (n. 44 above) 418 n. 3.

female protagonist, though that is uncertain.[47] The idea of staging an intrigue-comedy with a heroine may well be original with Aristophanes.

Thus at the outset something at once familiar and fantastic is occurring. As in *Acharnians* a character waits impatiently for others to arrive for an important meeting and gives us to understand that no one else seems to care about a most important matter. We are invited to sympathize with this character and are curious to know what business is at hand. But in this case the central character is a woman; moreover she waits for other women to leave their houses and meet with her for some undisclosed (contrast *Acharnians*) and unusual purpose. The opening words of the play make it clear that this purpose has nothing to do with women's usual intrigues and that the speaker is rather distinct from the others. Almost immediately we learn her name and that of her neighbor Kalonike (6). The significance of Lysistrate's name (Disbander of Armies) is a clue to the topic of the women's meeting; and Kalonike (Fair Victory) is propitious (cf. *Knights* 1254 ὦ χαῖρε καλλίνικε).

In the ensuing dialogue Aristophanes not only gives us further information about Lysistrate's purpose but also establishes her superiority to the others. This dialogue is static and expository in that its chief purpose is to give us information about the plot; the plot itself cannot be said to begin until the arrival of the other wives. This is the first extant play in which the exposition does not take the form of an explanatory monologue. Instead the information is delivered dramatically. Although the plot does not actually move forward, the audience, in suspenseful anticipation of a full account of Lysistrate's plan, must feel that it does.

Characterization is the second purpose of this dialogue. Lysistrate's first words to Kalonike (9–12) are distinctly elevated in their rhythm and diction, establishing a pattern that will continue throughout the play: Lysistrate will always, except for the purposes of climax, emphasis or shrewd generalship, speak like the high-minded leader she is. Kalonike by contrast plays the unenlightened buffoon and represents the kind of woman comedy (and satire) delight in portraying. We are perhaps also reminded of the prologue of Sophokles' *Antigone*, where an extraordinary and

47. Fr. 143, which contrasts the greater drinking capacities of women to those of men, is suggestive but not decisive for the presence of female main characters.

strong-willed heroine tries to explain her unheard-of plan to the naive and conventional Ismene.

Lysistrate begins by confessing her sorrow that the women are not living up to their reputation among men as clever rascals (12) but sleep through the meeting instead. When Kalonike reminds her that wives have domestic chores to do before they can leave the house Lysistrate replies that there are things more important than taking care of husband and children (20f.).[48] As we shall see, Lysistrate more than once in the course of the play displays impatience and indeed a marked insensitivity to the domestic feelings of the wives. This is of course necessary for the success of her plan, but it is important for Lysistrate's characterization that she finds it easy to divorce herself from the home and its concerns, whereas the other wives experience constant homesickness not exclusively connected with their longing for sex. Aristophanes wants to take every opportunity to satirize the conventional weaknesses of the female sex but does not want this satire directed at Lysistrate herself. Lysistrate will use the foibles of women to save Greece; but this noble ambition does not preclude hearty comic exploitation of the foibles themselves. As we will have occasion to observe later, the wives in *Lysistrate* are vehicles of the sex strike plot only; Aristophanes does not connect them with the nobler ideas concerning home and polis which Lysistrate will later expound. The importance of the young wives to the polis, an importance championed by Lysistrate and the Chorus of Women, is portrayed separately from the ludicrous character of the wives themselves.

Kalonike takes Lysistrate's claim that there are things more important than domestic chores as an opportunity to ask what Lysistrate's purpose is. Now begins a pattern maintained through much of the prologue: Lysistrate feeds details of her plan to us bit by bit. Whenever we near full revelation the dialogue shifts its course and delays exposition. Lysistrate is at first quite vague, giving Kalonike an opportunity to misunderstand her in obscene fashion (more characterization): (22–5) *Kal.* Why are you sum-

48. Read ἀλλ' ἦν γὰρ ἕτερα with Porson; τῶνδε refers to the domestic duties enumerated (and probably illustrated with gestures) by Kalonike. See J. C. B. Lowe, *Glotta* 51 (1973) 34ff. Note that Kalonike does not say that wives cannot leave their homes, only that they must finish their chores first.

moning us wives together? What kind of thing is it? How big? *Lys.* Big! *Kal.* And thick, too? *Lys.* Plenty thick, by Zeus! *Kal.* Then how is it that we've not come? *Lys.* That's not what I meant: if it were we'd all have been here[49] quickly enough.' This little exchange is of course ironic: for it is actually about the 'big, thick thing' that Lysistrate has summoned the wives, thought not in Kalonike's sense. What Lysistrate will demand of the wives will reach far beyond their basic desire for sex, will not be what they themselves would be capable of choosing, but nevertheless will ultimately lead back to what Kalonike has in mind here.

Lysistrate now divulges more of her purpose: the salvation of all Greece depends on the women (29f.), the very existence of Sparta, Boiotia, even (*absit omen*) Athens herself (32ff.). If the wives of Greece unite Greece might yet be saved (39ff.). Kalonike interjects jesting remarks as Lysistrate speaks (31, 34, 36) and then climactically demands to know what sensible or remarkable thing wives can do, who do nothing but sit around in their sexiest clothes (42ff.); of course she numbers herself among them. Here again we are reminded of Ismene's climactic testimony on women's weakness and inherent inferiority to men (Soph. *Ant.* 61ff.). Those sexy clothes are exactly what will save us, replies Lysistrate (46ff.). Notice that Lysistrate does not here or subsequently deny that the wives are frivolous and inferior. She emphatically says that these inherent weaknesses can be used as strengths when properly employed (or rather, not employed). She herself does not share in the weaknesses.

Kalonike is enormously pleased that her exaggeratedly sybaritic description of housewives is exactly what Lysistrate wants and she becomes a temporary convert. The audience, like Kalonike, are more anxious than ever to hear how the women plan to save Greece in this sort of way. But at this point Lysistrate again resumes her complaints about the women's tardiness: reference to the women of Salamis provides Kalonike with another sexual double entendre (59f.) and mention of the Acharnian women elicits a joke on female bibulousness (63ff.).[50] Thus we are returned for the moment to a less elevated plane.

49. Lysistrate speaks generically: cf. ἡμῶν 10.

50. Or, less likely, superstitiousness, depending on the reading in 64: see Wilamowitz and Coulon *ad loc.*

Women from Anagyrous enter (to still another joke from Kalonike, 67f.), led by Myrrhine. Lysistrate rebukes her for coming so tardily 'on a matter of such great importance' (71). This may imply that Myrrhine has already been told what the meeting is about. Note also Lysistrate's earlier remark about the Acharnian women: 'Nor have the Acharnians yet come, whom I had good reason to expect here first' (61ff.). Why would she expect them first? Wilamowitz thought that they are mentioned simply to yield Kalonike's joke, but the emphatic πρώτας has nothing to do with the joke. It might be thought that the Acharnians would not have had to travel as far as the others, but then again everyone from the outlying demes would have been within the city at this time anyway. Most likely women from such a traditionally warlike area (cf. *Ach.* 204ff.) would be expected to show particular interest in a question of peacemaking.

If some of the women (not Kalonike, who appears to be totally ignorant: 6ff., 21ff.) know what the meeting is about, why do they presently ask (94ff.)? This question has some bearing on the attribution of lines at 74–81. At 72f. Myrrhine protests that she had trouble finding her girdle in the dark. 'But if there is some urgency tell those present what it is.' At this point R (our sole witness for this part of the text) makes Lysistrate say: 'No, let's wait a while longer, until the Boiotians and Peloponnesians arrive (74–6a). *Myr.* That's a better idea. In fact, here comes Lampito now! (76b–77) *Lys.* Dear Spartan girl! Greetings, Lampito! (78)' If this is the proper attribution[51] Myrrhine must indeed know something of what is afoot, otherwise she would not know that Lampito is expected or know her name. She shows no surprise when Lysistrate mentions the imminent arrival of foreigners (75). Yet Kalonike, who clearly knows nothing, showed no surprise either at Lysistrate's similar announcement earlier (39–41).

Coulon (after Bake) gives Kalonike 74–6a and Lysistrate 76b–81, wrongly: Kalonike is not the one to determine how the meeting will be ordered, nor would we expect her to counsel delay. In addition 76b, 'That's a better idea', is illogical and ill-fitting to Lysistrate; it is most logical in the mouth of Myrrhine, whose

51. For a defense see P. Händel, *Formen und Darstellungsweisen in der aristophanischen Komödie* (Heidelberg 1963) 190 n. 3; Wilamowitz and Rogers adopt it.

demand for instant revelation has been denied. Süss[52] suggests following R but giving Lysistrate 77ff. But 77 ἠδὶ δὲ καὶ δή seems to require the same speaker as 76b: cf. *Ach.* 174ff., where Amphitheos' sudden return interrupts Dikaiopolis' laments over his lost lunch: 'But here's Amphitheos back from Sparta. Greetings, Amphitheos!' Amphitheos is just in time to provide Dikaiopolis with a way out of his despair. Following the traditional attibution here allows a similar comic effect, and the best: Myrrhine wants to know Lysistrate's purpose at once; Lysistrate tells her to wait; and just as Myrrhine is agreeing that Lysistrate's counsel is the wiser the sudden arrival of Lampito provides both confirmation of this and the expectation that her curiosity will at last be satisfied. It is dramatically best if Myrrhine herself announces excitedly that Lampito is coming. The audience will no more marvel here at how Myrrhine would know who Lampito is than earlier when Kalonike shows impossible knowledge of why the women have been delayed (58ff.) or when Lysistrate offers no explanation of (and Kalonike no surprise about) how women from all over Greece could possibly have made such a trip in the first place.

Lampito herself excitedly asks who has invited her to this meeting; by this she means, presumably, which one of you is Lysistrate (93f.). If we push the logic of the text as we have arranged it we must conclude that Lysistrate has summoned women from the important cities to meet on a matter of war and peace and has told them all as much. She has told none of them her actual plans and seems to have told Kalonike nothing at all. Kalonike's function in the opening dialogue, to provide the most basic exposition of the action (why are we waiting for the wives?), demands total ignorance. But perhaps logic is not to be pushed too far; Aristophanes often makes no special effort to distinguish what is appropriate for characters themselves from what is necessary for the plot at any given moment.

Lampito is greeted by Lysistrate's astonished description of her strength and beauty (79–81); as usual her language is rather formal. Kalonike[53] offers a further description (83) that contrasts

52. N. 43 above, p. 242.

53. With Bake; R has only a paragraphos. In addition to its suitability for a buffoon this line would lose much of its comic effect if given to Lysistrate, who has already assessed Lampito.

with Lysistrate's (in the now familiar pattern) in its colloquial indecency, 'What a beautiful deal of tits you've got!' This technique of a feed by Lysistrate and an offcolor punchline by Kalonike continues through the introduction of the Boiotian and the Korinthian, prominent features of whose homelands provide material for double entendres. Thus we give 88bf.[54] to Kalonike and also 91bf. (with Bentley and Bake respectively). Whether the latter should be given to Lysistrate depends upon our feeling about what would be 'in character': Lysistrate has not yet officially noticed the Korinthian; but then the joke is more Kalonike's style. If Kalonike speaks, argues Süss,[55] she would be in effect duplicating her joke of 88af. But why should she not? 87bf. might be Myrrhine's (van Leeuwen), since she has not yet spoken and the remark is offcolor. But here Lysistrate is doing the talking with Lampito and the other foreigners and (despite Süss) Kalonike usually speaks before Myrrhine.[56]

This routine with the foreigners' bodies of course depends upon ethnosexual prejudices (not to mention the amusement of Lampito's accent) and caters to the male audience's enjoyment of sexual humor. From the women's point of view Lysistrate's admiration of the foreign delegates has further ramifications: Kalonike and Myrrhine react purely out of envy; but this parade of feminine allurements strikes Lysistrate the way Oliver's good looks struck Mr Fagin. She is delighted that her domestic arsenal is so prettily stocked.

We notice a pattern. Each time it seems that we are close to hearing Lysistrate's plan something interrupts and the heroine's panhellenic fervor must temporarily give way to buffoonery. At this juncture Lampito, like Kalonike (21ff.) and Myrrhine (73) before her, asks why the meeting has been called. Kalonike eagerly seconds the motion for disclosure.[57] Again Lysistrate postpones her answer until she has asked two questions (99ff.). The first concerns the husbands, the second sexual fulfilment: (1) I know that each

54. A late corrector in R gives this to Lampito because of the erroneous τὰν in 89.

55. N. 43 above, p. 246.

56. There is no reason, with Wilamowitz, to give 87bf. to Kalonike and 88af. to Myrrhine.

57. With Wilamowitz and Coulon: see Süss (n. 43 above) 247. 98b is also Kalonike's: H. Kruse, *Quaestiones aristophaneae* (Flensburg 1874) 6.

of you has a husband, father of your children, away at war; don't you want them back? (Lysistrate says nothing about a husband or children of her own.) Kalonike, Myrrhine and Lampito[58] all affirm the absence of their husbands. (2) Furthermore, not only are there no adulterers in the city, there are no dildoes available, either, because of the defection of Miletos; don't you want to end the war that has caused these deprivations? Once again, the three affirm (with comically inflated oaths) that they do, in the order Kalonike, Myrrhine, Lampito (with Kruse (n. 57 above, pp. 6f.) and, independently, Coulon).

Let us take a moment to discuss this attribution. R gives 112b–114 to Myrrhine, 115f. to Kalonike. Arguments can be made for either attribution. A decision can be made on the basis of our attribution of 122b–135: whoever speaks 130 must speak 115f. Süss (n. 43 above, pp. 248f.) defends R on the grounds that Kalonike takes the interrupter's role at 122f., where she is tricked into swearing to do whatever Lysistrate demands. Her subsequent refusal (130), after she has heard the demands, motivates Lysistrate's outburst and prepares the way for Kalonike's predominance in the scene where Lysistrate must convince her and Lampito to accede to the plan. But this is weak. (1) It deprives this section of an established pattern of response in which Kalonike speaks first. (2) It robs Kalonike of a joke on bibulousness (112b–114) very much in her style. (3) It leaves 129 hanging: at 123 Kalonike swears that she will do whatever Lysistrate demands even if she must die for it; after Lysistrate announces what is involved, it is awkward if Myrrhine and not Kalonike says, 'I won't do it – let the war roll on!', leaving Kalonike with the follow-up (130), 'Nor I – let the war roll on!' οὐκ ἂν ποιήσαιμ' (129) is funnier if it is spoken by the speaker of ποιήσομεν (123), i.e. Kalonike. After Lysistrate's contemptuous reply to this (131f.) Kalonike breaks in (133–5) to defend her refusal. Thus, 129 to Kalonike and 130 to Myrrhine (Kruse, p. 7). A problem not hitherto discussed is who speaks 135b?

58. 102f. must be Kalonike's (with Brunck) on account of the jest about Eukrates; 104 must be Myrrhine's (with a late corrector in R, which has a paragraphos). Lampito, the only other candidate, speaks in dialect and Lysistrate cannot answer her own question, nor does Aristophanes wish to give us any information about Lysistrate's background. The fact that Myrrhine's husband Kinesias later appears does not prevent her from speaking of his absence here, as Brunck thought.

After both Kalonike and Myrrhine refuse, Lysistrate asks (135a), 'And what about you?' To which someone replies, 'I, too, would rather walk through fire.' R has a dikolon here; a later hand supplies Myrrhine. But why should Lysistrate demand an answer of a woman who has already given one? Brunck emended the line so as to make Lampito speak, but we immediately learn that she is reserving her decision (140ff.). We must, I think, give 136b to an extra, one of the other Attic wives: all the women, not only the ringleaders, are refusing. ἄλλη is in fact the attribution in ΓVp2H.

The two interpolated questions at 99ff. not only build suspense but establish an important prerequisite of the plan's success: sex outside marriage is impossible. The adulterers and dildoes – not to mention slaves and muledrivers – with which housewives are frequently said by comic poets to amuse themselves (e.g. *Thesm.* 491ff.) are not admitted in this play. We later learn that the same groundrule applies to the husbands: the slaves, boys and prostitutes who in other plays provide comic characters with sexual gratification outside the home are absent (cf. *Ekkl.* 311–47). If sexual outlets other than spouses were allowed here the sex strike would fail and Lysistrate would be unable to concentrate on the theme of the sanctity and security of married life, which forms the basis of her strongest arguments against the war in the prologue. This, of course, does not prevent Aristophanes from making it clear that the wives very much desire these illicit outlets; but he also makes it clear that they would prefer to have their husbands. The two questions do two more things: they further establish Lysistrate's tactical skills: she knows in advance that the women will be recalcitrant and, giving them the attractive part of the plan first, gets them to swear obedience before they know the unattractive part. And they set us up for the wives' mass refusal at 124ff.

Now Lysistrate announces her plan (120ff.): 'We must, if we are to force the men to treat for peace, give up... *Kal.* What? Tell us! *Lys.* You'll do it, then? *Kal.* We'll do it even if it means death! *Lys.* We must, then, give up...the cock!' This first outright obscenity in the play could not be more climactically placed. The shocked and reluctant behavior of the wives upon hearing this announcement provokes a paratragic address by Lysistrate (125ff.), followed by the refusals of Kalonike, Myrrhine and another wife (135b). Lysistrate bitterly reflects on the weakness and shamelessness of the entire female species and declares that the tragic poets have reason to denigrate it (137–9). Thus her fears of 10ff. are confirmed and further generalship is required if her dream is to be realized. Note how seamlessly and naturally exposition gives way to plot.

Let down by her countrywomen, Lysistrate finds a new resource in Lampito. The establishment of a call-and-response pattern of enthusiasm before and cold feet after Lysistrate's climatic announcement at 124 not only underscores in a most comic way the cowardly fickleness of the Athenians but prepares the way for this new tactic: Lampito, who before 124 answered third after Kalonike and Myrrhine, is silent here. She is therefore the only one left to turn to, for she has not yet made up her mind. 'My dear Spartan – for if you alone join me in this business the whole plan might yet be redeemed – vote with me!' (140–2). Lampito admits that sleeping alone is difficult for wives but if in the interests of peace this must be done she will go along. Lysistrate gratefully proclaims her 'the only real woman here' (145), comically using 'woman' where we would normally expect to hear 'man'. In reality, of course (that is, according to comic stereotype), not Lysistrate and Lampito but the others are behaving like real women. To be a real woman now requires that the wives act like men in one important respect and one only: they must remain their most female selves but resist what they as a sex were widely believed unable to resist: sexual temptation.[59]

Aristophanes has arranged things in such a way that Lysistrate's plan will be managed under the shared leadership of an Athenian and a Spartan; the development of the play will show that Aristophanes' vision of panhellenic peace sees the Greek world jointly led by her two preeminent states, just as it had been in the

59. Cf. Eur. *Andr.* 220f., 995. See K. J. Dover, *Greek Popular Morality in the Time of Plato and Aristotle* (Berkeley/Los Angeles 1974) 98ff., 208. Sexual desire, like pain and fatigue and hunger, is a threat to the well-disciplined personality and the Greeks admired and trusted those who could resist it. Cf. Plato, *Smp.* 196c3, εἶναι γὰρ ὁμολογεῖται σωφροσύνη τὸ κρατεῖν ἡδονῶν καὶ ἐπιθυμιῶν, ἔρωτος δὲ μηδεμίαν ἡδονὴν κρείττω εἶναι· εἰ δὲ ἥττους, κρατοῖντ' ἂν ὑπὸ ἔρωτος, ὁ δὲ κρατοῖ, κρατῶν δὲ ἡδονῶν καὶ ἐπιθυμιῶν ὁ ἔρως διαφερόντως ἂν σωφρονοῖ. In all fairness, however, women apparently had a harder struggle: for the story that they received ninety per cent, and men ten per cent, of the pleasure (according to Teiresias) see Dover, p. 101 and the sources cited by Pfeiffer, Callimachus Fr. 576 and Rzach, Hesiod Fr. 162.

glorious days of the Persian invasions. It is fitting that this ideal be mirrored also in terms of the women's fantastic conspiracy through which it is to be realized. Lampito will do in Sparta what Lysistrate does in Athens. Naturally, it is the Athenian who has the idea and is largely responsible for its success.

Lampito's support and the praise it elicits from Lysistrate draw a new and more open-minded response from Kalonike: while she still hopes that the wives will not have to give up 'what you say' (146: she cannot bring herself to use the actual word), she wants to know how peace might come if they did. This question gives Lysistrate a chance to expound her plan in detail, under close and typically buffoonish questioning by Kalonike. As already intimated (46ff.), the wives are to make themselves as alluring as possible and parade around the house (149), refusing their husbands sex until they agree to make peace, 'as I know they will'.[60] If the husbands force us against our will the result will be the same, for men have no pleasure in sex unless the wife does, too.[61] Having successfully answered Kalonike's questions,[62] Lysistrate finally wins the support of the Attic wives (167).

At last we have heard Lysistrate's plans for the wives: a sex strike to be carried out at home and that presupposes the presence of both husbands and wives (cf. 16ff.). But moments earlier we heard that the husbands have for some time been away from home (99ff.). Thus the complaint Lysistrate adduces (the war has disrupted family life by removing husbands from their homes) is

60. Here Lampito interjects the story of Menelaos' helplessness at the sight of Helen's breasts as supporting evidence (155f.). Wilamowitz thinks she is comically misinformed about the legend, but he overlooks Eur. *Andr.* 628ff., which is so close to Lampito's version that Aristophanes might be poking fun here at Euripides. Helen's fabled breasts are part of the tradition of this anecdote: Stes. 201 P, Ibyk. 296 P, *Little Iliad* 17 Allen = 14 Bethe; cf. L. Ghali-Kahil, *Les enlèvements et retours d'Hélène* (Paris 1955) 71ff., B. Ashmole, *JHS* 87 (1967) 13f. This 'historical' precedent is meant to strengthen Lysistrate's assertion that men need sex as much as women and in a real showdown will be unable to resist desire. Lampito's choice of precedent (in view of the Spartans' famed hardiness) is well chosen.

61. A remark drawn from life, not the usual comic stereotypes. Note Kinesias' behavior later, when even after he is deceived by his wife he still insists that he loves her and wants her back. See Dover (n. 59 above) 210, 212.

62. Lysistrate has no real answer to the plausible idea (157) that the husbands might actually throw the wives out; Aristophanes deflects the thought by introducing an obscene joke (158, contradicting 109).

to be remedied by a plan inconsistent with the complaint itself. Moreover, the objection of the wives to this plan (they cannot do without sex) is unintelligible if in fact the husbands are away at war: in that case the wives would already be doing without sex, as, to judge from Lysistrate's remarks at 107ff., they indeed seem to be doing. What part of the plan, if any, corresponds to the historical reality of 411? And why does Aristophanes go out of his way to flout dramatic logic? The same answer can be given to both questions. The war had indeed taken the lives of many men and left their wives husbandless, their children fatherless (the lighthearted prologue avoids explicit mention of death); still other husbands must have spent much time away from home. The disastrous Sicilian Expedition was a very recent event, and the rapid defection of Athens' allies required unprecedented vigilance by many such as Eukrates in Thrace (103). Family life has indeed been disrupted by the war. It is the importance of domestic life that will provide the major theme of the play and the strongest case against the war: Athenian society is to be viewed from the vantage-point of the happy home, where wives are the central figures. Aristophanes in the prologue wants to establish the sexual theme in terms of women at home. The plot will show the women turning the tables on the men and thereby demonstrating that in a choice between the happiness of home and the misery of war the men must choose the home. As far as husbands and wives are concerned sex and procreation are the strongest centripetal forces. Later on Lysistrate will operate as champion of the domestic front on other levels as well, for instance the role of the home as guarantor of traditional values, such as religious, social and political ones. To dramatize the alternatives of war and peace Aristophanes needs to stage both: he must show homes disrupted by war to motivate a plot in which homes will be disrupted by wives.

And so the wives acquiesce. But Lampito has an objection not based on sex: we Spartan women will be able to persuade our men to make a just and honest peace (this must have raised cackles in the audience) but how will you make the Athenian mob stop talking nonsense as long as they have their ships and their treasure (168–74)? Lysistrate has the answer: while we wives have been plotting our domestic initiative the oldest women have been instructed, on the pretext of performing a sacrifice, to seize the Akropolis (175–8). Thus we hear the full extent of Lysistrate's bold scheme: the women will act not only from the home but on the civic front as well, and not only wives but old women, too.[63] The audience will be very curious to see how Aristophanes will manage to show both of these plans in action.

All objections met, Lysistrate suggests that the wives seal their plot with an oath, an oath that lightheartedly recapitulates Plan A (the strike) and assumes that husbands and wives will be at home (212–36). The attribution of lines and proper visualization of the action immediately preceding the oath-taking itself deserve comment. Lysistrate first suggests a sacrifice into a shield, after the manner of Aischylos *Seven* 42ff. Kalonike objects to using a shield in an oath for peace (189f.: Kalonike is the natural interlocutor here, with a corrector in R). Here the warlike Lysistrate must be guided by her more feminine colleagues. 'What, then, will be our oath?' asks Lysistrate (191a). Kalonike, who raised the objection, now gets a chance to suggest an alternative: 'What if we get a white horse from somewhere and sacrifice that?' (191b–192). 'What do you mean, white horse?' objects Lysistrate (193a). This (with van Leeuwen and Wilamowitz) is the only satisfactory distribution. Coulon[64] gives 191–2 to Lysistrate and 193a to Kalonike. But (1) Lysistrate cannot make two unacceptable suggestions in a row, and (2) Kalonike cannot object to the white horse, since that would not be appropriate for a buffoon. Whatever Kalonike intended by suggesting a white horse – an allusion to Amazons (van Leeuwen) or simply an outlandish-sounding victim (Wilamowitz) – the reaction of Lysistrate relegates her suggestion to the ridiculous. It is probable that there is an obscene double entendre at work[65] and in that case the suggestion is even more firmly assignable to Kalonike.

63. Nothing is said in the prologue about the extent of Lysistrate's plans for the Akropolis. We are told only that this action is necessary to cripple the war effort. We are not told whether the occupation is temporary or permanent. The prologue confines itself to the strike and the wives involved in it; the seizure is mentioned only as an ancillary strategic move.

64. Following H. Hamaker: see A. Römer, *Zur Kritik und Exegese von Homer, Euripides, Aristophanes und den alten Erklärern derselben*, in *Abhandlungen der Kön. Bayer. Akad. der Wiss.*, Philos.-Philol. Kl. 22 (1905) 621.

65. See Henderson (n. 24 above) 126f.

Now it is Kalonike's turn to admit defeat and ask, 'So what will we swear by?' (193f.). Naturally we will not give this question to Lysistrate (Hamaker, followed by Coulon), since it duplicates her question of 191. Here someone makes the winning suggestion, one that appeals to all the wives: Let's upend a huge black drinking bowl and sacrifice into it a jar of Thasian wine, then swear... never to mix in water! Wilamowitz, Rogers and van Leeuwen give this to Myrrhine (after Bergk), but it is unlikely that the decisive idea will come from that quarter: there is no pressing need fully to involve Myrrhine in every phase of the prologue simply to give her something to do. Coulon (after Hamaker) gives the lines to Kalonike. True, they are more in her style, but do we want to give the winning sugggestion to anyone but the leader? The ms. rightly assigns these lines to Lysistrate.

It has been felt that the idea is beneath the dignity of Lysistrate, especially the final surprise in 197, 'never to mix in water', which Dover[66] feels might be 'an unreproved interruption' of Kalonike's. But later Lysistrate comically rounds off the oath (235) with the same joke, 'And if I transgress this oath, may the bowl be filled with...water!' The idea of sacrificing a huge amount of wine is not so far removed from the surprise in 197, and if Lysistrate is to make the suggestion about the wine in the first place (as she must) she should be allowed to go all the way to the final joke, which is not only unreproved but immediately and loudly extolled by no less a figure than Lampito (198). Obviously the entire suggestion has the dramatic effect of (for once) rallying all the wives in united enthusiasm. What better evidence of Lysistrate's consummate generalship than this stroke of genius? Lysistrate knows how to reach the hearts of her bibulous co-conspirators, and even the male audience would agree that she has struck the right note.[67]

Lysistrate now orders a slave to fetch the jar and bowl (199), upon whose appearance someone exclaims, 'Dear women, what a piece of pottery! Even to touch this (jar) would bring one instant pleasure!' (201f.). Then Lysistrate, 'Put it down and place your hand on the...victim with me' (202), whereupon she prays to

66. *Lustrum* 2 (1957) 93. The suggestion was anticipated by Dobree, who gave 194b–197a to Myrrhine.

67. See Süss (n. 43 above) 244.

Persuasion and to the power of the cup to provide solidarity.[68] Lines 200 and 201 could be spoken by the same person (R has a paragraphos at 200 over which a corrector writes Lysistrate). Rogers and Coulon (after Bentley) give them to Kalonike, but the action is livelier if two women react to the appearance of the wine, and it is clear that Kalonike must be the one who grabs at the jar. Thus 200 to Myrrhine (Reisig) and 201 to Kalonike.[69]

Immediately following Lysistrate's prayer (202–4) comes the following exchange: 'How beautiful the color of the... blood and how nicely it spurts out!' (205) 'And how very sweet it smells, by Kastor!' (206) 'Let *me* take the oath first, girls!' (207) 'Nothing doing, by Aphrodite, you must wait your turn!' (208) 'All of you lay hold of the bowl, and I mean you, Lampito:[70] let one of you on behalf of all repeat after me what I say, and all of you swear to abide by the oath.' (209–11) What is happening here? A quarrel has developed over who gets to drink first and Lysistrate must stop it before the oath-taking can begin. The wine Lysistrate holds like a carrot before a horse: the women must swear first, then drink (which they do at 238ff.). Lysistrate later uses a similar technique (1114ff.) when she dangles the ravishing Diallage before the lust-swollen husbands of Athens and Sparta, who must agree to a peace settlement before they can enjoy its fleshly rewards. In both these scenes Lysistrate is presented as a being of superior will.

Who are the speakers? 206 is guaranteed by dialect for Lampito and 209 for Lysistrate because she must lead the swearing-in. This leaves 205, 207 and 208. 207 and 208, accompanied by action (someone's attempt to drink followed by someone else's attempt to prevent this), are forceful responses to 205 and 206, in which the sight, sound and aroma of the wine are enticingly described. Our attribution of speakers will depend upon which of the possible choices is funniest. It makes better comedy if the speaker who tries to drink first here (207) is not Kalonike, who has already tried to do this and has already been rebuked (201f.). We should therefore

68. See H. Kleinknecht, *Die Gebetsparodie in der Antike* (Stuttgart/Berlin 1937 = *Tübinger Beitr. zur Altertumswiss.* 28) 49ff.; Wilamowitz *ad loc.*

69. With Süss (n. 43 above) 244. Not 200 to Kalonike and 201 to Myrrhine (van Leeuwen and Wilamowitz).

70. For plural verb followed by singular vocative see K-G 1. 85. The construction signifies that the speaker singles out the most prominent member of the group addressed: cf. *Frogs* 1497.

give this second attempt (following the prologue's established pecking order) to Myrrhine.[71] It seems to follow that Kalonike speaks 205.[72] Finally, who rebukes Myrrhine at 208? Lysistrate could do it herself, as she did at 202.[73] Or Kalonike could do it only to be silenced in turn by Lysistrate's imperative at 209. This in fact is better: at 205 Kalonike, chastened by Lysistrate's rebuke, keeps her hands to herself and confines her excitement to praise of the wine. At 206 Lampito leans over the wine and praises its smell. At 207 Myrrhine, as yet unreproved and imagining (perhaps correctly) that Lampito is going to take a drink, demands to be first. At 208 Kalonike protests.[74] Finally Lysistrate steps in (209) and tells them all to take hold of the cup at once. Her singling out Lampito in particular (see n. 70) is motivated both by Lampito's action at 206, which caused the trouble, and by her status as co-leader (she ought to be above drink-filching).

For all the hieratic and paratragic features of Lysistrate's preparations,[75] which give these proceedings just enough serious coloration to intensify the comedy (farcical action contrasted with inflated language),[76] the oath ceremony itself is played strictly for laughs (212–37). Kalonike repeats after Lysistrate a series of promises detailing sexual acts which the wives will no longer perform for their husbands (οἴκοι 217). The various acts mentioned are intended by Aristophanes to underline the lecherousness of the wives (Kalonike's knees tremble, 216), and Lysistrate's catalogue of all the sexual pleasures that the wives forswear amounts to a satirical setpiece on this theme, although it is not hostile in tone like the Relative's catalogue in *Thesm.* 466ff. Unlike the wives of *Thesm.* these women do not dissimulate their rascality or their

71. With Hamaker, followed by Rogers, van Leeuwen and Wilamowitz. The corrector in R impossibly assigns the line to Lysistrate. Coulon (with Lenting) gives it to Kalonike.

72. With the corrector in R and modern edd. Hamaker's attribution to Myrrhine is not impossible but weakens the dramatic effect gained by having three women instead of only two quarreling.

73. Thus Lenting and Coulon.

74. With the corrector in R and modern edd. Brunck's predilection for Myrrhine led him to give her 208, which is alien to her character.

75. See Kleinknecht (n. 68 above) 49ff.; for the wine, K. Kircher, 'Die sakrale Bedeutung des Weines im Altertum', *RVV* 9. 2 (1910) 1ff.

76. 'Der Kelch wird damit kein sogenannter Augenblicksgott, sondern die Macht, die in dem feierlich gemeinsamen Trinken liegt, ist immer etwas Göttliches und soll sich als solches jetzt bewahren', Wilamowitz at 203–4.

preoccupation with sex. On the contrary, they realize that sex is their only weapon. Thus the sexual humor here is gay and titillating. The adulterers said to be absent at 107 make an appearance at 212–14, but this is simply a joke (adulterers are mentioned before husbands) in the spirit of the satire.[77]

A cry is heard (240): Lysistrate explains that this is the signal that the older women have taken the Akropolis. Lampito is sent home, the foreigners are left 'here with us' as hostages (244)[78] and the wives are instructed by Lysistrate to assist those on the Akropolis in barring the gates. The locale changes to the area before the Propylaia (the wives move across stage to the door now representing these gates). Kalonike's question at 242f., 'Don't you think that the men will march against us straightway?', shows no surprise that the skene no longer represents houses or that the wives are not after all going home for the strike.

And so the wives, originally scheduled for a home-front strike, go to join the other women on the Akropolis and remain there for the rest of the play. When next we hear of husbands it is they who must sit at home alone. It would have been easy, since the wives perform no further function aside from the Kinesias–Myrrhine scene and the scene of attempted desertion, to have Lysistrate say, 'I shall go now to the Akropolis with these hostages and help the others; you return home', and later to stage a scene exemplifying the strike in front of a door representing a home. There are several reasons why Aristophanes prefers to tolerate some degree of illogicality in the plot.

First, Aristophanes wishes primarily to stress the importance of the domestic sphere to the polis as a whole. This sphere, the special realm of the wives, is fundamentally different from the public sphere of the men. In ordinary times the two function harmoniously together; the war has disrupted the harmony and threatened the wives on their own ground. The major disruption is the absence

77. At 238a Lysistrate finally gets the first drink ('ratification'). Now it is Kalonike's turn to warn her leader, 'Only your share, friend, so that we shall all be friends from the very start' (238bf.). J. Jackson's suggestion that 239 should be Lysistrate's final clause to the oath is refuted by S. Radt, *Mnem.* 27 (1974) 9.

78. The Boiotian and Korinthian wives (85ff.). Lysistrate and Lampito are the chief agents; the subordinate position of the allies is explicitly described at 1176–81.

of husbands and this provides the motive for Plan A, the strike, treated in the prologue and in the Kinesias–Myrrhine scene. The women turn the tables on the men at home. But to base the play on the domestic front alone would make it difficult to confront the war as an issue, since war is a phenomenon of the men's sphere – not to mention the difficulty of developing Plan A much beyond what we have in the prologue and in the Kinesias–Myrrhine scene. Plan A is farcical and unpolitical. Aristophanes therefore devises Plan B as a way to demonstrate the indispensability of the domestic sphere to those in charge of the city and to assert the superior value of domestic management in time of war. War is presented as fundamentally evil; the home is the one area of polis life untainted by war-madness. Plan A will ultimately force an end to the war by making the fighting men choose home over battlefield, but it cannot be used to confront the warmakers themselves. Plan B, which thrusts the women into the men's sphere, demonstrates that the women, representing domestic values, must take over when the city is mismanaged by its leaders, here represented by a Proboulos and a Chorus of old men who support and vote for the war policies. This merging of the home and the Akropolis, of sex strike and occupation, gives the play its thematic unity; allows the women for a time to manage the public realm in terms of the domestic; and demonstrates not only the importance to the polis of female activities but also the importance of the female psyche as a stabilizing factor in the Greek world.

It must be emphasized that Aristophanes does not argue for the superiority or even equality of women. Their takeover of the polis and disruption of homes are temporary measures aimed at bringing the fighting men to their senses and confiscating the financial base of the warmaking leaders. Lysistrate alone is a superior being, and Aristophanes takes care to differentiate her from the wives. The wives succeed not because they are women but because they represent the good things of peace – food, drink, festivals and sex – and force the husbands to admit that they would rather enjoy these things than fight. The wives do not protest their lot as women, but long to be safely back at home where they belong.

Making the wives ascend the Akropolis has in addition the virtue of allowing Aristophanes to keep all the participants in the action in one place, to give all the women – young wives and old fighters – a united front with Lysistrate at the center of both parts of the plan. She cannot be at home and on the Akropolis at once. By herding everyone onto the Akropolis Lysistrate can simultaneously keep the men from the Treasury and the wives from the husbands. Private sexual obstructionism is presented in terms of open political obstructionism and both are thematically merged in the symbol of Athena's citadel. As we shall see, Plan A and Plan B are conceived and developed quite separately despite their thematic connection.

Let us take a moment to consider some social and political implications of the prologue. We have seen that Lysistrate is portrayed as essentially different from and superior to both her allies from among the Attic wives and her Spartan counterpart Lampito. She possesses superior charm, will, vision, political insight, strategic and diplomatic abilities. She is also free of the stereotyped weaknesses of her sex: inability to resist the need for sexual and other sensual pleasure; ignorance of and lack of concern about anything outside the home; preoccupation with trivial matters. Unlike the wives (16ff., 72)[79] she moves about at will and must in fact be reminded by Kalonike that not every woman enjoys the same freedom. In addition, Aristophanes carefully avoids mentioning a husband or children or any other detail about her private life: contrast 99ff., 829ff. All this reinforces the impression that Lysistrate is in a class by herself. In fact we may be able to specify her class more precisely. Alan Sommerstein has recently shown[80] that there are only four instances in Aristophanes of a respectable woman being named publicly by a free man:[81] Lysimache, priestess of Athena Polias (the most important female priesthood), at *Peace* 992, and Lysistrate (1086, 1103, 1147). D. M. Lewis (*ABSA* 50 (1955) 1ff.) showed that Lysimache was still in office in 411 and suggested that our heroine was modelled on her. Note that at 554 Lysistrate virtually calls herself Lysimache. This assumption, if correct, would explain the 'nameability' of Lysistrate: ordinary women would not have a public personality or a public role. Lewis' conjecture in fact best explains the extraordinary portrayal of Lysistrate that we have examined thus

79. And unlike Praxagora, *Ekkl.* 35ff., 54ff., 510ff.
80. 'The Naming of Women in Greek and Roman Comedy', forthcoming.
81. For a similar protocol in the orators, see D. Schaps, *CQ* 27 (1977) 323ff.

far and should be borne in mind later in the play, where Aristophanes develops definite thematic connections between Lysistrate and Athena (a goddess partaking of both male and female attributes; immune to sexual temptation; a warrior and at the same time patroness of the domestic sphere), and underscores the importance of the older women's religious services on behalf of the city. Perhaps features of Lysistrate's costume aided in this identification, and it is possible that the real Lysimache held views similar to those attributed to Lysistrate.

The social and political orientation of the prologue establishes patterns that will be worked out consistently in the course of the play. Lysistrate must be thought to move in quite high social circles:[82] the priesthood of Athena Polias, like that of Poseidon Erechtheus, was a traditional preserve of the Eteoboutadai. She is in contact with women from other states as prominent as herself: Lampito was a name borne by King Agis' mother, the Boiotian is πρέσβειρα (86: cf. *Ach.* 883), and the Korinthian is χαΐα (91). All the wives are agreed that negotiations for peace, begun on Athenian initiative, must be consummated and that the principal cities involved will be Athens and Sparta. No one disputes the assumption that the war is folly for all combatants and that the Athenian demos and its radical leaders must be forced to stop fighting. There are unmistakable hits at prominent democratic leaders: Eukrates (103) may be the demagogue attacked at *Eq.* 253f.; the reference to the loss of Miletos (108) must be a hit at Alkibiades (Th. 8. 17); and Lysistrate has anticipated Lampito's concern about the 'Athenian rabble' (168–79).

There is nothing here that contradicts the summary of Aristophanes' political position recently formulated by de Ste Croix.[83] No supporter of oligarchic reaction, Aristophanes was doubtless a patriotic democrat; the whole of *Lysistrate* is in fact a celebration of the traditional Athenian democracy. But like Lampito and Lysistrate he held 'an essentially paternalist attitude' toward the lower orders; 'he clearly resented the political power the demos was beginning to exercise' and 'betray(s) the irritation felt by the upper-class Athenian at this innovation of the radical democracy'. Aristophanes' irritation was directed in particular at the new

82. Perhaps like Aristophanes himself: S. Dow, *AJA* 73 (1969) 234f.
83. *The Origins of the Peloponnesian War* (Ithaca 1972) 357f.

leaders of the demos, men not belonging to the old leading families, who, in his view, duped the people for their private gain. The demos itself, as Thukydides also saw, too often acts from passion rather than from reasoned intelligence, too often forgets its best values and traditions. On the question of the war de Ste Croix's remarks are worth quoting in full:

> (Aristophanes) was very much against the war: he thought it should never have been allowed to break out in the first place, and that any chance of bringing it to an end and making peace with Sparta should be eagerly embraced; the admirable situation which had existed before the coming to power of the radical democrats could then be restored, and Athens and Sparta could dominate the Greek world jointly. In this last respect, as well as in his general political position, Aristophanes can be described as a 'Cimonian'.

As we shall see, this summary may be said to describe the views of Lysistrate as well.

The prologue sets the stage for these potentialities of plot but does little more. It is played mostly for laughs, the subject of the war introduced primarily to motivate the more farcical aspects of Lysistrate's initiative. At 29–41 there is ominous talk of the destruction of Greece, but this is liberally sprinkled with jokes from Kalonike and soon turns into a discussion about wives' fitness for any kind of sensible action. From this point on the war is mentioned only as a force that keeps husbands and wives apart, and the emphasis is on sex. These arguments are the only ones Lysistrate needs in a discussion with the young wives; the larger issues must be reserved for her confrontation with the politicians. How different are Lysistrate's opening complaints from those of Dikaiopolis! The humor of the prologue depends mainly on the exploitation of conventional stereotypes of feminine weakness, in particular the wives' inability to resist sexual temptation and their lack of will. Aristophanes does not attack these stereotypes but exploits them. Lysistrate must see to it that the women are uncharacteristically strong until the question of the war is resolved. When the men have had a failure of will the women temporarily take their place. Whether Lysistrate's will will prove strong enough to overcome the congenital weaknesses of the wives is a question to be answered in later scenes.

Parodos (254–386)

The parodos begins a series of epirrhematic scenes (254–705) in which the Chorus – divided into semichoruses of old men and old women – takes a large and important role. In plays featuring a united Chorus this role usually ends after the parabasis, when an argument has been settled, the Chorus thereafter assuming no further decisive responsibilities. In this play the antagonistic semichoruses continue their dramatic role well after the epirrhematic section of the play, since their differences are not settled by argument. Their role is to dramatize the men's resistance to Lysistrate's occupation and to enact the hostility between the sexes that has come about as a result of the pressure of the war on the domestic sphere and the women's having taken an anti-war stance. The old women help defend the Akropolis and bolster the stance taken by Lysistrate with arguments of their own.

The epirrhematic section of the play is entirely devoted to Plan B: Lysistrate defends the occupation and demonstrates the superiority of traditional democratic and domestic values to the warlike values of current leaders. Her opponent, the Proboulos, represents the Athenian government; the women's opponents, the old men, represent the anti-Spartan hardliners who ratify Athenian policy and are temperamentally inclined to make war. Sex is not an issue here, for these men are old; Lysistrate's helpers (both the women on the Akropolis and in the Chorus) are also old. The wives of the strike are temporarily forgotten, as are the husbands against whom the strike is directed. The goal of an end to the war is not furthered in this section, for neither the Proboulos nor the Chorus of Men is convinced by Lysistrate's arguments. We do however feel that the plot moves, since new arguments are made and the Proboulos and the old men are rendered impotent.

The episodes of the sex strike actually turn out to move the plot; but these are essentially farcical and do not touch the question of war and peace. It is this epirrhematic section, essentially static, that provides the play's thematic ballast and that gives Aristophanes a forum for his arguments against the war. Comic exploitation of the foibles of the female sex is centered entirely on the wives, not on the older women of these epirrhematic scenes. The wives represent the happy home but are themselves presented ludicrously;

the defense of their importance to the polis is carried through by Lysistrate and by older women who are not sexually caricatured.

The Chorus of Men enter to iambic tetrameters, a rhythm evidently suggesting slowness and effort appropriate to the very old (especially when they are lugging a large battering ram and other siege equipment). The same meter is used elsewhere in Aristophanes' parodoi for the same purpose (*Wasps*, *Wealth*). As elsewhere the Koryphaios begins by urging his companions on (*Ach.* 204, 301; *Wasps* 230). He names Drakes (254) and is answered by the Chorus by his own name, Strymodoros. Drakes is evidently a common name (*Ekkl.* 294, cf. Soph. *Ichn.* 177) and Strymodoros seems to be appropriate for an extremely old man (*Ach.* 273, *Wasps* 233), like 'Methuselah'. Naming of individual choreutai is apparently a feature of comedy and satyr-play but not of tragedy. Here it serves to introduce characters who are for much of the play (even in trimeter sections: 387ff., 706ff., 1107ff.) as prominent as the actors. Much of the unusually extensive agonistic portion of the play is centered in the orchestra, the only opposition to Lysistrate's occupation coming from these oldsters and from the aged Proboulos whom we meet presently. As in *Acharnians* the official opposition of the polis to the protagonist's initiative, which threatens the status quo, takes the form of a group of bellicose oldsters whose negative characteristics show the war in an unfavorable light and whose opposition is easily overcome; later they admit the error of their ways. Also as in the earlier play they find a champion onstage (Lamachos, the Proboulos) who is also easily defeated but who never admits the error of his ways. But unlike *Acharnians* our play adds a new opposition to the orchestra: Lysistrate and her helpers rout their enemies on stage, while her partisans hold up their part of the action in the orchestra. Thus this Chorus plays a more prominent role in the protagonist's schemes than in any other play.

The old men display typical features of a comic type as old as Homer's Nestor: they recall and exaggerate incidents from their glorious youthful days (271ff.), incidents which make them well over 100 years old; they consider the past superior to the present (256ff.); they are angry and bellicose; they do much complaining (286ff.); they feel unappreciated by the current generation of fighters (313). Their attitude towards women is traditional and unfavorable: for these old men, who are beyond the power of eros, women are a manifest evil reared up in their own homes to the woe of the city (260f.).[84] They alone have the energy to deal with the crisis and they intend not merely to put the women back in their place but actually to burn them up in one great bonfire if need be.[85]

Fire, smoke and battering rams (symbols of anger and perhaps phallicism) dominate the first half of the parodos; the old men consider the women's occupation (whose purpose they do not know) a threat sufficiently grave to call for the attention of the generals on Samos (313). They recall their own participation in repulsing grave threats of the past: the occupation of the Akropolis by the Agiad Spartan King Kleomenes (273) and the Persian invasions themselves (285, cf. 318). For the moment these recollections are left unconnected with specific political issues; they serve only to characterize the oldsters as anti-Spartan and anti-Persian patriots, loyal (like the Acharnians) to the current leadership, as eager to press the war effort as energetically as anyone else, and prepared to resist any threats to its efficient functioning. Despite their status as decrepit emeriti and troublesome curmudgeons (blocking figures like the Proboulos), they are not unsympathetic. No doubt many in the audience shared their attitude, and in some respects (e.g. their feelings about tradition and about the Persians) they share Lysistrate's own views. It will be up to the women, as it was up to Dikaiopolis, to demonstrate to them that their patriotism is misdirected. But a debate cannot be held until their violence has been dampened: Dikaiopolis too must first disarm his pursuers. The aim of the parodos is to highlight the passions underlying the war-psychology and it does so by means of much colorful action.

Noteworthy is the way Aristophanes transforms theme into physical action and metaphor into concrete form: the battering ram with which the oldsters hope to force the 'closed gates' of Athena's citadel (Plan B) cannot fail to remind us of the domestic sex strike (Plan A). Phallicism in the form of siege is a concrete

84. For this sentiment in tragedy cf. A. *Cho.* 249, 292, S. *Ant.* 531, E. *Ion* 1262, *Andr.* 271, Fr. 429.

85. For oldsters in comedy see W. Kassies, *Aristophanes' Traditionalisme* (Amsterdam 1963) 63ff.

image emphasizing that the act of love, in which the women will no longer acquiesce, has been replaced by acts of war. As warfare by men disrupts home life, so disruption of home life by women leads to warfare in the city at large.

Anger is symbolized, as in the parodos of *Acharnians*, by fire. But here Aristophanes presents warfare differently. The parodos traditionally furthers the plot by enacting the Chorus' reaction to the protagonist's initiative. But in this parodos the question of the war does not directly come up; the Chorus does not know the reason for the women's behavior and, unlike the Acharnians, cannot take a position on the issues discussed in the prologue. Their actions – and their anger – are disengaged from any specific political stance and their embodiment of a warlike psychology is presented purely in personal terms.

The fire and smoke carried by the oldsters cause them more pain than they do their enemies: at 296ff. the smoke is like a mad beast biting their eyes (δάκνει, ἔβρυκε). δάκνειν is an old metaphor for the infliction of suffering (*Il.* 5. 493) both physical and mental (*Ach.* 17ff.).[86] Here the action gives unusual resonance to the metaphor: like anger and warfare themselves, the smoke is uncontrollable in its destructive force, turning back on those who wield it and causing them pain. The beast in the eye, symbol of anger, remains alive until late in the play, when its removal by the old women forms the basis for the final reconciliation of the semichoruses. And the idea that war and its psychology is madness will reappear. Thus in the parodos, as in the prologue, the war is not attacked from a partisan angle but more universally: the suffering it causes all citizens.

The women enter carrying water and to brighter, quicker iambochoriambic rhythms. Their leader is not named but Nikodike, a lady whose tardiness threatens to imperil the lives of Kalyke and Kritylla (two of the women on the Akropolis with Lysistrate), is told to get a move on. The women have been delayed in their defensive action by the crowd at the well: it is a humorous touch to mention in such an extraordinary context an ordinary morning's bustle to fetch water (cf. Eur. *Hipp.* 121ff.), but it also draws attention once again to the domestic front and to the disruptions

86. See J. Taillardat, *Les Images d'Aristophane*² (Paris 1965) 153f.

occasioned by war. Traditional domestic routines like water-fetching parallel the men's recollection of their traditional services to the city. The women have heard that the 'crazy old men' have come with fire and rams, and pray to Athena not to let them incinerate the women. The men have already beseeched 'Lady Victory' to grant them as signal a victory as their earlier one over Kleomenes. The women's prayer is designed to outdo the men's: 'Goddess, may I never behold these women in flames, but rather let me see them rescuing Greece and all her citizens from the insanity of war – it was for this, O golden-crested protectress of the city, that they seized your citadel. I call upon you as an ally, Tritogeneia – should any man try to burn them up – to help us carry the water!' (341–9).

The prayer is humorous, its formal style[87] contrasting with the ridiculousness of the situation and culminating in the bathetic 'help us carry the water'. But it is surely meant to touch the audience, too, by its naive and simple trust in the great goddess and by its appeal for an end of the fighting. The women see the men not only as mad but impious, too: ἔρρειν (336) is often used of going where one is not supposed to go (*Knights* 4, *Thesm.* 1075, *Frogs* 1112), and as the Koryphaia says at 351, 'Good and pious men would never have done these things.' The men, representatives of Athens at war, have compounded their violation of the home by attempting to violate Athena's citadel, now the women's sanctuary.

The rushing and the prayers at an end, the two semichoruses square off for a battle. But it is not much of a battle, for the men cower at the sight of the women (354) and their own feeble threats are answered by positively blood-curdling threats from the women. When the Koryphaios threatens to scorch his opposite number with his firebrand, he and his companions are drenched with water and taunted about their decrepitude. The Koryphaios is called a 'tomb' (372), 'Acheloos' (381), told that the drenching is a wedding shower (378) and advised to take a bath (377). Although drenching and burning are standard slapstick routines[88] the action of the parodos – an archetypal opposition of fire and water – is a fitting thematic development of the basic opposition

87. See Kleinknecht (n. 68 above) 69ff.
88. See L. Campo, *La dramma satireschi della Grecia antica* (Milan 1940) 198f.

of warlike men and peace-loving women. The domestic forces have won their first victory under the auspices of Athena. The old men are humiliated and their fighting spirit, along with their fire, considerably dampened.

Lysistrate and the Proboulos (387–613)

At this juncture the Proboulos, representing the Athenian government, enters with a retinue of police. Aristophanes has arranged things in such a way that the most unsympathetic possible male character – old, unreasonable, boastful – should represent Athenian leadership and submit to the triumph of Plan B. The husbands who actually fight the war and who are vulnerable to the strike are thus disengaged from actual responsibility for warmaking. When they appear later, gripped by intolerable sexual deprivation, we see them as sympathetic victims not only of men like the Proboulos but also of the disaffection occasioned by war itself. By the time of their entry the war has been made to seem a nuisance from which everyone with any sense longs to be liberated. The Proboulos is an ideal scapegoat, an authority-figure calculated to win little sympathy from the audience.

Like the Chorus of Men the Proboulos is ignorant of the reasons for the occupation and blames it on female lewdness. But at the start (387ff.) he has, like the Chorus of Men earlier, an historical precedent on his mind, and a recent one: the disastrous Sicilian Expedition. At the time when the Assembly was deciding to send the ill-fated armada on its way, the women were bewailing the death of young Adonis from the rooftops – the worst kind of omen when the flower of Attic youth was about to go into battle. As at 108 there may be an implicit hit at Alkibiades, the most eager and influential proponent of the expedition. In any case the Proboulos unwittingly reminds the audience of a recent disaster in which the forebodings of the city's women turned out to be more accurate than the confident predictions of the politicians. The implication is that the proponents of the expedition proceeded in the face of explicit divine warnings. And, incidentally, it was primarily to this disaster that the Proboulos owed his present position of authority.

The Chorus of Men quickly draw the Proboulos away from this touchy issue to their own risible predicament: the women have made them look like codgers unable to control their urine

(399–402). This provokes a long denunciation by the Proboulos of the wantonness of women and the gullible acquiescence of their husbands: a humorous set-piece written strictly for laughter but also reemphasizing the Proboulos' complete misunderstanding of the situation he faces. It is not women's wantonness but their strict self-control that has resulted in the occupation. The Proboulos has been outflanked. Here lies the women's advantage: they have, under Lysistrate's leadership, turned their weaknesses into strengths. The Proboulos acts on impulse and misinformation. Aristophanes' tactic is to isolate and expose this kind of mentality and demonstrate that the sane members of the Greek world do not share it. The confrontation Lysistrate/Proboulos reminds us of Diodotos/Kleon in Thukydides and Dionysos/Pentheus in Euripides' *Bakchai*.

After his speeches the Proboulos and his police attempt to break down the gates but are halted by the voluntary emergence of Lysistrate herself: 'What need of rams? This is no matter for rams but for intelligence and rationality' (431f.). But before Lysistrate has a chance to engage the Proboulos in an argument she must disarm him as her partisans had disarmed the old men. After Lysistrate and three of her stouter allies have chased the police who try to tie them up,[89] there is a battle between Lysistrate's market-women and the police that ends in the utter rout of the latter (456–61). The Proboulos, unreasonably clinging to his outmoded stereotypes, grumpily remarks that the women must be drunk to show such spirit (465f.). It is indeed a humiliation to be bested by women in a fight. But the real men of Athens must be beaten by their own desire (presented in terms of domestic sex) for a peaceful way of life; the Proboulos may simply be beaten.

Now that the Proboulos is defenseless the action narrows to an agon between him and Lysistrate.[90] Each semichorus delivers a brief and unusual speech in tetrameters (467–75), the men re-

89. The speakers of 439f., 443f. and 447f. are older women, not the wives of the prologue. At least one of them (addressed as γραῦς at 506) remains onstage to play the role of buffoon (as Kalonike had in the prologue) during the agon (505, 515, 535, 556, 561, 603, 604). Two of these women (Kritylla and Kalyke) are friends of the Chorus of Women (320). I have discussed the staging of 424–62 in *ZPE* 34 (1979) 31ff.

90. For the agon see T. Gelzer, *Der epirrhematische Agon bei Aristophanes* (Munich 1960 = *Zetemata* 23) 24ff., 57ff., 64, 130ff.

iterating their outrage and demanding further physical action, the women promising to be courteous as long as the men refrain from brawling. The divided Chorus cannot render a verdict but continue their squabbling during and after the agon. The agon itself is less a real argument on both sides of a question than a kind of rowdy news-conference in which Lysistrate, who has the upper hand to begin with, defends her actions and lectures the Proboulos on the insanity of war, the confusion of the polis and the impotence of its leaders. The Proboulos offers no counter-arguments; he merely asks indignant questions and delivers piqued responses to Lysistrate's arguments.[91]

Lysistrate's arguments in the first half of the agon are general; in the second half she provides the detail. The first half traditionally belongs to the losing side, and so the Chorus of men begin it by addressing encouragement to the Proboulos. They do not tell him to present arguments (for they do not know what the issue is) but to demand straight answers from the women about the occupation of 'our citadel', 263. Each half of the agon closes with a pnigos in which Lysistrate and her older companions on stage humiliate the Proboulos: first the Proboulos, who is unwilling to listen to anyone wearing a veil,[92] is equipped with a veil and a woolbasket (the latter anticipating the dominant metaphor in the second half of the agon). This physical reversal of sex-roles dramatizes the actual situation: the domestic sphere has taken over the civic, and the women now give orders to men; and the men must, like the women previously, listen quietly on pain of a beating. At the end of the agon the still recalcitrant Proboulos is dressed like a corpse and storms off in a rage, vowing to display himself thus humiliated to his fellow Probouloi. But in fact the Proboulos is no more useful than a corpse and disappears forever like one dead and gone.

For the first time in the play there is an opportunity to debate about the war analytically. But instead our heroine limits herself to an explanation of the rationale behind the seizure of the Akropolis (what the Proboulos demanded to know): the women will control the money needed to finance the war and purge the city

91. The development of this sort of 'Darlegungsagon' is visible also in *Birds* 462ff. and *Ekkl.* 583ff.

92. The Proboulos' attitude towards argument with a woman resembles that of Kreon at S. *Ant.* 484f., 678.

of warmongers like the Proboulos by employing methods formerly confined to the home. Her program for peace is formulated in terms of the domestic and therefore hits at the war from a point outside the traditional political structure. Aristophanes obviously feels that the time has passed for rehashing the origins and history of the war; perhaps he also feels that too direct a confrontation with the issues and persons involved would be offensive and even dangerous. And so women are the representatives of the arguments for peace: they alone, without resort to politics, can force the fighting men to acknowledge their truer instincts. The Proboulos and his kind are isolated as troublemakers. Thus is the argument against the war cast in universal rather than particular terms.

This is true even of the one particular political reference in this section (489–93): '*Pr.* So it's because of the money that we're at war? *Lys.* Yes, and that everything else was thrown into confusion, too. For it was for opportunities to steal that Peisander and those aiming for positions of power always kept stirring up some tumult. Let them do what they want about it, for all I care, because they're no longer going to be making off with this money.' The imperfects of Lysistrate's response refer to the whole course of the war from its inception; the reference to Peisander must refer to his history as a radical, pro-war democrat (*Peace* 395, Fr. 81 (*Babylonians*)), not to his current dealings with the oligarchs. 'Those aiming for positions of power' covers not only oligarchic hetaireiai (see 577f.) but all responsible for continuing the war. This is a standard Aristophanic pitch: no one benefits from the war except the corrupt politicians. Lysistrate does not care whether the warmakers are radical democrats or oligarchic plotters: whoever makes war must be stopped so that decent people may once again go about their business.

Lysistrate's opening argument is as follows: We women have taken over the Treasury to prevent the continuation of the war and to end the official corruption, political confusion and civic strife that the war engenders. We are entitled to do this because you leaders have clearly demonstrated your incompetence at managing the city. We have long experience in handling the domestic economy and can do equally well with the state economy. Thus you will be saved despite your own self-destructive instincts.

We long sat quietly at home observing your disastrous decisions;[93] our suggestions were rebuffed by blows. But as the ranks of male citizens steadily dwindled we decided to act together to save Greece. If you are willing to sit quietly, as we used to, you will hear good advice.

The Proboulos is of course unwilling to sit quietly; Lysistrate has him dressed like a woman and proceeds with her advice (551ff.): 'If Eros and Aphrodite grant us charm and afflict the men with sexual longing Greece will be saved.' This is the only reference to Plan A in the agon; the Proboulos cannot understand its meaning, so the reference is for the benefit of the audience. In fact this part of the agon sounds much like the sort of address to the audience that in other plays forms the anapestic section of a parabasis. Lysistrate's full exposition of her plans for the future must include mention of the fighting men themselves, as well as their leaders: 'Men will no longer act like madmen, roaming the market-place in arms and terrifying the people who work and shop there' (555–64; with the mention of Thracian mercenaries here cf. the Odomantians at *Ach.* 136ff.).

Then, suddenly shifting her exposition from the men to the management of the state, Lysistrate develops an extended metaphor from woolworking,[94] the climax of the play's merging of domestic and political: 'When a ball of wool becomes tangled, like the city at war, we use our spindles to put in order. In the same way, through embassies, can the tangled threads of the war be properly arranged. We must wash the filth from the city as from a ball of wool, beating out the bad and useless parts and picking away the burrs – those who clump in caucuses and knot themselves together to obtain positions of power must be combed out and their leaders plucked away. Then the wool must be carded into the basket of peace and goodwill where all useful people shall be: citizens, metics, friends. And all of our colonial cities, now strewn like fragments of a whole, must be drawn into the common ball and woven together into a mantle for all the people.'

93. 513 is an example of a general event wearisomely repeated; it does not refer particularly to the repudiation of the Treaty of 421 (Th. 5. 56. 3).

94. See W. M. Hugill, *Panhellenism in Aristophanes* (Chicago 1936) 39ff. for an extended (perhaps overextended) interpretation of the metaphor.

We shall see later that when Lysistrate comes to the actual negotiations, which must be ratified by the men of Athens and Sparta, she does not touch upon any of the really thorny problems that in real life would have to be settled. Instead she appeals to sentiment, to the idealized past and to the good things that can be enjoyed only in peacetime. So here, instead of arguing for any particular policy or strategy, Lysistrate merely instructs the Proboulos on how the city itself can be made stronger through healthy internal and external purgation. The 'sending of embassies' Lysistrate has already covertly arranged; later we shall see her brand of international diplomacy in action. As for the internal tangle, she refers to all troublemakers en masse: oligarchic conspirators, democratic warmongers and everyone else who cannot or will not benefit the city.

Aristophanes does not wish to recommend a particular internal policy or the possible concessions Athens would have to make before a peace could be arranged. But he does argue that Athens should make herself as strong as possible, so that when negotiations do come the city will be in the best position to bargain. Aristophanes takes a similar line at *Frogs* 686ff. Thus the clearest advice Aristophanes has for Athens in *Lysistrate* concerns the management of the city: eliminate all who seek private advantage and encourage everyone else to work together. It is a message couched in general terms but, as subsequent events were to prove, an important one.

The Proboulos' reaction to all this is to reiterate his opinion that women have no right to talk of war. Lysistrate answers that women bear more than their share of war, since they produce the men who fight and...Here the Proboulos silences Lysistrate, and this once she allows it, for she had indeed touched very close to home.[95] Note how drastically Lysistrate has pushed home this argument here, essentially the same argument made in a more lighthearted way before the young wives. Lysistrate follows it up by describing the plight of the young girls who remain unmarried and childless, growing old in their lonely chambers. Even old men can find brides, but a woman past her prime is useless. Thus Lysistrate's exposition returns full circle to the ravages of the war upon the homes and their custodians, to the annihilation of Athens' future.

95. A good discussion is in O. Seel, *Aristophanes oder Versuch über Komödie* (Stuttgart 1960) 79ff.

Epirrhematic scene (*614–705*)

The departure of the Proboulos rouses the Chorus of Men to a renewed attack on the Propylaia that is again repulsed by the women. On formal criteria this section is a doubled syzygy: the men deliver a strophe and their leader an epirrheme consisting of ten trochaic tetrameters; this is followed by an antistrophe and an antepirrheme from the women; then the structure is repeated. Because the Chorus is still at odds there can be no proper parabasis, that is, no address in anapests by the Chorus leader to the audience. Much of what might have been said in such a parabasis was said by Lysistrate in the agon. Instead each leader delivers two epirrhemes, a total of twenty tetrameters each, thus preserving in a fashion a common feature of parabases in which anapests are in multiples of four. Although these are agonistic each contains 'advice' to the audience based upon the leaders' different interpretations of the present crisis. Aristophanes gives another new twist to a standard parabatic feature: instead of the Chorus divesting itself (literally or metaphorically) of its choral persona in order to speak directly to the audience, Aristophanes has these semichoruses strip for battle (615, 637): an important dramatic motif, since the Chorus' undress plays a part in its final reconciliation (1019ff.). Thus this 'parabasis' contributes fully to the ongoing action although it does not itself move the plot forward.

The theme of this section is again the women's seizure of the Akropolis; the strike is not mentioned, nor is the domestic sphere. Its purpose is to conclude and summarize the defense of Plan B which has occupied Lysistrate during the confrontation with the Proboulos. The women justify their actions by claiming to be more reasonable than the men about the present plight of Athens and by stressing the importance of women's public role in Athenian life. The men reiterate their opinion that the women's action is a pro-Spartan plot to take over the city and criticizes the women for their innate wantonness. As in the parodos and agon the men offer no positive position but simply obstruct. Only the women offer positive advice.

The men's opening strophe (614–25) accuses the women of trying to set up a tyranny at the instigation of Spartan fifth-columnists. Their leader warns the audience that this is a real threat to the city and vows to be as vigilant as Aristogeiton in opposing it, even if it comes to...punching an old lady in the jaw! (626–35). The charge of plotting tyranny (a criminal offense) is, as always in earlier plays, a reference to the hated tyranny of Hippias. This kind of charge is always ridiculed by Aristophanes as a scare-tactic used by the radical democrats to discredit their opponents; it is often combined with charges of lakonizing. No doubt oligarchic movements were in fact smeared in this way. Although it is in character for the oldsters, constantly harping on the good old days, to sniff out tyranny everywhere, and although the occupying women are a ridiculous target for such charges, this kind of fear was not entirely groundless in 411. Many in the audience must have feared (not without reason) oligarchic plots in the city; Lysistrate has already made pointed allusions to secret societies and political cabals. Many had seen in Perikles and still saw in Alkibiades a new Hippias.[96] Events were soon to demonstrate the dangers of secret dealings with the enemy by Athenian factions. Nor is the reference to the oldsters' pay (624f.), which they accuse the women of trying to steal, entirely self-serving: the oldsters earned this pay, lived on it and rightly considered it an essential feature of traditional Athenian polity. But nevertheless the oldsters are thoroughly mistaken, just as the Acharnians and just as Philokleon were mistaken. The men who support the war or sit on juries get little benefit from their pittances and are only being used to line the pockets of their leaders. Lysistrate has already pointed the way for removal of these abuses.

The women do not answer the charge of conspiracy in their antistrophe (636–47) but stress their loyalty to the city by emphasizing the role of women in the city's most important cults; this may be taken as indirect support of the assimilation of Lysistrate to Lysimache. Here the women have a chance to dilate on an aspect of women's usefulness to the city hitherto not discussed. That they address this song to 'all the citizens' (638) signifies that they are saying something serious. The Koryphaia's epirrheme (648–57) further justifies the women in advising the city on a

96. But note that the references to tyranny are still jocular: by the time of the City Dionysia Aristophanes is much more seriously concerned about the possibility of a tyranny of Alkibiades (*Thesm.* 338f., 1143f.): see Sommerstein (p. 153 above) 122.

question of war and peace: much of the argument here develops what Lysistrate has already said to the Proboulos: 'Then do I not owe it (προὐφείλω) to the city to offer it some good advice? And if I am a woman do not resent me for contributing (εἰσενέγκω) something better than the current state of affairs. For I take part in making contributions (τοὐράνου), for I contribute men. But you miserable codgers take no part and make no contribution of your own (a pun on εἰσφορά = 'contribution' and 'property tax'), even though you have squandered the fund (ἔρανος) established from the Persian Wars and said to be ancestral. Thus we are still in danger of being ruined by your foolishness. If you object to being saved you will get a punch in the jaw!'

The women do not claim to be better than the men, only that good advice ought to be heard regardless of its source (we perhaps hear Aristophanes' voice, too). In this case the women have a further right – in fact obligation – to speak: from the point of view of the city they are citizens who make contributions as important as taxes and therefore have a right to protest misuse of their contributions. They will not be silenced by those who make no contributions of their own. This argument takes Lysistrate's on Plan B farther than she herself took it in lecturing the Proboulos: there the emphasis was on the superiority of the domestic in time of war and on the fact that the women were the only citizens not involved in the instigation and prosecution of the war. The women's contribution of men to the war was only briefly mentioned. Here the Chorus of Women develop that justification for the occupation and link it with women's role in cult and the right of every citizen to determine how the ancestral wealth of the city is to be spent. The reference to the Persian Wars rebuts the (mis-)use of the same patriotic allusion by the men. The old women thus strengthen in the audience's mind the connection between the traditional values of the home and the traditional values of the just polity. Again the war is attacked not in terms of international politics but from the point of view of internal disorder and its deleterious effects on traditional ways of life.

The men's response is an outraged accusation of hybris (note their similarity to the Proboulos), and another call to the attack. Their leader delivers a speech comparing the women to Artemisia and the Amazons, warning of a naval and equestrian attack and promising resistance should this occur (671–81). The speech is largely a humorous development of sexual double entendres[97] and the argument resembles the Proboulos' words at 387ff.: sexual criticism of the women is again ironic in view of the self-control that will ultimately ensure their victory. The inability of the men to answer the women's charges, and their reliance on inapposite sexual and political insults, is by itself a confession of failure and a further humiliation, just as it was with the Proboulos. Note that the men's words are written humorously; the women's are not. This is evidence for the actual alignment of the poet himself.

The men's return to the sexual level gives the women another opening and they land yet another telling blow to the men's position. After an antistrophe capping the men's threats, the Koryphaia concludes this section by celebrating the panhellenic solidarity of all women: as long as Lampito and Ismenia (the (Boiotian representative) are active you men will never win, no matter how many decrees you pass, you (poor wretch!) who are so universally hated even by our neighbors. The old men stand for all Greek men as warmongers; they ratify the decrees of leaders like the Proboulos. Divided, they cannot long oppose the united front of the women. Again, Aristophanes is at pains to distinguish the leaders from the ordinary folk who fight and suffer; these oldsters are their dupes. This is a whiff of the arguments extensively developed by Dikaiopolis against the Acharnians. The harmful consequences of current international politics are then illustrated by a droll anecdote: 'Just yesterday I planned an entertainment in honor of Hekate and invited as a companion for my daughters a nice playmate from the neighborhood[98] – an eel from Boiotia! But they said they could not send her on account of your decrees. And you will never stop passing such decrees until somebody grabs you by the leg and puts you down for the count!' (700–5). The domestic encompasses the political: a neighborhood pinic becomes a frustrated exercise in international diplomacy and peaceful coexistence. This anecdote is another time-bomb in the plot: later

97. See Henderson (n. 24 above) 161ff. As in the parodos the oldsters recall the Persian invasions.

98. Meaning the immediate neighborhood: C. Austin, *Menandri Aspis et Samia II* (Berlin 1970) 14.

we see that the women of Greece finally have their diplomatic feast, and this time it is a resounding success.

Attempted desertion (706–80)

The seizure of the Akropolis finally established and secure, the plot as envisioned by Lysistrate in the prologue resumes with the sex strike. We now learn that Lysistrate, so successful at managing the political part of her scheme, is having further difficulties with the domestic part. The young wives (the trusty older helpers of the epirrhematic section are gone) weaken in their resolve and are attempting to go back on their oath and rejoin their husbands. Lysistrate ruefully confides in the Koryphaia and mentions several comical escape attempts (717–27). Three wives emerge, each with an excuse for a furlough. The first complains that her fine linens are being ruined by moths and begs to be allowed only 'to spread them out on the bed' (728–35). But the linens must be sacrificed (734). A second wife complains that her flax needs scutching; Lysistrate gently explains that if she grants one leave she will have to grant them all (735–41). Sex is here disguised in the form of housewifely tasks, the very ones that formed the basis for Lysistrate's political recommendations to the Proboulos; thus Aristophanes adumbrates Plan B even while developing Plan A. He also reminds us that though the strike will drive the husbands wild it will also desolate the homes. The performance of domestic tasks has been suspended, or rather transferred to the political sphere and its center on the Akropolis. The premature return of the wives threatens to ruin both the domestic and the civic initiatives. These references to domestic disruption will continue during the coming Kinesias–Myrrhine scene, which has mainly to do with sexual deprivation.

The third deserter claims to be on the point of childbirth (742ff.) and demands to be dismissed on the grounds that she must not defile the holy precinct. It soon emerges that she has put Athena's helmet under dress:[99] the humor consists of a ridiculous use of a central feature of Athena's sanctuary, a pun on κυνῆν/κυεῖν, and a familiar (cf. *Thesm.* 637ff.) routine in which a character caught redhanded sticks to an untenable story. But there is a deeper

99. Thus τὴν in 751, not τήνδ' with Wilamowitz and Coulon.

symbolic significance. The scene recalls 588ff. and 648ff., where Lysistrate and the Koryphaia emphasize childbirth as their special justification for speaking out on the war and as the crucial factor in the maintenance of the Athenian state. Here maternity is an excuse for sexual indulgence that threatens the whole plan to reform the city and that would confirm the Proboulos' opinion of the female sex. But the desire for sex – dissimulated in the hollow helmet-baby (750) – also shows that the war has replaced husbands as the wives' principal concern. Athena here is the Athena of battle and resistance to eros. Lysistrate rallies the weakening wives: in a short while the men will give in. To bolster her authority she adopts a trick of the skilful politician, producing a comic oracle that convinces the wives (770–80).

Choral interlude (781–828)

Here the semichoruses continue their scurrilities; each threatens the other and jokes about the other's nakedness. To document their stance each tells a story of the once-upon-a-time variety (cf. *Wasps* 1182). The men tell of the youth Melanion, who eschewed marriage and lived in the wilderness hunting and trapping (recall Hippolytos); we are no less misogynistic than he! To the women's taunts about their unkempt pubic hair the men reply with the examples of Myronides and Phormion, whose hairiness was proof of their valor in battle. Now the women tell their own story: Timon lived in the wilderness and hated evil men, but was most friendly to women. Thus the women champion a man and stress that only evil men are to be cursed. Likewise the women hate only warmongers, not the husbands whom they desire and attempt to recall to city and household. Everywhere Aristophanes advocates removal only of troublemakers; all decent citizens, men and women alike, desire peace.

Kinesias and Myrrhine (829–979)[100]

This scene, in which Kinesias is tormented by Myrrhine, who plays the role of ridiculously dutiful wife, is pure ribald farce. For the first time Plan A is exemplified and its initial success is proven by Kinesias' huge erection. Since the plot prevents Aristophanes from

100. For the staging see above, pp. 158f. Possible analogues are *Wasps* 1208ff., Eur. *Kykl.* 544–65.

staging this as originally formulated (at home), Myrrhine must enact it in the environs of the Akropolis. This necessity of staging has a thematically happy by-product in that the transformation of the civic center into a household run by women (Plan B) continues as Plan A takes over. Unlike the Proboulos and the old men, Kinesias and the other husbands who follow him in these final scenes are desperate and do not care why the women have occupied the Akropolis. The old men worry only about Plan B; the husbands only about Plan A. Aristophanes thus dissociates the latter from the war and shows that they are eager for the pleasures of peace and for the normality of the home: someone to care for the children, run the house, provide sexual fulfilment. But they must agree to make peace first. Myrrhine successfully demonstrates this to Kinesias, who stands for all the husbands, and, just before her sudden departure, forces him to promise that he will vote for peace (951).

Aristophanes portrayed the Proboulos and the old men as unsympathetic obstructionists, but takes just as much trouble to present Kinesias rather sympathetically. His physical affliction is enough by itself to draw a derisive but understanding response from the audience. And his little soliloquy (885–8), which he delivers as Myrrhine makes her way down from the battlements, is almost touching: 'This wife of mine appears to my eyes to have become even younger and more ravishing! Even if she causes me trouble and acts haughtily, these are the very things that make me burn with desire for her!' Earlier (865ff.) he had complained to Lysistrate that he no longer enjoys life, hates to go home where all is empty, cannot even eat his food.[101] These outspoken sentiments of a man who misses his wife display real feeling that goes beyond the conventional desire for sexual satisfaction so typical of the men in Old Comedy. In Kinesias' longing for the return of Myrrhine we catch a glimpse – rare in Aristophanes – of the affection between man and wife that must have been true of many couples. The pertinence of such a glimpse to Aristophanes' present message is obvious and flows from the themes of the play. Here there is no room for the usual salacious and fantastic sexual aggrandizement that is the goal of so many Aristophanic protagonists. Kinesias must

101. These laments recall Admetos, E. *Alk.* 941; Theseus, E. *Hipp.* 1408; Medeia, E. *Med.* 226f.: cf. [Lys.] 6. 28.

represent the desire for the status quo of real-life households. But for the rest of the scene the poor man must play the unwonted roles of defendant pleading with heartless authorities; excluded lover; even the prostitute's client who must pay the bawd for his favorite (862f.: cf. 871 κάλει, a verb used to mean 'summon a lover' at *Ekkl.* 915).

After Myrrhine's final departure Kinesias and the Chorus of Men sing a duet parodying tragic laments. Kinesias stresses his despair and the Chorus answers sympathetically, if with an I-told-you-so air, adding a few hostile comments about Myrrhine. Kinesias, however, emphatically rejects this disparagement (970): 'She's not disgusting and terrible, but a darling and a sweetie!' Kinesias has been won for peace; the stubborn hostility of the oldsters will not move the husbands who fight the war. Just as Lysistrate had earlier taken away the money needed by the warmakers, so Myrrhine takes away her husband's will to fight. The Koryphaios' final prayer – may a great storm carry Myrrhine aloft and then deposit her squarely upon Kinesias' phallus – is a yearning for the impossible. The situation of the warmongers is now past hope. This is a deft employment of the kind of prayer uttered in tragedy by characters or Choruses on the eve of a great calamity.

The Spartan Herald (980–1013)

As the Chorus finishes its prayer a Spartan Herald enters and asks an Athenian onstage where he might find the Athenian Senate and Prytaneis: 'I have something important to tell them!' When asked whether he is a man or a Priapos he identifies himself and says he has come about a peace treaty. Aristophanes contrives to make the Spartans the first to buckle and sue for peace, just as he arranged to have an Athenian woman the instigator and commanding general of the peace plans. There is some byplay in which the Herald tries to conceal and then explain away his erection (compare the 'pregnant' wife earlier). Finally he admits his plight and informs the Athenian that all Sparta suffers from the same affliction. 'And whence came this evil upon you? From Pan?' 'No indeed: Lampito was ringleader, then all the Spartan women together devised a plan to keep the husbands away from their . . . twats until we all vote for a general peace' (997ff.). On hearing this the Athenian produces a fair anagnorisis in the tragic mode (1007ff.): 'This business is a universal conspiracy of the wives! I see it all just now! But you, go as quickly as you can and tell your countrymen to send ambassadors with full power to treat for peace; and, displaying this cock of mine, I'll tell the Council to choose ambassadors on our side.'

Who is the Athenian? The mss. attribute the lines to the Proboulos but this is a bad guess: the aged Proboulos (this Athenian is a young man, 983) has nothing to do with the strike nor does he have a reason to sport an erection (1012). Wilamowitz and Coulon follow a suggestion of van Leeuwen's, that 'Proboulos' was a mistake for 'Prytanis'. The only justification for this attribution is Wilamowitz's feeling that the speaker must be of sufficient stature to represent the Athenian state and call a meeting of the Council. What a time to be thinking of dignity and protocol! In any case, any Athenian could advise the Council (1011) about something important, even the lowly Blepyros (*Ekkl.* 311ff., 520ff.): cf. *Eq.* 647, Lys. 13. 21, Andok. 2. 3. 20. Furthermore, the speaker is not announced as a new arrival and should therefore be someone familiar to the audience, someone already onstage. Finally, a Prytanis would be introduced to receive the Spartan, not ask who or what he is.

As Bentley concluded from the scholion at 1014 (ἐν ἄλλῳ Κινησίας ὁ λέγων) the speaker must be Kinesias. He has not yet exited but has been sitting dejectedly where Myrrhine had left him. As representative of Athenian husbands Kinesias is dramatically and psychologically the perfect character for the initial meeting of Spartans and Athenians. After his defeat by Myrrhine he is ready to sue for peace; in further confirmation of Lysistrate's predictions he immediately meets a fellow-sufferer from Sparta. The sequence is reminiscent of tragic scenes in which the hero's laments and forebodings are terribly confirmed by the arrival of fresh bad news. Thus only Kinesias can now exclaim 'I see it all now!' (cf. Eur. *Alk.* 940, *Bakchai* 1296), and, realizing that the game is up, decide at once to set the peace negotiations in motion. There is no talk of hatred here, as there was from the Proboulos and the Chorus of Men, but only mutual recognition of a plight shared by both sides. It is surely best if the politicians initially have no role in the peace initiative, only the husbands.

The Choruses reconciled (1014–42)

Now that the fighting men have set aside their differences the antagonistic semichoruses engage in a last confrontation before they are united. The old men are the last Athenians to be brought around for peace. Since they cannot be reached by Plan A the old women must somehow soothe their anger. The Koryphaios begins by reacting to the events onstage: 'There is no beast more indomitable than a woman, not even a fire, and no panther more dangerous!' To which the Koryphaia: 'If you realize that, why keep fighting me, you naughty fellow, when you might have my friendship?' 'Because I am an eternal hater of womankind!' 'Well, that's your affair. In any case I'm not going to let you remain naked; look how ridiculous you are! But I shall walk right up to you and replace your cloak.' (All the women follow suit.) 'You women haven't done an evil thing in that, by Zeus, but no matter: it was from evil anger that I removed it in the first place!' The men are not yet mollified, though they grudingly admit the women's kindness. But they cannot hold back their tears when the women remove from their eyes the bug (symbol of mad anger since the parodos) that has been biting them. In their own way the old women show the old men what they are missing as a result of the war's disruption of normal life, just as the wives had shown the husbands. As the old men admit at 1039, 'women are impossible to live with but you cannot live without them'. The reconciliation is sealed with a kiss, which the women plant on the men 'whether you like it or not' (1036, echoing Lysistrate's words to the Proboulos at 499ff.). A metrical effect strengthens the impact of this moment: the trochaic tetrameters, hitherto resolved in the fourth foot, suddenly become regular at the moment of the kiss.

Choral interlude (1043–71)

The newly united Chorus sings a responsional song in four stanzas that concentrates on private life and anticipates the coming peace. They begin by announcing their intention to say nothing bad about any citizen but to say and do only nice things; 'for we have had enough bad things already'. This is a point in Old Comedy at which Choruses frequently sing abusive songs about people in the audience. Here Aristophanes wishes to call attention to his unwillingness to do so on the eve of his reconciliation of Athens and Sparta. The use of ἄνδρες at 1043 underlines the seriousness of this appeal for goodwill. These songs develop not abusive jokes but a (to our taste) rather simple joke: whoever wants anything from us may come and claim it – only he won't get it! Apparently this was successful, for Aristophanes uses it again at 1189ff. and in *Ekkl.* 1141ff. These songs serve only to bridge episodes and provide a bit of relief from the wild action preceding. Their focus on home and family draws our attention to the blessings that will follow the panhellenic reconciliation.

Spartans and Athenians reconciled (1072–1188)

The Koryphaios announces the entry of a distended Spartan ambassador and engages him in a brief conversation in which it emerges that the Spartan men are ready to agree to peace terms. Again the Spartans make the first move. A similarly afflicted Athenian ambassador arrives[102] and the two former belligerents, under teasing by the Koryphaios, compare notes on their desperate condition. Both agree that Lysistrate must be summoned at once to arrange the treaty. But she is already on her way (1106f.). As she had earlier (431) Lysistrate has been watching events and takes the initiative. The Koryphaios,[103] eager for a smooth conclusion of the ceremonies, hails her arrival and bids her use on the audience she has made captive all her formidable qualities of charm, cleverness and grandeur, for the Athenians and Spartans are ripe for a settlement (1108–11).

Lysistrate begins by bringing out the beautiful Diallage, symbol of reconciliation.[104] 'It won't be difficult to agree on a settlement if the men are thinking of their own desires and not fighting' (1112f.), says Lysistrate, recalling the logic of her original prediction. Diallage will keep the men's attention on sex and the

102. There is no reason to call him Prytanis (with Wilamowitz and Coulon). The mss. have 'Athenian'. He is an ambassador chosen, we suppose, by the Council on Kinesias' advice.

103. At 1093 he makes a joke about the Hermokopidai: since serious matters are to be discussed the negotiators are advised to cover their phalli. I do not see in this jocular passage any reference to Alkibiades, *pace* Sommerstein (p. 153 above) 123.

104. See H.-J. Newiger, *Metapher und Allegorie* (Munich 1957 = *Zetemata* 16) 107f., and compare the similar devices in *Ach.*, *Knights*, *Peace*, *Birds*.

longed-for return to the tranquil pleasures of peace. She is told first to take hold of the Spartans 'not roughly or highhandedly or (as our husbands are wont) boorishly, but, as is fitting for women, very homily' (οἰκείως πάνυ 1118). She repeats the conciliatory gesture already employed by the Chorus of women (1021ff.). In addition to sex, women offer gentleness and kindness. Then Diallage is instructed to do the same for the Athenians. Lysistrate jokingly suggests that if the negotiators do not offer their hands Diallage should take hold of the most convenient alternative; but the phalli have already been covered up (1093ff.).

Throughout the reconciliation scene Lysistrate's arguments are punctuated by this sort of risqué foolery and by indecent interjections by the men. Wilamowitz thought this a 'truly offensive' aspect of the scene.[105] But Aristophanes is merely fulfilling the thematic logic of the play in a concrete way; he is also easing the tension of a potentially overcharged moment. It is normal for serious speeches to be interrupted by jokes: recall Kalonike in the prologue and the old lady in the agon.

Lysistrate's proposed settlement is formulated along familiar lines: peace is viewed in terms of an idealized past and emphasizes the personal, the traditional, the nostalgic, the sensual. International politics and their complexities are best viewed, according to Aristophanes, from the vantage point of a happy city conscious of its best traditions. Diallage keeps the audience's attention on the pleasurable side of peace and makes the real-life morass seem far away. Lysistrate's speech is not at all humorous and is therefore intended to be taken seriously; her audience is the party given to humor. That they think more about Diallage than about politics is the natural outcome of Lysistrate's plan.

After justifying her claim to address leaders ('I am a woman but I, too, can reason. I have managed on my own to acquire no mean judgment; from listening often to the words of my father and other older men I have become fairly well-educated', 1124–7, cf. *Ekkl.* 473f.), Lysistrate begins her tripartite speech. First she rebukes the Spartans and Athenians alike (1128–35): although the two states have always enjoyed the religious and cultural unity represented by the great panhellenic festivals, and although the

105. P. 59, cf. at 1136.

Persians are their traditional enemy, Athens and Sparta go on fratricidally (ξυγγενεῖς 1130) destroying each other's men and cities. This program has been well prepared in the course of the play. Lysistrate and the Chorus of Women have consistently emphasized (and in a sense embodied) both the supreme importance to Athenian democracy of its best values and traditions and that the present war amounts to impiety and cultural self-destruction. Earlier the focus was on internal disorder; now the same lesson is applied to international relations. Mention of the Persians continues an important theme of the play. All the major battles of the Persian invasions (τὰ μηδικά 653) are mentioned: Marathon (285), Salamis (675), Artemision and Thermopylai (1247ff.).[106] As a tradition the Persian invasions represent the good old days when all Greece stood united under the joint hegemony of Athens and Sparta against barbarians. As a political reality the Persians represent for Aristophanes a continuing threat. The present passage rebukes both sides[107] for angling for Persian gold as a way to prolong and win the war. No doubt many Athenians hoped to replace Sparta as Persia's ally; secret negotiations were already underway (Th. 8. 53. 2–3). Aristophanes had expressed the same opinion ten years previously (*Peace* 108, 406ff., 1082); now he suggests that a return to the old arrangement will solve the present crisis. The reply of the Athenian (1136) rounds off this first *logos* (1135): he is not really listening but thinking only of his lust, as Lysistrate had planned (1112f.).

Now Lysistrate turns to the Spartans (1137–56). After what has preceded it is not surprising that she mentions Kimon here: how can you desolate Attika after Kimon once saved all Sparta when earthquake and revolt threatened her annihilation? The reference is to the hoplite army Kimon sent to relieve the embattled Spartiates in their siege of the revolting Messenians on Ithome (*c.* 462).[108] Kimon was a faithful friend of Sparta, whose proxenos he was, and his embarrassing dismissal from Ithome spelled the end

106. Not Plataia, where the Boiotians (included in Lysistrate's peace) played what would have been considered an embarrassing role.

107. Dover (n. 6 above) 170 sees 1133f. (with the scholiast) as self-congratulatory in the mouth of an Athenian. But in the present context the criticism must tell against both sides (κοινῆι 1129).

108. 'Four thousand hoplites' might be an exaggeration (1143) like 'six years' at 280.

of his policy of an Athenian–Spartan hegemony. In fact his dismissal was a milestone in the history of enmity between the two states.[109] Lysistrate urges the Spartans to rectify that wrong now and embrace the Kimonian ideal as the securest foundation for their foreign policy.

At 1147 the Athenian says, 'By Zeus, they're in the wrong, Lysistrate!', to which the Spartan replies, 'We're in the wrong; but what an unspeakably pretty ass-hole!' (1148). Then Lysistrate, beginning a new *logos* (1149), 'Do you think I'm going to let you off, Athenians?' What is happening here? As at 1136 the men ogle Diallage and hardly listen. The Spartans, notorious for their fondness for anal intercourse, think of Diallage's hindquarters: thus at 1152f. the Spartan says that he has never seen a χαϊωτέραν woman (cf. 91), to which the Athenian replies, 'And I've (never seen) a lovelier cunt!' This ethnosexual joke forms the basis for the arrangement of peace terms to come and is a leitmotif of the entire scene. Wilamowitz, observing that line 1149 is awkard after the Spartan speaks, assigns 1148b to the Athenian. But that ruins the joke. I suggest instead that 1147 and 1148 were reversed in the copying by homoiarchon (ἀδικου-): following the speech of Lysistrate rebuking the Spartans, the Spartan admits wrongdoing; when the Athenian chimes in his agreement Lysistrate turns on him with 'Don't think *you're* going to get off!'

Now Lysistrate lectures the Athenians (1149–56): don't you remember how the Spartans helped you free yourselves from the yoke of Hippias' tyranny and replaced your servile rags with the cloaks of free men? Here Lysistrate answers the charge of tyranny leveled by the Chorus of Men: the Spartans are tyrant-haters too! Again, an incident from the past is made the basis for present policy: just as Athens helped Sparta in her perennial effort to maintain Spartiate rule, so Sparta helped Athens in her establishment of democracy. Lysistrate thus appeals to the deepest-rooted fears of both states: overthrow of Spartiate rule, overthrow of democracy.

Her speech at an end, Lysistrate turns to the settlement itself, negotiated by means of sexual double entendres and therefore

109. See de Ste Croix (n. 83 above) 180–3.

entirely farcical.[110] Aristophanes has no desire to bring up strategic difficulties that would have to be faced in real life, but instead focuses on sexual pleasures and the allurements of a happy normality said to be characteristic of the days before the war. The close of *Archarnians* presented a similar focus.

After the two sides assure Lysistrate that their allies will go along with the terms of the treaty ('Aren't we all eager to fuck?' says the Athenian, 1178f.), Lysistrate in the name of all the women invites the ambassadors to a banquet on the Akropolis for the official ratification. By a typical Aristophanic stroke all the wives (including the Spartans') suddenly appear with picnic baskets (*kistai*). The food is carried in these and this reminds us that the homes will soon function again. The pun on *kistai* (also female genitals) provides thematic cohesion. As Vaio remarks,[111] 'For the last time the Acropolis (ἐν πόλει 1183) functions as the setting for their political regime. Soon wives and husbands will return to their homes, now made safe by the women, who have succeeded in turning the conduct of public life into an expression of their own domestic wisdom.' As all exit through the Propylaia the Chorus sings another bridging song quite similar to the song at 1143ff.

110. The Spartans ask for and get the hindquarters (ἔγκυκλον, Πύλος 1161–3: see p. 164 above); the Athenians get the pubic hair (ἐχινοῦς) and vagina (Μηλιᾶ κόλπον) behind it (τὸν ὄπισθεν), as well as the 'Megarian legs' (1168–70), despite a Spartan objection that the Athenians want everything. Perhaps this is a lighthearted allusion to Athenian imperial rapacity. For the details see J. Henderson, *AJP* 96 (1975) 344ff. This settled, the Athenian announces his intention to strip down and start plowing. The Spartan is ready to gather dung (a joke about anal intercourse), 1173f. Lysistrate tells them they may do this as soon as they ratify the settlement. Hugill's interpretation (n. 94 above) of the reference to Megara is worth quoting: 'In this remark Aristophanes gives himself a final opportunity to urge that Megara and her walls be allowed no longer to disturb the peace of Greece. The mention of Megarian legs by the Athenians is a pathological symptom of vestigial recalcitrance, and their demand is meant to illustrate the long pursuit of wrong ambition and inveterate error which Lysistrate now finally succeeds in eradicating' (pp. 32f.). But as de Ste Croix (n. 83 above) has shown, the 'Megarian Question' was less an actual cause de guerre than a propaganda issue; by the time of *Lysistrate* a reference to the Megarians may well have struck the audience as an amusing recollection of an issue that had lost its power.

111. Vaio (n. 1 above) 379f.

The final scenes

At 1216ff. the text has suffered corruption and the action is difficult to reconstruct. Certainly the Athenian speaker who enters carrying a torch has come from the banquet now ending. There is no reason to call him Prytanis (Wilamowitz and Coulon). He is followed at 1221 by another Athenian with, it seems, less authority. We will not go far wrong by imagining the first Athenian to be the ambassador of the previous scene (still responsible for his Spartan guests) and the second to be one of the other delegates; actually he is introduced simply as an interlocutor. The first Athenian threatens and probably assaults[112] a gatekeeper standing watch outside the Propylaia (1216) and then menaces a crowd of slaves (cf. 1240) which has gathered, ready to escort their masters home. The bullying of slaves is a tried and true crowd-pleaser (sometimes even in tragedy: Eur. *Or.* 1369ff.) and appears elsewhere in Aristophanes (cf. *Wasps* 1326ff., *Wealth* 1052ff.). The poet, realizing the low level of comedy yielded by such a trite device, sometimes apologizes for using it (*Ekkl.* 888f.) and sometimes denies using it at all (*Clouds* 543). So here Aristophanes makes selfconscious reference to his own technique: *Ath. I* (From inside to the gatekeeper): Open the door! (The gatekeeper obeys and is shoved out of the way by the speaker) You ought to have got out of the way! (A group of Athenian[113] banqueters emerges with torches) (To the slaves) You there – why are you sitting here? Want me to set you afire with my torch? (The slaves scatter) (To the audience) What a clownish device! I won't do it! (At least some in the audience shout encouragement) Well, if we *must* we'll take the trouble of doing you all that favor. *Ath. II* (To Ath. I): Yes, and we'll gladly help you take that trouble! *Ath. I* (Again menacing the slaves): Make way! Your hair will surely suffer! Get away so the Spartans can come out and go home happily after their dinner. *Ath. II*: I've never beheld[114] such a party in all my born days! Yes,

112. This would explain 1216b, which must be emended to give the sense, 'You ought to have got out of the way.'

113. The Spartans first emerge at 1241.

114. ὄπωπα 1225 is taken by Wilamowitz (and Dover, n. 6, above, p. 11) to indicate a Spartan speaker. But the Spartans have not yet emerged and if 1225 were spoken by a Spartan it is strange that the remark is ignored by the speakers

these Spartans were quite charming: and we are pretty clever ourselves when there's plenty of wine at the party!

The Athenian ambassador now reports on the banquet (1228–40). Impressed by the Spartans' charm and the ease of the negotiations, he vows to persuade the Athenians to conduct all future foreign policy drunk:[115] 'We don't show good sense when we're sober!...For as it is whenever we go to Sparta sober we start looking for trouble to stir up; we don't listen to what they say and suspect they're saying what they don't say and as a result we're always at cross-purposes. But now everything is fine.' An excess of food and drink, the common reward of successful comic schemes (*Ach.*, *Peace*, *Birds*, *Ekkl.*), are to be elevated henceforth to the status of official protocol.

The first Athenian once again routs the crowd of slaves to make a path for the emerging Spartans, who are accompanied by a special flute-player (cf. *Thesm.* 1175ff.). This flute differs from the Attic aulos and the novelty is part of the fun: compare the ostinoi of the Boiotian at *Ach.* 863. To the accompaniment of this player and at the command of the Spartan ambassador one of the Spartans performs a dance (the dipodia) and sings a song recalling the exploits of Athens and Sparta as together they expelled the Persian foe from Greece and prays that the newly negotiated friendship between the two cities will be a happy one (1247–72).

At this point the text must be rearranged (van Leeuwen):[116] lines 1273–94, which ought to end the play (1292ff. is identical with the close of other comedies), were inserted by the archetype in the wrong place. The Spartan's first song should be followed by 1295–1321; 1273–94 end the play. There is no need to assume the loss of the ending.

Impressed by the Spartan's song and dance the Athenian ambassador requests yet another song (1295). This time he sings in praise of Sparta, the happier Sparta of bygone days when the banks of the Eurotas resounded with music and dancing, and hymns Athena, protectress of both cities and inhabiter of the

of 1226ff., who discuss among themselves the favorable impression made by the Spartans at the banquet. Most likely the word is a colloquial elevation of speech; it is found in tragic dialogue.

115. For the joke, cf. *Ekkl.* 139, *Wealth* 1047f.

116. Also S. Srebrny, 'Der Schluss der Lysistrate', *Eos* 51 (1961) 39ff.

citadel before which the play has largely taken place. Now the Athenian ambassador bids the Spartans reclaim their wives (1273) and every couple stand together again, 'now that everything has worked out so well'. Wishing everyone good luck, he asks that all exit dancing in a hymn to the gods and hopes that no one will again transgress against his neighbor. To a hymn from the Chorus praising Athena and Aphrodite, all march off, a mute Lysistrate among them.

War and peace in the comedy of Aristophanes

HANS-JOACHIM NEWIGER*

The successful production in recent years of the so-called peace plays of Aristophanes in a number of German theaters provides a challenge for classical scholars to renew analysis of these comedies.[1] Peter Hacks' adaptation of *Peace*, which opened in Berlin, has been a popular success in many theaters. *Acharnians*, in the adapted translation of Wolfgang Schadewaldt, was accepted much less readily, but *Lysistrata*, for many years the most frequently performed comedy of Aristophanes, has since 1972 had outstanding success in a new translation by Schadewaldt.[2] In this essay I shall attempt to answer the challenge posed by these theatrical successes primarily by examining the differences between the three comedies in their treatment of war and peace. In addition, I hope to demonstrate an aspect of *Lysistrata* that has until now received scant notice.

Accordingly, let us turn directly to the question of exactly how Aristophanes represents war and peace in his peace-plays and how he brings the concept of peace to dramatic life on the stage; for while he manages to accomplish peace in all three comedies, the nature and presentation of peace differ greatly from play to play.

* Translated by Catherine Radford (= 'Krieg und Frieden in der Komödie des Aristophanes', ΔΩΡΗΜΑ: *Hans Diller zum 70. Geburtstag. Dauer und Überleben des antiken Geistes* (Athens 1975) 175–94).

1. This essay represents the abridged draft of a lecture which I gave apropos of the new production of W. Schadewaldt's adaptation of *Lysistrata* in the winter of 1972 at the Deutsches Theater in Göttingen, and afterwards before different associations in Berlin, Bremen, Hamburg and Konstanz, as well as at the Universities of Bern and Kiel – this last on 20 November 1973 in the presence of Hans Diller, to whom I therefore dedicate this essay. In keeping with the original design, the scholarly references are very selective.

2. Aristophanes is frequently performed in Greece. In 1974 the festival program featured performances of *Lysistrata* at Epidaurus, *Thesmophoriazusae* at Philippi and Dodona, *Birds* at Philippi, Dion and Athens, *Frogs* at Athens – in the ancient theaters themselves. I do not know how many presentations fell victim to the crisis in Cyprus, but in Athens on 20 September I had the pleasure of witnessing *Frogs* performed before a vivaciously sympathetic audience.

The action of *Acharnians*, produced in 425, the sixth year of the Peloponnesian War, is highly political from the very opening scene. The farmer, Dicaeopolis, is shocked that all attempts to deliberate about peace in the Assembly have failed. During the Assembly (represented as exceedingly grotesque) he sends a certain Amphitheos (whose name means 'divine on both sides [of the family]') to Sparta to negotiate a private peace solely for himself and his family. At the end of the Assembly Amphitheos has already returned and offers Dicaeopolis three kinds of peace, or, more precisely, three kinds of peace treaty embodied by three types of wine. 'Treaty' in Greek is αἱ σπονδαί, an offering, consisting of libations solemnly poured at the conclusion of a treaty. The designation 'five-', 'ten-', or 'thirty-year' can thus be as accurately attributed to the wine itself as it can to the treaty. Dicaeopolis naturally chooses the thirty-year wine and with it the thirty-year treaty, as it had existed before the outbreak of the war between Athens and Sparta.[3]

If we have already seen in the Assembly-scene that peace is in no way desired by the majority of Athenians, we are again made aware of its unpopularity when the chorus of Acharnians appears in the following scene. They are looking for the wretch who brings peace with Sparta (Amphitheos) in order to stone him, but instead come upon Dicaeopolis. This situation requires some historical background. The Acharnians, who form the chorus of the play and give it its title, are the inhabitants of the most thickly populated deme of Attica, which alone provided 3,000 hoplites.[4] They had especially suffered from the invasions and pillaging which the Spartans carried out in Attica almost every summer. The country population, having retreated according to Pericles' war plan into the city during these enemy incursions, had to surrender their land to destruction. Athens had formed behind her famous 'long walls' a single fortified area including the harbors of Piraeus and Phalerum. Here the country population had been dwelling on and

3. Here as elsewhere in this essay my explanations, as the expert will recognize, are based upon the interpretations given in my book *Metapher und Allegorie* (Munich 1957) 52f., 104–27, and appear without reference to specific passages.

4. Thucydides (2. 20) gives this number, but it may need to be corrected to 1200. See A. W. Gomme, *A Historical Commentary on Thucydides II* (Oxford 1956) 73f. *ad loc.*

off for a few months, miserably and to some extent without proper housing. Many remained in the city, since their farms had been irreparably destroyed and their farm work either constantly interrupted or rendered useless altogether. In addition, there was frequent military service and guard duty. These people, forced by cruel circumstances to endure a city life quite alien to them, were of divided minds. They wanted to return to the country to rebuild their farms in peace, but they were also filled with rage at the enemy who had injured them so grievously. They were now frequent participants in the Assembly, whereas in peacetime, because of their work and their distance from Athens, they had exercised their political rights only sporadically. They were less experienced in politics and therefore perhaps easier to influence.

The farmer, Dicaeopolis, personifies the desire for peace and the impulse to return to the countryside and its ancestral way of life. The Acharnians, rough charcoal-burners sorely distressed by the war, confront him; hatred for the enemy prevails among them and with it the will for war. Now Dicaeopolis alone has his peace and is celebrating his Dionysus festival in the country with a phallic procession when the Acharnians assail him. He succeeds in obtaining a hearing only by saying that he holds hostages, that is, pieces of charcoal, which by comic metaphor become valued countrymen of the charcoal-burners from Acharnae. He stakes his head, which he promises to lay on the chopping-block, on the assertion that he has convincing arguments for peace. This metaphor is presently made literal. The chopping-block comes onto the stage; he lays his head on it; but for a while he does not present his arguments. On the contrary, he first wants to dress up as a tragic beggar-hero, since otherwise he would not appear pitiable enough. We are thus diverted from the arguments against the war for over a hundred verses by an exquisite scene in which our hero borrows a tragic costume from none other than the tragic poet, Euripides. Tragic parody displaces politics, and we are made aware that in this comedy the poet is parodying a series of episodes and dialogues from Euripides' *Telephus*.[5]

Now Dicaeopolis, his head on the chopping-block, makes his great political speech. But, leaving to one side the affirmation that

5. Cf. P. Rau, *Paratragodia* (Munich 1967) 19–50, who cites the earlier literature.

'even Comedy stands up for truth and right', he brings forth no serious discussion but instead represents the causes of, and responsibility for, the war in a manner at once highly flippant and highly literary: the cause of the war was the kidnapping of women, and the audience is meant to recall not only fair Helen and the Trojan War, but most of all the reciprocal rapes at the beginning of Herodotus' history! This is the argument (524–39):[6]

> But some young tipsy cottabus-players went
> And stole from Megara-town the fair Simaetha.
> Then the Megarians, garlicked with the smart,
> Stole, in return, two of Aspasia's hussies.
> From these three Wantons o'er the Hellenic race
> Burst forth the first beginnings of the War.
> For then, in wrath, the Olympian Pericles
> Thundered and lightened, and confounded Hellas,
> Enacting laws which ran like drinking-songs,
> *That the Megarians presently depart*
> *From earth and sea, the mainland, and the mart.*
> Then the Megarians, slowly famishing,
> Besought their Spartan friends to get the Law
> Of the three Wantons cancelled and withdrawn.
> And oft they asked us, but we yielded not.
> Then followed instantly the clash of shields.

Although Dicaeopolis' speech brings half of the chorus over to his side, the other half calls in the war-hero, Lamachus, as their supporter. This Lamachus, who comes forward in a martial manner, is lustily ridiculed by Dicaeopolis, and here another metaphor is made literal: the farmer manages to get hold of the officer's helmet and a feather from its plume, tickles himself in the throat with the feather and vomits into the helmet, because to him helmets are, if the expression may be excused, only for puking into.

Finally, by emphasizing the great gulf that separates officers and office-holders on the one side from the mass of have-nots (to which the Acharnians belong) on the other, Dicaeopolis brings the rest of the chorus over to his side. In the parabasis that follows the chorus praises the courage and merit of the young poet and laments the ill-treatment of old people in the city, particularly in the courts. This we may pass over.

6. The English translations are those of B. B. Rogers.

The remainder of the play represents the contrast between war and peace in scenes simultaneously comical and symbolic. We see chiefly how Dicaeopolis, with his private peace, can obtain a succession of bodily pleasures from hostile foreigners, since he now has a kind of open market. His behaviour, however, is shown to be purely egotistical, and neither in a bourgeois-political nor in a personal sense does he behave in an altruistic or social manner. He refuses to give a share of the profits he has gained to anyone else.[7] The opposition between war and peace reaches its climax (and the comedy its conclusion) in a sequence of scenes which contrast the separate destinies of Colonel Lamachus and the carousing farmer Dicaeopolis. Peace is manifested exclusively in bodily pleasures of an erotic as well as a culinary nature. Lamachus receives an order, now, in the middle of winter, to garrison the passes to Boeotia, where an enemy invasion threatens, but Dicaeopolis is invited to a banquet and drinking contest at a great festival. In a section of stichomythic dialogue both men make their separate preparations. The chorus concludes the scene with the following suggestive strophe (1143–9):

> Off to your duties, my heroes bold.
> Different truly the paths ye tread;
> One to drink with wreaths on his head;
> One to watch, and shiver with cold,
> Lonely, the while his antagonist passes
> The sweetest of hours with the sweetest of lasses.

This fundamental opposition of war and peace is maintained in the closing scene.[8] Once more our heroes, their concerns as different as their destinies, return: Lamachus from battle, wounded in the leg and supported by two soldiers; Dicaeopolis from feasting, thoroughly drunk and supported by two girls. Both heroes express their condition in parallel verses (1190–1202):

> Lamachus: O lack-a-day! O lack-a-day!
> I'm hacked, I'm killed, by hostile lances!
> But worse than wound or lance 'twill grieve me
> If Dicaeopolis perceive me
> And mock, and mock at my mischances.

7. Cf. K. J. Dover, *Aristophanic Comedy* (London 1972) 86ff.

8. I have intentionally overlooked the messenger's speech (1174–89) with its notorious textual and interpretive difficulties. For the various interpretations cf. A. M. Dale, *BICS* 8 (1961) 47–8 (= *Collected Papers* (Cambridge 1969) 170–2; cf. also pp. 292f.); P. Rau, *Paratragodia* 139ff.; M. L. West, *CR* 21 (1971) 157f.

Dicaeopolis: O lucky day! O lucky day!
What mortal ever can be richer,
Than he who feels, my golden misses,
Your softest, closest, loveliest kisses.
'Twas I, 'twas I, first drained the pitcher.

The sexuality becomes still more apparent in the following section, but I believe that even here the contrast between war and peace is evident. The comedy ends with the departure of an exceedingly dissipated Dicaeopolis, with his retinue of female companions and the chorus, to accept a wine-skin, his victory prize. The exuberance of a country Dionysus-festival thus provides the conclusion.

Through supernatural and magical means a single dissatisfied person obtains an utterly unreal private peace whose joys, portrayed from the standpoint of the farmer, are of a primarily culinary and sexual nature; these joys are then contrasted with the unpleasantness ('horrors' would be too strong an expression) of war. There is no talk of the preservation of the fatherland or even of the extension of this private peace to other sufferers.[9]

War and Peace do not appear as characters on the stage in this comedy as they do in the next peace-play, *Peace* of 421; rather, the peace treaty is symbolized concretely in the wine of the drink-offering accompanying the treaty. But in the poet's words and in the songs of the chorus, war and peace (or more precisely, war and reconciliation) are in fact already represented as characters in *Acharnians*; we can thus find a bridge to *Peace* as well as to *Lysistrata* purely in the play's imagery and the poet's conceptions. Of Πόλεμος, War, it is said in *Acharnians* (978–87):

War I'll never welcome in to share my hospitality,
Never shall the fellow sing Harmodius in my company,
Always in his cups he acts so rudely and offensively.
Tipsily he burst upon our happy quiet family,
Breaking this, upsetting that, and brawling most pugnaciously.
Yea when we entreated him with hospitable courtesy,
Sit you down, and drink a cup, a Cup of Love and Harmony,
All the more he burnt the poles we wanted for our husbandry,
Aye and split perforce the liquor treasured up within our vines.

War is an evil table companion, a drunkard who in spite of every attempt at appeasement dashes to pieces all that is dear to the peasant. This is less than a depiction of the actual horrors of war,

9. Cf. Dover, *Aristophanic Comedy* 87f.

but more than a description of the inconveniences involved in military service, wretched lodgings in the city and the renunciation of many bodily pleasures. It must be stressed, however, that in the representation of war in *Acharnians* a high propriety holds sway: no mention is made of the dead and Lamachus' injury is represented as a ridiculous mishap.

Of Διαλλαγή, Reconciliation, the chorus sings (989–99):

O of Cypris foster-sister, and of every heavenly Grace,
Never knew I till this moment all the glory of thy face,
RECONCILIATION!
O that Love would you and me unite in endless harmony,
Love as he is pictured with the wreath of roses smilingly.
Maybe you regard me as a fragment of antiquity:
Ah, but if I get you, dear, I'll show my triple husbandry.
First a row of vinelets will I plant prolonged and orderly,
Next the little fig-tree shoots beside them, growing lustily,
Thirdly the domestic vine; although I am so elderly.
Round them all shall olives grow, to form a pleasant boundary.
Thence will you and I anoint us, darling, when the New Moon shines.

Reconciliation, like 'treaty' another word for peace, is portrayed as a longed-for bride. Agricultural metaphors paraphrase love-making and procreation – a connection obvious to an Athenian audience, for the official Attic wedding ceremony contains the phrase 'for the ploughing of legitimate children' (ἐπὶ παίδων γνησίων ἀρότῳ).

The bride of the wine-grower Trygaeus, who brings about the peace in *Peace*, is not the goddess of peace herself (that would be, according to Greek thought, hybris and sacrilege)[10] but her attendant Opora ('Οπώρα), the Harvest, a happy invention of Aristophanes and a personification typical of those which occur abundantly in this comedy. In a manner immediately clear to those of an anthropomorphic cast of mind, the poet creates in these personifications partners for the plot, or even characters participating in the action whose symbolic names emphasize the main issues of the plot. If the Harvest is intended for the farmer Trygaeus, so another attendant of the goddess of peace, Theoria (Θεωρία), which I might translate 'Festival', is designated for the Council of Athens. We are to understand that as a result of peace it will become possible to hold festivals outside of Athens, and that

10. Cf. Alcman Fr. 1. 16f. P.: 'No man should seek to fly to heaven, nor to marry Aphrodite...'

the Council must concern itself with them as part of its authority. And the manner in which the Council could 'concern itself' with the young female character, Theoria, embodiment of the festival, is reflected once more in sexual imagery made possible by Theoria's sex. Thus in Theoria and Opora, Festival and Harvest, the spiritual union (the Council is concerned with the festival, the farmer with the harvest) is represented as carnal union and sensual activity. I might add at this point that as early as *Knights*, performed the year after *Archarnians*, the peace treaty, symbolized in the previous year concretely as wine, is now procured for the rejuvenated Sir Demos (Δῆμος), the embodiment of the Attic people as politically sovereign, in the guise of two maidens (Σπονδαί, in accordance with the plural *feminini generis*), and thus as actual characters. The nameless girls with whom Dicaeopolis appeared at the end of the play as a sign of his joyousness and as objects for his delight have now, in *Knights* and *Peace*, become maidens with symbolic names that impart immediate significance to the action of the play. A metaphorical manner of speaking is thus taken literally and represented symbolically on stage.

This transformation of the metaphorical into the literal also underlies the scenes of the first half of *Peace*, which I consider to be among Aristophanes' most brilliant conceptions. Trygaeus wants to fetch from heaven the peace which has disappeared, and rides there on a dung-beetle. A metaphor – 'to fetch from heaven', which ought to express an impossibility – is actually staged, and for the fantastic and ingenious art of comedy the impossible turns out to be thoroughly possible. Moreover, because the ride on the dung-beetle also parodies the ride of a tragic hero on the winged horse Pegasus, the scene gains another stratum of meaning and a further dimension.[11] The task of bringing back peace (which in Greek is feminine, Εἰρήνη) in the form of a statue of the goddess of peace naturally proves to be difficult. The difficulties of peace negotiations are symbolized by the stones heaped up before the cave in which the goddess of peace has been confined by War, and by the labors of Greeks from all tribes and cities as they try to haul the goddess back into the light. The farmers, having an especially strong interest in peace, finally succeed in recovering the goddess together with her companions, with whom we have already become

11. Cf. Rau, *Paratragodia* 89ff.

acquainted. Here again is a marked complexity of dimension: the recovery of an object by means of a chorus pulling on a rope has its prototype in a satyr play of Aeschylus in which the satyrs drag a chest, in which the heroine Danae has been abandoned with her little son Perseus, from the sea by means of a rope.[12] I believe that we can here recognize remarkably well the workings of the poet's fantasy and the comic technique by which he transposes important and meaningful models and ideas into a grotesque-comic plot.

To return, however, to War. He (Πόλεμος) and his companion Tumult (Κυδοιμός) appear, before the rescue of the entombed Peace from her cave becomes at all possible, *in persona* on the stage, not, as in the lyrics of *Acharnians*, as evil houseguests, but as a cook and his handyman. This cook is much more dangerous than the drunken guest in *Acharnians*; he wants to pulverize in a mortar the belligerent cities, which are symbolized through their agricultural products: cheese for Sicily, onions for Megara, honey for Attica, and so forth. But his handyman Tumult can no longer procure for him a pestle or pounder to carry out the destruction. The Spartans as well as the Athenians have lost their pestle, and thus the war-cook is deprived of his craft – he can make nothing without a pestle. Trygaeus seizes this opportunity to drag Peace out into the light. The pestles are of course the generals of both sides, Cleon and Brasidas, who until now (to continue the metaphor) had served as tools for war; but now they have fallen in the same battle. With the pestle Aristophanes resumes a comparison he has used before: in *Knights* the detested Cleon was compared to a pestle by which everything is tossed into confusion and mixed up. What was previously expressed in metaphorical language is here enacted in a scene on stage.

In conclusion we can say of this play that the peace brought about here is both real and truly panhellenic. Trygaeus does not obtain a private but rather a universal peace, and, totally unlike Dicaeopolis, deserves well of his city and of all Greece. The chorus, appearing on behalf of all the Greeks, represents the common struggle for peace. Peace might be seen here again predominantly from the perspective of the farmer; the spirit of a panhellenic conception, however, of a peace for all cities and classes, imbues the first part of this comedy. On the other hand, in contrast with

12. Cf. Rau, *Paratragodia* 194.

Acharnians, the play is less a protest against the war than a celebration of the official conclusion of the peace treaty[13] which followed at most ten days after the performance. A British colleague formulates, 'Thus Trygaios is not the mouthpiece of a far-sighted minority lamenting the continuation of an apparently unending war, but a man who performs on a level of comic fantasy a task to which the Athenian people had already addressed itself on the mundane level of negotiation.'[14]

Ten years later in 411, four years after the second outbreak of the war and in a time of great tribulation, Aristophanes produced *Lysistrata*.[15] In the autumn of 413 Athens had not only lost vast numbers of troops in Sicily, almost her entire fleet and her most capable generals, but since the spring of 413 the Spartans, on the advice of the turncoat Alcibiades, had established themselves under King Agis in Decelea,[16] only fifteen miles from Athens, and from there maintained continuous control over the Attic countryside. The conditions of the Archidamian War, so monstrous for the country folk, but during which it had only been necessary to withdraw behind the city walls for a few months at a time, now became permanent. Provisioning the city-dwellers also became more difficult because command of the sea was no longer certain, and it was believed throughout Greece that Athens would soon be forced to capitulate. Slaves deserted to the enemy in droves, the silver mines at Laurium had to be shut down, and most of the allies were becoming disaffected.

But Athens continued the war with unbelievable obstinacy. Through the introduction of new tariffs and the expenditure of her last financial reserves she built a new fleet, and in the autumn of

13. Even C. M. J. Sicking, 'Aristophanes laetus?' Κωμῳδοτραγήματα (Amsterdam 1967) 115ff., will not deny that it has happened thus *de facto*; that, however, a better peace than that of Nicias was desired is certainly correct. When Sicking finds it 'more correct to interpret the majority of Aristophanic comedies as imaginary solutions to a menacing state of affairs perceived by the poet as problematic', and stresses the ἀδύνατον in his comedies, he must be certain of universal agreement.

14. Dover, *Aristophanic Comedy* 137.

15. At the Lenaea, as I assume in spite of Th. Gelzer, 'Aristophanes der Komiker', *RE Suppl.bd.* 12 (1971) 1467–9, 1473–5; cf. also Dover, *Aristophanic Comedy* 150, 169–72.

16. On the hill, in fact, on which the cemetery chapel of the former Greek royal house stands today.

412, at approximately the time when Aristophanes was putting the final touches on *Lysistrata*, over one hundred ships, based on Samos, stood off the Ionian coast of Asia Minor. In Athens, the saying resounded just as it had fourteen years earlier, 'Let the war continue!' The women at the beginning of *Lysistrata* also use this saying (ὁ πόλεμος ἑρπέτω, 129f.) as they hear what they must do to end the war.

Athens' perilous external situation went hand-in-hand with an extremely threatening domestic situation. The military failures of the democratic administration gave the oligarchs their opportunity to restrict and perhaps even eliminate the democracy which since Pericles' death had become more and more radical and whose leaders were the driving force behind the continuation of the war. The oligarchs were also intent on a settlement with Sparta for reasons of internal politics. The establishment of a new governing body of ten probouloi (to which the so-called 'Councillor' appearing in the first part of *Lysistrata* belongs) represented the first restriction of the democracy, for these probouloi curtailed the rights of the prytaneis and the Council; Sophocles, incidentally, was one of them. These tensions existed even in the fleet on Samos, and from there the oligarchic rebellion, which followed a few months after the performance of *Lysistrata*, gained significant momentum. Thus the conception and performance of this comedy took place in a constantly worsening situation which threatened Athens (and this must be stressed) in both the internal and external political spheres.

The greater universality with which Aristophanes now treats the old theme of war and peace stems to some extent from the tendency of all the extant plays after *Birds* to be less limited to a particular time and situation. The explanation is, however, also to be sought in the political situation, which would scarcely have tolerated any partisanship on the part of the poet. Such partisanship might not only have proved dangerous, but would certainly have deprived him of any possibility of influence as a poet and would have diminished the validity of his declarations. This the chorus of *Lysistrata* announces explicitly (1043ff.):

> Not to objugate and scold you,
> Not unpleasant truths to say,
> But with words and deeds of bounty

Come we here to-day.
Ah, enough of idle quarrels,
Now attend, I pray.

A plot summary will show how the old theme of war and peace is handled here. Under the leadership of Lysistrata, married women from Athens as well as Sparta, Boeotia and Corinth meet and form a conspiracy, after Lysistrata has persuaded them that the only plausible method of obtaining peace must be a refusal to perform their conjugal duties. That this ticklish theme is treated coarsely and explicitly is quite understandable, given the nature of Old Comedy. In particular, the women doubt their own ability to hold out, but finally take a pledge not to surrender themselves to their husbands willingly, but in fact to excite them through provocative behavior. Employed in all the warring states simultaneously, this method has an immediate success. Hand in hand with this plan, however, comes a sort of coup d'état in Athens.[17] While the younger women plot the marriage strike, the old women occupy the Acropolis (which shelters the treasury of Athens in its temples) in order to shut off the main source for the continuation of the war, that is to say, the money.

The next scene shows the attempt of the chorus of old men to gain forcible entry onto the Acropolis by assailing the barricaded gates of the Propylaea with fire. The chorus of old women confronts them and extinguishes the fire, which again is not without symbolic force. Then one of the new probouloi approaches to take funds from the Acropolis; his attempt to break in forcibly also fails, and he must instead engage in a long discussion with Lysistrata, after his attempt to have her arrested is frustrated by the women. She takes this opportunity to say several things: first, she identifies the money as the source of the war; the women want to manage it exactly as they manage money in their homes. Second, she stigmatizes the political failures of the high-handed men: they should have obeyed the reasonable counsel of their wives who were so hard-pressed by the war. Third, the heroine

17. Since this was written J. Vaio has carefully illuminated the two 'planes' or 'themes' (marriage strike – uprising) and their interaction in the whole play: *GRBS* 14 (1973) 369–80. Vaio frequently supports the position I have developed here concerning comic technique, without expounding the distinction, essential to our study, between external and internal politics.

explains in a simile that the women plan to handle politics and the state like wool: they will clean it, unravel the threads and weave everything beautifully again into a cloak for all the people. The central idea of her statement is obviously more concerned with internal politics, with civic harmony and the reconciliation of opposing factions in Athens than with external politics and war, and (like the famous parabasis of *Frogs*) recommends inner strength through disentanglement of the complicated domestic situation.[18]

A later scene shows how Lysistrata, who feels no temptations herself, manages to prevent the weakening women from rushing to their husbands, and finally, the scene between Cinesias and his wife Myrrhine (notorious on account of its explicit sexuality), demonstrates how a woman, seemingly ready to surrender, excites her husband to the utmost in order to deny him fulfilment – all according to plan.

After it has been made clear through the appearance of a herald from Sparta that the Spartans are also in a state of high sexual excitement and for that reason ready for peace negotiations, the choruses of the old men and women of Athens are the first to be reconciled. As the deputies from Athens and Sparta, manifestly *in statu erectionis*, proceed to peace negotiations, Lysistrata summons Reconciliation to the stage in the form of an attractive girl, and with this symbol of the attainment of their fervid desires before their eyes, both sides quickly consent to easy terms. Lysistrata invokes the days of the Persian War and other earlier times when Athens and Sparta stood together, and refers to that national unity of all Greeks manifested in the panhellenic religious festivals at Delphi and Olympia. The rest of the play portrays a peace festival at which the Spartans in particular have their say, thus showing how beautiful peace among the Greeks could be.

The means by which peace is brought about here seems to us, as compared with *Acharnians* and *Peace*, less fantastic and impossible. The marriage strike requires neither the magic of enchanted wine nor a ride to heaven, but only good intentions. But it is doubtful

18. Cf. Dover, *Aristophanic Comedy* 161: 'her recipe...insensibly passes into what is a recipe not so much for peace as for strength (574–86, in many respects comparable with Frogs 686–705), implying that from a position of strength one can get a peace which is to one's own advantage'.

whether at that time this was a less fantastic means than the wine or the ride to heaven.[19]

The poetic means of bringing peace and reconciling the hostile sides turns into a main theme what was in the earlier plays a subsidiary theme. In the earlier period there also appeared, as part of that full enjoyment of life made possible by peace, the sexual aspects of life, in *Peace* (and *Knights*) symbolically emphasized through the significant names of the female characters. Here the sexual (or as I would prefer to say, erotic) desire is made the means by which readiness for peace becomes possible. If, in a poetic simile in *Acharnians*, the chorus imagined Reconciliation (Διαλλαγή) as a longed-for bride, now Reconciliation actually appears on stage, embodied as a desirable woman and naked[20] like the companions of Dicaeopolis, the Spondai (Treaties) in *Knights*, and Festival and Harvest in *Peace*. The great Wilamowitz, in his 1927 commentary, took the strongest offense at this scene with Reconciliation which depicts the peace negotiations. He wrote, 'The terms of the peace could not of course have been treated seriously. The poet had to wriggle through dangerous reefs. The way he did it is more unbearable than the ithyphalloi. He has introduced Διαλλαγή as a naked girl and transformed the yearning for peace into lascivious desire for this wench's charms. The vulgar obscenities accompanying Lysistrata's admonitory speech are truly shocking' (58f.). Now, shocking or not, Wilamowitz overlooked the fact that the women's scheme, and with it the essential poetic idea of the whole play (if we may formulate it less aggressively), is the transformation of the yearning for peace into the yearning of men for women. The scene with the personified Reconciliation again makes this most emphatically clear, and thereby the peace negotiations are actually trivialized. Peace negotiations with moderate terms for Athens

19. For further discussion, see Gelzer in *RE*, col. 1479, and Dover, *Aristophanic Comedy* 159f.

20. Cf. J. Vaio in *GRBS*, 379 n. 48: '...such roles were played by extras wearing female masks (cf. Hippocr. *Lex* 1) and exaggerated female σωμάτια with painted genitalia but without chitons. Holzinger argues cogently from the weather at the time of performance and the physical requirements of the theater: the spectators in the last rows should be able to see something of the described particulars. One might add the tendency of Old Comedy not to reflect reality but grotesquely to distort it.' I agree. [But see now my 'Drama und Theater', in *Das griechische Drama*, ed. G. A. Seeck (Darmstadt 1979) 481f.]

were at that time certainly impossible, and the people preferred to continue the war to the bitter end of capitulation.[21]

The men's yearning after women – and thus also after peace – is certainly more deeply founded than is commonly recognized, because it centers around their own wives, and the yearning is mutual, so that this droll and audacious play is actually a celebration of conjugal love and companionship.[22] In the scene in which the hostile choruses are reconciled, the women are clearly represented as more understanding, sympathetic and mature than the men, who are possessed by fixed ideas (1014f.). That the representation of the war is also more deeply founded is expressed clearly when it is said that the mothers must give up their sons, and when the losses suffered by the women, whom the war has cheated of their most beautiful years and the meaning of their lives, are expounded (587ff., 648ff.).

This comedy, as opposed to the earlier peace plays, thus acquires a deeper human dimension. It seems to me that, to the extent to which its utopian conception distances it from the political reality of a conceivable peace, the play acquires a more human reality. That must be the reason why of all Aristophanes' plays this one moves us the most today, even (and especially) if we free ourselves from the false notion that the play is pacifistic. In particular the scenes in which the choruses of old men and old women dominate bring a new note of understanding humor; and they are reconciled even without the erotic means which reconciliation requires in the external political sphere.

I venture to speak at this point of a domestic reconciliation within this play, and to work out an element which has been almost completely overlooked: the domestic reconciliation, the mediation between opposing factions within Athens, and I offer for consideration the possibility that the play has a much weightier and less theoretical significance than the propagation of what was at that time a practically impossible peace.

The peace striven for in *Acharnians* and *Peace* (and in *Knights* as well) can be fixed historically as the Thirty-Year Peace by which

21. That they had unfortunately rejected a possible peace in the summer of 410, and after the Battle of Arginusae in the late summer of 406, does not fall within the scope of this discussion.

22. Cf. Dover, *Aristophanic Comedy* 160f.

Athens and Sparta were bound before the outbreak of the war. It is the representation of the possibilities of attaining peace that is fanciful and unreal in these plays; the possibilities themselves are thoroughly real. This much is clear from the settlement of the so-called Peace of Nicias immediately after the production of the comedy entitled *Peace*. If the peace striven for and represented there is the state of affairs before the outbreak of the war, the *status quo ante*, so in *Lysistrata* it is a distant happy past in which Athens and Sparta stood side by side, the time of the Persian Wars; indeed, there are allusions to events of one hundred years earlier, because they show the present enemies as allies (271ff., 664ff., 1149ff.). It is a Golden Age, and thus this peace is a utopian conception. But a reconciliation of domestic factions struggling among themselves seems to me to be not a utopian conception but a plausible aspiration, bringing internal strength to Athens. This alone could perhaps still avert the threatening doom. That such a reconciliation between oligarchs and democrats was possible became evident a few years later when after the reign of the Thirty Tyrants and after much bloodshed and open civil war, such a domestic reconciliation actually occurred, and the idea of amnesty, of forgetting wrongs suffered, became so significant. Such pardoning and domestic reconciliation for the strengthening of Athens is recommended in the famous parabasis of *Frogs*;[23] we know that on account of this parabasis the rare honor of a second performance was accorded to this play. If we see this as the true goal of *Lysistrata* as well, then we shall better understand a few especially significant passages in the play.

I have already pointed out that the choruses of old men and women are reconciled without recourse to the marriage strike or to Lady Reconciliation. These choruses, however, had fallen out over the coup d'état of the old women who were occupying the Acropolis, while the younger women plotted for the denial of intercourse. Thus, to put it simply, external and internal politics go hand in hand. Lysistrata's great discussion with the proboulos concerns war and peace, the role of money and the political failure of the men, but the main point of her exposition is represented by the simile of the handling of the wool, which is clearly intended to refer to domestic politics. If the cleansed and unraveled threads are to be woven into a cloak for the entire populace, this must be

23. *Ran.* 686–705, but also 718–37, where the idea is continued.

an exhortation for civic harmony, for the reconciliation of domestic differences (565–86) and the strengthening of Athens, just as is recommended in the parabasis of *Frogs*.

In the parabasis of our play, the role of women in cult is stressed, specifically the cults of Athena and Artemis on the Acropolis, before which the action takes place (638ff.):

> Right it is that I my slender
> Tribute to the state should render,
> I, who to her thoughtful tender
> care my happiest memories owe;
> Bore, at seven, the mystic casket;
> Was, at ten, our Lady's miller; then the yellow Brauron bear;
> Next (a maiden tall and stately with a string of figs to wear)
> Bore in pomp the holy Basket.
> Well may such a gracious City all my filial duty claim.

When Lysistrate, perhaps armed with shield and spear, appears on the citadel (706ff.), she, who feels no temptation herself, reminds us of the virginal goddess who protects the city, Athena Polias. We now know that the priestess of Athena Nike (Victory) in these years was named Myrrhine, like the woman who excites her husband to the utmost while she herself remains steadfast and thereby provides an example of how the women could be victorious. The priestess of Athena Polias, on the other hand, was at that time a certain Lysimache.[24] Her name is not only similar in sound to that of Lysistrata, but in meaning as well: the priestess's name means 'Disbander of Battles', our heroine's 'Disbander of Armies'. The women will some day be called Disbanders of battles, Λυσιμάχας, says Lysistrata to the proboulos (554), in an obvious pun on her name. I believe that this double coincidence of the names of characters in the play with those of actual priestesses of Athena on the Acropolis should not be explained away as even Dover has done (*op. cit.*, p. 152 n. 3). I would prefer to see this as evidence not only of how seriously the poet takes the fate of his native city, about which Athena Polias herself (as it were) is concerned, but also as evidence for the new stature which the play, in spite of all its madly audacious activity, gives to women,

24. Cf. D. M. Lewis, *ABSA* 50 (1955) 1ff., and further literature in Gelzer in *RE*, cols. 1480f., with whose judgment I largely agree. It is significant in this connection that Lampito, the name of the Spartan woman in the play, is also the name of the mother of the Spartan king Agis, who was at that time in command at Decelea.

although they are politically without rights. The significance of the names must be taken together with the emphasis on the women's interest in the ἔρανος (648ff.) and their role in cult (638ff.) – the cult on the Acropolis; it must be taken together with the proposal, given in the form of a simile, to clean and untangle the matted and soiled wool of the domestic situation and weave it into a cloak for the demos, the people (567ff.). Thus the meaning of this play is internal unity and the strengthening of Athens as a precondition for peace with external enemies.

I would like to add a word about pacifism, which is nowadays frequently attributed to Aristophanes, and not only in theater programs and newspaper reviews. In my opinion, pacifism was unknown to the Greek of that time, least of all the free, self-confident citizen of democratic Athens. It went without saying for him, not only that he should fight and, if necessary, die for his fatherland and his gods, but also for his political ideals, rights and achievements, for the freedom and equality of his democratic state. For even these were being threatened in this war; measured against Athens, Sparta seems almost a totalitarian state, whose aim in war was not only the destruction of Attic power, but also the elimination of democracy. A peace from which the government and the constitution would not emerge even half-way intact was not acceptable to the citizens of Athens. Thus one can hardly speak of pacifism, which views life as the highest good.[25]

Of course it also goes without saying that the Greeks, and Athenians in particular, preferred peace to war, but not peace at any price, and least of all peace at the price of democratic freedom. The peace for which *Lysistrata* strives is a peace among the Greeks, such as had existed at the time when they waged war together against the Persians. The peace which the sophists and their pupils preached in their speeches is also a peace among the Greeks, often precisely in order to be able to wage war against the barbarians even more effectively.

I am certainly far from trivializing Aristophanes' frequent advocacy of peace,[26] but one should not forget that he could only appeal to one of the warring sides, Athens. Pacifism can be spoken

25. Cf. Dover, *Aristophanic Comedy* 84f.

26. He seems to surpass the other comic writers in this, and to have taken it especially seriously; cf. Gelzer in *RE*, cols. 1458f., 1481f.

of least of all with reference to *Lysistrata* if the poet was here encouraging domestic strength, as he did in *Frogs*. His democratic and patriotic sense of duty, his concern as man and citizen are nevertheless remarkable, when on the eve of the oligarchic coup d'état he stood before both political factions and advocated a civic harmony and a true democratic settlement within the state that can no more be ignored than the famous parabasis of *Frogs*. Only a year after the performance of *Frogs* came the capitulation of Athens and the loss not only of 'the splendor and glory of the Attic empire' (Wilamowitz) but also (much worse) of democratic freedom itself. The Thirty Tyrants, behind the screen of a quasi-totalitarian occupation, seized the helm of state. I am sorry that I must close with the tragic feelings which Aristophanic comedy evokes in us because we know the outcome of this war. But we have known since Plato's *Symposium* that it should be possible for one and the same man to create both comedy and tragedy; indeed, comedy by itself is often very serious, and that was quite true even before Plato.